MEDIEVAL PORTRAITS FROM
EAST AND WEST

Medieval Portraits
from
East and West

—————

Eleanor Duckett

Ann Arbor
THE UNIVERSITY OF MICHIGAN PRESS

To my friend
HELEN L. RUSSELL,
Professor and Dean of Students, Smith College,
Northampton, Massachusetts
I dedicate this book.

PREFACE

From information gathered through letters, historical records, biography, codex, chronicles, and verse, enlightened by the work of modern scholars, I have drawn these portraits for the interest of those who are not specialists in medieval research but enjoy the reading of history. Here they will find medieval emperors, empresses, popes, archbishops, bishops, monks and nuns, military generals, philosophers, and poets, in their human relationships, standing as the Byzantine historians pictured them. From these relatively simple pages the student, having grasped his background, secular and religious, may gladly pass to more impersonal details of trade and commerce, concerning those who form the multitude: the laborer, the poor and lowly, in their various crises and conflicts.

Once again I give warm thanks to the librarians of Smith College and of the Hampshire Inter-Library Center in America; to those of the University of Cambridge in England. To Helen Russell, Dean of Students in Smith College, I have dedicated these pages in gratitude for comfort and counsel in my own conflicts and crises.

E. S. D.

November, 1970
Northampton, Massachusetts

CONTENTS

Theodosius the Great

Early in September 394, Theodosius the First, known to us as Theodosius the Great, ruler of the Roman Empire, arrived at Milan in Italy. He was weary to death, and, as he himself felt, his last sickness was already at work within him. Yet joy was in his face; his road as he entered the city was lined with crowds of his subjects, shouting to heaven their eager praise of one who came to tell them of victory and of peace.

At Milan the Emperor remained four months, resting in its Imperial Palace, thinking back to the past and forward to the future.

Spain had seen his birth about 346; in his early twenties under his father, also Theodosius, he was fighting the Picts of Britain; a few years later he was winning his own battle against barbarians in the land of the lower Danube. About 376 the elder Theodosius, who for some two years had carried on a fierce campaign against rebel Moors in Roman Africa, was put to death by unjust accusation from jealous authority in Carthage. Shock of grief and apprehension forced his son into retreat upon the family estate in Spain.

The Roman Empire in 376 was under three rulers, nominal or actual. The East was governed by Valens, with his capital at Constantinople; the West held as co-Emperors at Milan his two nephews, Valentinian the Second and Gratian. As Valentinian, son of Valentinian the First and his second wife, Justina, crowned Emperor upon his father's death in 375, in 376 was a child five years old, the Empire in the West was under the direction and command of his half-brother Gratian, son of Valentinian the First by his first wife, Severa, also known as Marina. Gratian himself at this time was but seventeen.

The situation for both Valens and Gratian was dangerous; barbarian peoples—Huns, Alans, Alamanni, Goths from West and from East—were constantly attempting to invade Roman territory. In 376 Visigoths, "Goths of the West," gained after long entreaty permission from Valens to cross the Danube and settle in Thrace, land under his rule.

This leniency proved fatal. In 378 the inhabitants of Constantinople were in rebellion against him, caused by barbarian threat to invade even their own city; Thrace already had been laid waste by its wild occupants. Valens was forced by this deep discontent to march out to war, only to meet near Adrianople in Thrace disaster indescribable and his own death. Tradition cites that, wounded by an arrow, he fled from the field of battle to shelter in an outlying hut. There the Goths found him, shut him in, set fire to his fragile defence and left his relics lost in ashes with utter unconcern, not knowing who he was.

Gratian at nineteen could not hope to hold alone his control over both East and West; his brother was now only seven years old. He sorely needed military support, and he sent envoys to Theodosius. Would Theodosius share with him rule of the Roman Empire and assume the Imperial Crown of the East?

Lying on his bed in 394 at Milan, sixteen years later, Theodosius remembered still his long hesitation, his final resolve to serve the Roman Empire thus, if need must be. In January 379, he was crowned as Gratian's fellow-ruler; Gratian also added now to the Empire of the East the rule of Eastern Illyricum in the Balkans.

Long and skillfully, supported by the generals of his armies—Bauto, Arbogast, and Saturninus—he first fought and then negotiated with the Goths in the East; at last he won peace from battle. Far more, indeed, than peace; he knew how to hold those he had conquered. These Goths who year after year had invaded territory of the Empire he now made her allies—*foederati:* bound by treaty, settled in Thrace on their own holdings with their families, sworn to defend and to promote Roman interests.

Four years Theodosius of the East shared Imperial government with Gratian of the West, and the sharing gave him fear. Envoys brought to him disturbing reports of this co-Emperor: so promising in his youth, so hopelessly unable to meet the demands of rule, the duties of his Crown; so partial to some, and these not Roman, but barbarian; so heedless of policy and tact; so keen on sport and merriment. True, he was a devoted Christian, ever ready to serve and uphold the orthodox faith laid down at Nicaea. There were still, however, pagans and heretics in plenty who liked him little for this firm stand. Had not Gratian refused to wear the pagan robe of Pontifex, which his predecessors, Constantine and Valentinian the First, Christian though they were, had accepted? And, when he rejected it, had not the Chief Priest among the heathen present drily observed: "If the Emperor is not willing to be named Pontifex Maximus among us, right quickly Maximus will be Pontifex himself!"

The story, true or not, comes from Zosimus, a Byzantine historian and one resolutely loyal to his pagan creed. It may well have foretold what was to come. During 383 soldiers of the Imperial forces in Britain, resenting favors showered upon barbarian cohorts, rose against Gratian and declared Maximus, a Spaniard, Emperor in his place. As Emperor, Maximus crossed the Channel to fight with Gratian in Gaul and to win sure victory. Gratian fled southward, only to be caught at Lyons, on its bridge over the Rhône, and murdered by will of the man who had taken his crown.

At once Theodosius turned to think of protection for Valentinian the Second, his surviving co-Emperor in the West, a boy twelve years old. With a judgment doubtless wise and politic, he left Gaul in the hands of Maximus: a usurper, but one seemingly content to enforce peace and safety there as an Imperial colleague. Italy remained nominally under the sovereignty of Valentinian; but its actual rule was held by his mother Justina, a woman of keen intelligence, spurred on by a strong desire for power.

So history progressed as quietly as one could expect until 387. Then the hungry ambition of Maximus drove him to invade Italy; terrified lest her son be captured and killed, Justina took him and his sister Galla with her overseas to beg help from the Emperor of the East in the Macedonian city of Thessalonica.

Zosimus, who as a pagan held no deep admiration for the Christian Theodosius, flavors his description of this visit with romance. Justina, he tells, found the Emperor reluctant to start operations against Maximus. Civil war, he maintained, brought death and destruction to a land; it would be far better to send envoys to Maximus, bidding him for his own security to resume the *status quo* as co-Emperor in Gaul and leave Italy to Valentinian and his counselors. Of course, should Maximus refuse, war must follow.

Justina, however, had decided for war at once; next time she had audience with the Emperor she took her daughter Galla with her. Theodosius had lately lost his wife, Flaccilla; Galla was a girl of loveliness and charm. Promptly, rebuked by Justina for his lack of gratitude to Gratian who had given him his crown, and touched by the appeal of beauty in helplessness, he prepared for battle.

Doubtless this was due to his own sense of responsibility. But Theodosius and Galla were married the same year, and he sent his bride to await his return safe and sound at Constantinople; on the way she narrowly escaped capture by Maximus. In 388 Theodosius was in Italy, marching with his officers Arbogast and Promotus to punish the usurper.

Maximus felt confident and secure; he had even occupied Rome, a city fiercely hostile. His success was brief. Theodosius and his army defeated him in two pitched battles, and in all haste he fled north to Aquileia. There he was caught as he sat on his throne, handing out gifts of money to his soldiers. His captors tore from him his Imperial robe and carried him off for judgment; after a few scathing words on his crime against the Empire Theodosius delivered him to the executioner. Then he sent off Arbogast across the Alps to depose and to slay Victor, the son of Maximus, appointed "co-Emperor" with himself.

Here the Imperial wrath ended. Pardon without penalty was given to all others concerned in the rebellion; mercy to the mind of Theodosius was the guardian of peace. He stayed in Italy from 388 until 391, ruling that land for Valentinian, to whom he gave the charge of Gaul.

His rule, mostly held by him in Milan, was marked by events which he was never to forget. They had their beginning in that Thessalonica which he knew so well.

In the summer of 390 its people were unhappy; they bitterly resented the crowding of their city by rough and rude barbarian soldiers enrolled in the Roman army for the protection of Roman leaders. Resentment rose to rage when Butheric, commanding officer of these unwelcome guardians, sent to prison the best charioteer the Thessalonicans had, idolized by all, and continued to keep him there in spite of constant petitions for his release. One day Butheric was found lying dead, hacked to pieces by their wrath.

The Emperor and all in Milan heard of this murder with horror. All knew that he would be angry, and Ambrose, bishop of Milan, hastened to the Palace to plead with him for these rebels of Macedonia, guilty of killing one in the Imperial service. Again and again the bishop begged Theodosius to show mercy. But the Emperor, wise, shrewd, kindly and just as he was, held curbed within him a passion of anger which under strong provoking he seemed unable to control. His secular advisers urged stern measures, and easily he yielded. An edict went out from Milan, ordered by him; capital punishment was to be the fate of the rebels. Barbarian soldiers interpreted the order as they would; the historian Theodoret declares: "They say that seven thousand of Thessalonica's citizens fell before their swords and spears." This may well be an exaggerated rumor, and, indeed, Theodoret cared more for color than for accuracy.

The edict was soon followed by two events which showed Imperial wrath chastened by panic of conscience. One was the hasty issuing of a second edict, which commanded repeal of the first. It arrived too late; the streets of the city, we are told, were strewn with bodies of the dead. From Verona, where Theodosius was staying when he realized what he had caused, came a law, now recorded in the *Codex Theodosianus* (IX,40,13), against the date August 18, 390. It declared that a period of thirty days must pass between the issuing of sentence of death for a criminal, and its actual carrying out. Both Sozomen, another Byzantine historian, and Theodoret mention this law, and Theodoret adds: "Thus decisions, made in moments of sudden anger, through reason may be judged as just or unjust. "

Both writers also give a dramatic story. Once again in Milan, shortly afterwards, Theodosius went, as was his custom on feast days, to its Cathedral for prayer. At the doors, we are told, stood Ambrose, its bishop. Out went his hand to grasp the Emperor's robe of Imperial purple, and before all the congregation gathered for Mass, "Stop! he said. "To a man foul with sin, his hands stained by blood unjustly shed, there is no entrance here! No approach to this holy place, no communion with sacred mysteries, until due penance be done!"

Nevertheless, a letter written by Ambrose himself to Theodosius (No. 51) shortly after the massacre, shows the bishop in a very different light.

"In the city of Thessalonica," Ambrose wrote, while the Emperor was still unreconciled to the thought of penance, "a deed has been done unknown in the memory of man; a deed beyond recall by me; a deed which, before it was done, I called most savage in so many petitions to you; a deed which, once done, I could not forgive, even though you yourself held it harsh, and tried, too late, to revoke its sentence. . . .

"I have written to you, not for your confusion, but in hope that the examples of kings may urge you to wipe out this crime from your reign; and you will wipe it out if you humble your soul before God. Human you are, and temptation comes to you. Conquer it! Sin is blotted out by tears and penitence, nothing else. No angel, no archangel can remove it, only God; God alone can say 'I am with you'. If we have sinned, He shows mercy only to the penitent.

"I pray you, I ask you, I exhort you, I warn you! For it is pain and grief to me that you—you who were our ideal of most singular love and duty toward God, you who outdid all men in mercy, you who would not allow the guilty, one after another, to run risk of undue punishment—that you should not grieve at the death of so many innocent souls. . . .

"There is no arrogance, no pride in my mind. There is fear for you; I dare not offer the Holy Sacrifice in your presence." . . .

The letter, from which only a few words are given here, ended in affection:

"I love you, I respect you, I follow you with my prayers. And if you believe this, follow me; if, I say, you believe me, accept what I say. If you do not believe, forgive me that I place God before you. Blessed and happy may you be with your children; may you enjoy a peace that shall last for ever, August Emperor."

Until Christmas Theodosius the Great lived in misery, excommunicated. Then he recognized this command of justice and duty. Publicly in the Cathedral of Milan he acknowledged his sin and faithfully he fulfilled penance laid upon him by the Church. Augustine wrote in his *City of God:* "The tears of the people who saw the Imperial Majesty bowed to the earth were more real than their fear of his wrath against their own misdeeds" (*De Civitate Dei* V, 26).

In 391 the Emperor returned to his capital city of Constantinople. Valentinian the Second remained in Gaul. But, as he was now nearly twenty years of age, Theodosius gave over to him as Emperor of the West the charge and rule of Italy, Gaul, and Africa, with Arbogast as supreme commander of his army and his adviser in military tactics.

The following year tragic news came from Gaul: Valentinian was dead, killed by violence. History has left us various versions of this disaster; from them, however, we can at least gather reasonable evidence.

The Chief Commander, Arbogast, was of barbarian race, a Frank at birth who had enlisted in the Roman army and had risen to be second in rank to Bauto, also of Frankish origin, a general under Gratian and Theodosius. After Bauto's death Arbogast had stepped into his place as *Magister Militum,* "Master of Soldiers." He was extremely able, well skilled in strategy; he was honest, scorning to gain success by bribery and corruption; his men adored him and accepted readily all he said or did.

It mattered little to them that promotion had swelled his pride; they held him their Commander, rather than the youthful

Emperor. Valentinian, it is true, was said to yield readily to the
faults of youth; yet after his death Ambrose of Milan loyally defended him. "He delighted overmuch in the public games of the
Circus, and met this accusation by repudiating them; he spent too
much time in hunting, and, when accused of this, he abandoned all
thought of sport; those who disliked him declared that he loved to
eat, always hungry, and he met this charge by frequent fasting.
Perhaps, had he lived longer, he would have shown a character
more resolute. Meanwhile Arbogast, confident in his own standing
and contemptuous before a sovereign whom he did not respect,
spoke and acted rudely in his presence; so often that Valentinian
at last became obsessed by bitter sense of inferiority and shame.
Zosimus tells that one day, when the Emperor was sitting in state
to give audience, he saw this Chief Commander approaching his
throne. Now was the time, Valentinian suddenly decided, to do
what he long had wanted to do. As Arbogast came near he held
out to him a roll of paper; it gave order for his immediate dismissal
from Court and from the army in Gaul. The general read it, tore it
into pieces, and tossed the fragments to the ground. "*You* never
gave me my command," he said, "nor can you take it away!" With
this he left the hall. It was Theodosius in the East whom Arbogast
recognized as Emperor; one who could control and rule Roman
and barbarian alike. Philostorgius, another historian of this period,
shows Valentinian in storm of wrath, snatching a sword from a
bodyguard near his throne and only just prevented from bringing
it down on Arbogast standing before him. But here he tried to
explain his passionate anger. "It was really myself," he said, "that
I wanted to destroy; because, Emperor though I am, I am allowed
to do nothing that I want to do!"

He seems in these days to have feared for his life, and it is
to his credit that he did not hurry for safety to Milan or to
Constantinople. Stubbornly he held his post. But often he wrote
to Theodosius, his brother-in-law, crying for help. A sense of peril
may also be seen in his letters to Ambrose of Milan: Would Ambrose
come quickly to Gaul and give him baptism of the Church? Perhaps his thought went back to that courageous officer, Theodosius,
father of the Emperor now in Constantinople, who, doomed to die
at Carthage sixteen years before, in his last moments had sought,
in this baptism, cleansing from all sin and thus had gone to his fate
with peace of mind.

During May 392, Valentinian the Second was at Vienne in
Gaul, on watch against barbarian hordes gathering in the Alps.
Doubtless they were planning assault upon Italy. There at Vienne

in a lonely spot near his Palace he was found one day, killed by strangling. Whether this was done by his own act in a moment of despair, or whether by an enemy's will, is not certain. Evidence points to Arbogast; it would seem probable that either he himself or men under his command fell upon the Emperor, taken by surprise, and left a towel tied fast around his neck, his body hanging from this noose, as a suggestion of suicide.

Other evidence also points to Arbogast as the murderer. A barbarian Frank, he could not hope himself to seize the Imperial throne of the West; he had therefore decided to choose, for this usurping, one whom he could make his tool. This was Eugenius, once a master and teacher of rhetoric in Rome, and now in Gaul as secretary of Valentinian and his Court. To him, after much flattery and show of warm friendship, Arbogast had revealed his plan: Valentinian must be removed and Eugenius would sit as Emperor. Eugenius naturally was horrified; he was also immensely frightened. But Arbogast knew how to persuade; was he not head of the army in the West? The murder, we may think, was carried out; it was called suicide.

But at any rate, whether murder or suicide caused the convenient death of Valentinian II, in 393 Eugenius was declared Emperor, and the soldiers of Arbogast each and all supported the deed, confident of reward.

With Eugenius and a strong force of Gothic fighters in 393 Arbogast marched for Italy; an envoy had been despatched to Theodosius, asking for recognition of this secretary as co-Emperor in the West.

News of murder, usurpation and invasion struck the Court at Constantinople with bitter consequence. Galla, Empress of Theodosius, died in childbirth. Nevertheless action against the invader could not wait. "After Homeric custom," Zosimus writes, "Theodosius gave one day to tears." Then, leaving in Constantinople his two sons, Arcadius, now about sixteen, and Honorius, nearly ten, both already co-Emperors with himself, he marched for Italy with an army which held a large force of Goths. It was May, 394.

Near Aquileia and the Julian Alps in the north of Italy Theodosius encamped, high upon a hill, looking down upon the vast horde of the enemy below. Without delay he gave order for attack. Thus began that famous struggle known in history from the river nearby as the battle of the Frigidus.

By nightfall the Romans were in despair. Bravely they had

fought, and they had held their ground; but elsewhere there was disaster. A multitude of the Goths had been killed; the survivors were scattered in flight; all on the Gothic side of the army seemed lost. In joy of victory Eugenius was handing out donations to those who had done most to win his victory; from his tents the sounds of revelry and feasting came to Theodosius, sitting alone. Alone in the darkness he stole away up the hillside to find a secret place among rocks and trees, and there, hidden from all, he spent the hours of that night in prayer to the Lord Christ: "Thou, Who canst do all things for good, if my cause is just, come to us! Stretch forth Thy right hand to aid Thine own, lest the heathen say 'Where is their God'?"

At dawn—it was the sixth of September—he rose, put on his armor, and called aloud to his men to renew the battle. Astonished at his courage, they plucked up their own; few as they were, they ran forward once again. Suddenly, as they fought, hoping for nothing but speedy death, there came a rush of wind in fury, driving at their backs and in the faces of the troops of Eugenius and Arbogast. Borne by its force, the little army of Theodosius dashed forward; the soldiers of Arbogast lost their spears, torn from their hands; baffled and bewildered by the gale blowing against them, they fell back, their shields knocking upon their breasts, their arrows, aimed against the enemy in front of them, flying in reverse to pierce their own bodies, their eyes blinded by the dust coming straight in their path.

Victory for Theodosius was complete; among those taken prisoner was Eugenius himself. As Maximus in 388, he was led before the Emperor; while he crouched at his feet in terror, one of the Imperial guards leaped forward and struck him dead. Arbogast escaped into the mountains of the north; finding there no shelter, certain of capture, he put an end to his life. To all others Theodosius once again granted full amnesty.

It was his last battle in defence of the Empire. Now he was in Milan, nearing his own end. He did not fear for himself; he had faced death too often. Long before, in 380, when critical illness had seized him in Thessalonica, he had sought Christian baptism from his bishop, and firmly he had upheld its creed; too firmly indeed. As Emperor he had insisted upon orthodox practice for all his subjects. Against heathens and heretics he had threatened to issue grim laws with a determination fortified by the condemning of Arianism in 325 at Nicaea. There bishops of the East, assembled in the First General Council of the Church, had proclaimed her creed:

We believe in One Lord Jesus Christ,
Son of God,
Very God of Very God,
Begotten (from all eternity), *not made,*
Being of one substance with the Father;
Who for us men and for our salvation
Was made man (in human time).

By Imperial will of Theodosius pagan temples remained closed; heretics were not permitted to celebrate their own ritual in public places. The Emperor held it his Imperial right to summon his bishops to meet in Council; as also it was for him, he declared, to decide which of the candidates favored by them should be appointed Patriarch of his capital city of Constantinople. In 381, through his choice, that office had fallen to one Nectarius. The same year had seen Theodosius assembling at Constantinople the Second Oecumenical Council of the Church. This had reaffirmed the ordering of Nicaea against the heresy of Arius, priest of Alexandria (holding that the Christ as Son of God was not in true reality God in fullness, not co-eternal with the Father nor of the same essence or substance); and against that of Apollinaris, bishop of Laodicea in Syria (holding that the Christ was not completely genuine Man). Both these men lived and taught in this fourth century; Arius had died in 336, Apollinaris, about 390. The same Council of Constantinople had also declared its episcopal see next in favor to the primacy of Rome. From this time onward Arianism no longer held its former cult among men of Roman birth. It lived, however, a vigorous life among the Gothic, barbarian peoples, implanted among them in this second half of the fourth century by a missionary bishop, Ulfilas, who, an Arian Christian himself, taught them his faith and made for them his famous translation of the Bible into their Gothic tongue.

In 382, by command of Gratian, the altar of Victory, reverenced by pagan worshippers, had been removed from the Senate House at Rome. Valentinian II and Theodosius had forbidden its restoration. Eugenius, that usurping Emperor of 393, was a zealous pagan; he had not only allowed the altar to be replaced and its honoring fully re-established, but in 393 and 394 he had revived the various ritual ceremonies connected with heathen deities; he ordered their temples once again opened for worship; he freely saw around him the practice of divination, the sacrifice of animals and the inferring of omens from their organs. In all this he was enthusiastically supported by Flavian, Praetorian Prefect of Italy, and by Arbogast, who had placed him on his throne. Had not Flavian, himself of great experience and fame as diviner of the future, declared to him that victory would be his, that the Christian religion would in his reign yield to pagan rites? Had not Flavian and Arbogast promised as they left Milan, just before the battle of the Frigidus, that when they returned victorious they would stable their horses in its Cathedral and send its clergy out to fight in the ranks of their army? Such memories must eventually have added to the joy of the Christian Theodosius, conqueror of Eugenius and Arbogast in 394. Augustine of Hippo was to describe this Emperor's work for religion in these words: "From the very beginning of his reign he did not cease by most just and merciful laws to aid the Church in her struggle against the impious: that Church which the heretic Valens had deeply injured by his favor shown to Arians; that Church of which Theodosius would far rather know himself a member than reign as any king on earth" (*De Civitate Dei* V, e. 26).

It is a partial and prejudiced judgment, and Theodosius as Emperor was certainly not just to all his subjects. We remember him, however, as one of strong and determined mind, one who conquered usurpers, punished those who plotted crime and forgave those who followed their lead. His constitutional reforms were born of intense thought and care; his policy toward barbarian peoples was wise. On the other side we remember those uncontrolled waves of passionate anger which caused so great evil, not only at Thessalonica in 390, but also at Antioch in 387. The citizens of Antioch had risen in rebellion against special and heavy taxation levied upon them. Theodosius had been planning high days of holiday to mark the years of his own Imperial sovereignty and that of Arcadius, who had been crowned co-Emperor with himself in 383. Moreover, war had been costly; hence the taxing to meet special need. Riot in Antioch had led to most grave offence; the statues of the Emperor and Empress had been thrown down and broken to pieces. Punishment had quickly followed: Antioch, it was decreed, was to remain silent and dark, its places of entertainment empty and barred; trials of the accused had been held by Imperial authority, and the officers sent to Antioch for this purpose had used force to induce confession. Magistrates of the city had gone further; they had put to death the leaders in this rebellion. Zosimus, ever ready to attack Theodosius, declared that, since in his reign morale was so low and "nothing tending to virtue won praise but every kind of luxury and licence was steadily increasing, the great city of Antioch could not endure this enforced payment to public funds, mounting higher day by day." Antioch, it is true, was magnificent;

its people lived in full comfort and enjoyment of life, and therefore they found hunger, terror and suspense, destruction and death, the more appalling. Their Patriarch, Flavian, old and weary, gathered up his courage and journeyed to Constantinople to plead for them.

Then, as Libanius wrote, that well-known professor of rhetoric in Antioch: "Men were lying helpless in prison, and their kinsfolk were coming to give them their love, to kiss and to cry over them before they must die; when suddenly, as the sun conquering the clouds with its rays, there came the light of a letter, driving away the dark. In a moment all that was hateful had slipped away and all that brought good cheer had entered in. Once again we had our friendly greetings to one another, again we had our sights and shows, our public baths. Once more our city had its own world, and the poor man his meat!"

Flavian had done his work, and Theodosius had sent full pardon to all his flock in Antioch.

It is of interest to watch the doings of a mind practical and stern in matters of State, whether political or religious; yet ready and willing itself to change at the command of conscience. It is interesting, also, to remember that this same Emperor who ordered his prelates to attend Councils and decided their elections, could listen humbly to the words of a hermit in time of crisis. Before he went out to war against Maximus in 388 Theodosius sent word to John, a recluse of great repute in Egypt and throughout the East for his ascetic life and his gift of prophecy: Would John tell him what he might expect, should be march against the usurper? Answer came that he would conquer Maximus and put him to death. Saint Augustine himself here commended this Emperor: "Facing a fear of dread victory of Maximus, in anguish of responsibility, he did not stoop to impious and unlawful peerings into the unknown, but sought out one to whom God had given power of prophecy for His own service" (*D.C.D., ibid.*). Again in 394—so the historian Theodoret writes—Theodosius sent to inquire of John before his battle with Eugenius, and the answer came: "Victor truly will you be, but after much slaughter."

At Milan in 394 the Emperor, as his sickness increased, sent for his second son, Honorius, left by him at Constantinople with Arcadius, his brother. Honorius came, a boy of about ten, and his father, in a burst of new hope for life, decided to celebrate his victory over Eugenius by games within the Circus at Milan. He seemed well and strong when he appeared with his son for the morning's sport; that same night he died. It was the seventeenth of January, 395.

Philostorgius calls the man "impious" who accused the Emperor of "excessive indulgence in luxury: the source of his suffering and his death from dropsy."

Ambrose, bishop of Milan, gave farewell to Theodosius amid his people, in the Cathedral that he had known so well. "It was this," the bishop said, "this, to which those dread quakings of the earth in their menace recently were pointing; this, of which constant floods of rain warned us; this, which strange, dense fog falling upon us foretold: that our most kindly Emperor was to go forth from this world. The very elements were mourning his departure from our midst. . . .

"Yet not altogether has he gone. He has left us his sons, in whom we shall know him still among us; in whom we both see him and feel his presence here."

CHAPTER TWO

The Empress Eudoxia and Saint John Chrysostom

I

Unhappily Saint Ambrose was here to prove no true prophet. Theodosius, sole ruler of the Roman Empire at his death, had left his elder son, Arcadius, as Emperor of the East, and the younger one, Honorius, as Emperor of the West. The East included Moesia, Thrace, Boeotia, the Peloponnesus, Asia Minor, Syria, Palestine and Egypt; the Empire of the West held Italy, Gaul, Britain, Spain, and Africa. Illyricum, territory of the Balkans, was now divided between East and West; soon began the long struggle between East and West for its possession.

Arcadius, now in January, 395, about seventeen years old, and Honorius, who was only ten, had both been born to Theodosius by his first wife, Aelia Flaccilla; he hoped that they both would find a friend in Stilicho, general in his army.

We will look first at Arcadius in Constantinople, capital city of the East. Twelve years had passed since that nineteenth of January, 383, when by decree of his father its citizens had acclaimed him, a little boy of six, as co-Emperor; in 385, at eight, he had been honored, together with Bauto, a military officer, as consul of the Empire.

What was he like at seventeen? Our source here is the historian Philostorgius: "Arcadius was short in stature, thin in body, dark of hair and complexion, listless and languid in manner. He was also dull and sluggish in mind, as you could tell from his eyes, ever sleepily blinking as though he could not keep them open."

That is bad enough; but, worse still, he was completely under the influence of his chief minister of State, Rufinus, Praetorian Prefect in the East. Rufinus, we learn from the same authority, was "tall in body, and masculine in character; his shrewd, hard-headed mind was seen in his alert eyes, his quick and able manner of speaking."

In character, however, Rufinus was an utter scoundrel, and we need not hesitate to accept the picture given us by Zosimus: "In very truth all power throughout the East was in his hands. All disputes there were settled by him, by his authority; that man won a quarrel who bought decision of him by money, or earned favor from him as judge by some agreement between them. . . . Whatever wealth dishonesty had earned for any man flowed finally into his house, plunging into poverty, here, there, and everywhere, those who once had been rich. Of all this the Emperor knew nothing; whatever Rufinus ordered, Arcadius at once made public in writing as his own command."

So the Praetorian Prefect amassed immense resources; men bowed before him, flattered, feared, and detested him. Some even suspected him of aiming at the Imperial throne itself. What did he care? He was obsessed by a vision of eminence and rank.

Moreover, he had planned a path to the glory for which he longed. Arcadius was now of age to take a wife who would share his throne as Empress, and Rufinus had a daughter ready for marriage. What could profit him more than to see them duly wedded? Casually he threw out hints of such a possibility in secret conversation with his fellow-ministers of the Court; and, of course, though he did not realize it, rumors began to circulate.

One of these whispers reached the ears of a man whom he despised as infinitely beneath him: one Eutropius. Eutropius could not, it is true, hope for a marriage of the Emperor with one of his own family; he was a eunuch. Nevertheless he had toiled hard, for his ambition matched that of Rufinus. Once a slave, he had at last been appointed Chamberlain in the Sacred Palace of the Emperor. As such, in intimate and daily service, he was of constant use to Arcadius. There was no mean, shifty, subtle act which he could not, would not, carry out. Possessed himself of riches, he aimed at attaining a high place in the society of Constantinople, among those in Imperial favor; at his luxurious house men and women of noble line feasted well, while to one another they reviled their host. Yet did he not know everyone and everything, and could he not serve their needs? Was he not hand in glove with the Emperor? Zosimus even wrote that "Eutropius lorded it over Arcadius as though the Emperor were a fatted head of cattle."

Naturally, when Eutropius heard that Rufinus, his rival in ambition, was thinking of an Imperial marriage for his daughter, he decided to do all he could to disappoint him. In the house of Promotus, once general of Theodosius but now dead, there was living with his widow Marsa and her sons a girl named Eudoxia. She was a daughter of Bauto, the barbarian Frank, fellow-soldier with Promotus; her father's death in 388 had brought her to the hospitality of Marsa. The historian Philostorgius describes her as "holding within her no little barbarian boldness"; at any rate, she was far different from the languid, indolent Arcadius. Moreover, her face and figure were of rare charm and beauty.

All this with tact and skill Eutropius mentioned to Arcadius, and impressed him even more by showing him the girl's picture. The plot thickened when he was ordered to bring her to the Palace. Not a word was said to Rufinus. When he saw the Imperial Chamberlain making preparations which indicated that an Imperial marriage was in the mind of the Court, he was sure that they concerned his daughter. A holiday was proclaimed, and a procession was marshalled, of attendants from the Palace carrying bridal array, dress, garland, veil and jewels. As it marched through the streets of Constantinople citizens followed it in crowds, highly curious, but sure that it would go straight to the splendid mansion of Rufinus. It turned to the far humbler home of the family of Promotus, and all waited breathless with excitement until Eudoxia came out to meet her escort for the Palace. On April 27, 395, Arcadius received her as wife and Empress in the Cathedral of Saint Sophia.

From this time Rufinus was filled with bitter jealousy of Eutropius. And not only of Eutropius; the power of Stilicho was rising in the West. Was not Stilicho a barbarian, of Vandal birth? And yet he was far nearer the Imperial throne than Rufinus himself. By Theodosius the Great he had been appointed Chief-in-Command of both infantry and cavalry; he still held this high office under Honorius, now his Emperor. The same Theodosius, who had admired him greatly, had given him in marriage his own niece, Serena. Serena, too, kept her eyes upon the politics of the West; she was as ambitious for their two daughters as Stilicho for their son. Stilicho was said to be hoping that this son, Eucherius, would marry Galla Placidia, step-sister of Honorius. Philostorgius declares, indeed, that both Rufinus and Stilicho had designs upon the Imperial throne, Rufinus for himself and Stilicho for Eucherius.

The reputation of Stilicho has been pictured for us by the poet Claudian, who was his contemporary. Born in Alexandria, Egypt, Claudian had come to live in Rome during these years, to write of Stilicho as hero, and of Rufinus and Eutropius as villains of the deepest dye. A few words from his poem on Stilicho's consulship in 400 will sum up his thought of this guardian of the West:

> In truth, since mortal man dwelt on this earth, never full-hearted fate was man's, granted to any one.
> For thee, joys flow in flood. Others, receiving part, rejoice; thou hast the whole!
>
> *De consulatu Stilichonis* i, 24ff.

On the other hand Rutilius Namatianus, in the elegiac verses which tell of his return in 416 from his service as Prefect in Rome to his native land of Gaul, wrote of Stilicho as one "who betrayed the sanctuary of Empire" and sent "barbarian arms forward for Latium's death."

The truth lies between these two poles. Stilicho attained exalted honors and to some extent he deserved them: a great soldier, a skilled politician. But his devotion to his own cause was greater than his thought for Rome; for his own profiting he allowed himself action, and also lack of action, seemingly akin to treachery. Especially is this to be remembered in regard to Illyricum, which, at the death of Theodosius I in January, 395, had been divided between the Empires of East and West; it was Stilicho's great and persistent aim that all Illyricum should be under the rule of Honorius, Emperor of the West, and therefore under his own power.

For a moment now we turn to the wild barbarian peoples of the East, ever ready to ride in search of plunder. Before the winter's ice of 394–395 had disappeared, Huns in hordes were crossing the lower Danube to ravage and ruin Roman territory. Through Thrace they spread, working destruction in their path; multitudes of others descended upon Armenia, Syria, and Cilicia, killing their inhabitants and laying waste their lands. Socrates and Sozomen, Byzantine historians, told of a rumor which now passed from man to man in Constantinople. These barbarian invaders, it was said, had been called into action by secret word from Rufinus; he was hoping that the Empire of the East, distracted by raid and slaughter, would call him to its throne. Claudian painted both his mind and his work:

> Rufinus (for cruel crimes allow no tranquil rest, and jaws dripping with filthiness refuse to dry) to kindle in our lands a war unspeakable begins; with wonted tumult he disturbs our peace.

He opened straight the road to wars; and that no land be
spared, spread in due portion his foul deed worldwide. Across
the savage Danube's solid ice now rushed the foe, breaking
with wheels the stream once touched by oars.

> *In Rufinum* II, 7ff., 24ff.

In the same late winter months, early in 395, came an army of
Visigoths, Goths of the West, hurrying eastward into Macedonia
and Thrace. They were led by Alaric, a Visigoth of high ambition
who had served under Theodosius the Great against Eugenius in
394. From Thrace they turned to ride for Constantinople itself.

Their coming, to the terror of its citizens and the joy of
Rufinus, in his soaring desire for himself glad to see destruction
brought even upon his capital city, is also told for us by Claudian:

That very city, known as rival of great Rome, which proudly
looks toward Chalcedon's sanded shore, is shaken now by no
far distant fear of war. Before its face the torches flare; raucous
the sound of screaming horns; its homes fast flying weapons
wreck, though citizens with constant vigil guard their walls,
though many haste to ring their port with anchored ships.
Fiercely Rufinus now rejoices in the siege, triumphant in evil;
from summit of high tower he looks upon the wicked spectacle
below.

Pleasure immense he feels; often he laughs; one grief alone is
his, that idle lies his hand alone. Lands far and near ravaged by
fire he sees; only his own are safe; happy in crime, he calls
the city's foes his friends.

> *In Rufinum* II, 54ff., 68ff.

The last words refer to a meeting of Rufinus and Alaric. The
Praetorian Prefect of the East went out from Constantinople in
secret and, disguised as a Gothic barbarian, sought out Alaric in
his camp outside its walls. There he persuaded Alaric by offer of
friendship and support to march with his Goths into Macedonia.

For two provinces, Dacia and Macedonia, formed Eastern
Illyricum, and Rufinus and Stilicho both eagerly coveted possession of this land: Rufinus for the Eastern Empire, Stilicho for the
Western, since possession by one or the other would increase his
own power of dominance.

Therefore Rufinus asked Alaric the Goth to enter Eastern
Illyricum, to occupy it, and Alaric actually did invade its territory.

But Stilicho was in no mood for yielding to Rufinus and the
Goths. Promptly he marched from Italy to face them in Thessaly

of Greece. The year was still 395, and his army held two forces: one of men, including many Goths, who had come the year before from the East to aid Theodosius in his defence of Italy against Eugenius; and the other of Stilicho's own soldiers from Italy.

Report of Stilicho's move gave Rufinus deep misgiving. Was this rival of his to earn fame and promotion, to hold Illyrian land which he, Stilicho, thought of as his own for rule?

Rufinus hurried to his Emperor, Arcadius, and wrung from him an order to Stilicho: Stilicho was at once to start on his return to Italy with his own soldiers and to send on the road homeward to Constantinople all who had come from the East in 394.

How did this order affect Stilicho, now facing the battle lines of Alaric in northern Thessaly? Claudian, the poet, dwells upon a fierce struggle in his hero's mind: on the one hand, his longing to conquer the Gothic army, now so near, and thus to save Illyrian land for the West; on the other, his fear of offending Arcadius by disobedience.

At last, in Claudian's words, he decided that he must obey, and quickly delivered the order as given, to the intense discontent, even rebellion, of both divisions of the army before him. At once he rebuked them and bade them march on their differing ways:

> Then, "No!" cried Stilicho: "Cease, I pray! Drop now your eager hands; let fall that vast ill will which threatens me! What care I for a victory, won by me doubtless for myself? My loyal men, Depart, my fellows once in war!" No more he spoke, but went his road alone.
>
> *In Rufinum* ii, 247ff.

His thought and his purpose were in fact far from this philosophy. Eastern Illyricum now might, he feared, be lost to the West through this command of Arcadius. Yet, no doubt, refusal to obey would cause serious dissension between the two parts of the Roman Empire. Concord in their working was essential. Did not he, Stilicho himself, desire intensely to be leader of both East and West, linked together by him in politics and in the field?

Of course, he told himself, it was Rufinus who had induced the Emperor of the East to issue the order. That was clear. It was equally clear that, if Rufinus were removed from the scene, relations between Italy and Constantinople would be far easier to control.

Autumn was setting in and he acted quickly. He placed the men returning to Constantinople under the leadership of Gainas, a Goth who had deserted his own people to serve the Roman

Empire. Before Gainas gave order to begin the march Stilicho secretly entrusted to him certain definite instructions concerning Rufinus.

All arrived in due course at Constantinople, where great preparations had been made to welcome them home. Outside the city, on November 27, 395, the Emperor awaited them with the Praetorian Prefect, Rufinus, who was rejoicing that his intrigue had succeeded so easily. Into an open field marched and rode soldiers on foot, soldiers mounted; there they drew up in order of rank for their reception in ritual of state. It is again Claudian who recalls the scene in his savage verses against Rufinus. First Arcadius came forward in all dignity to salute the defenders of his Empire; then Rufinus, "with that approach so cunning, so calculated, so sure to deceive." He praised their devotion; he called each man by his name; all those awaiting them in their homes, he was glad to tell them, their fathers and their sons, were safe and well. Even as he spoke, while the men on foot and on horse were keeping his eyes fixed upon them by plying him with questions, a circle was gradually closing in around him. Suddenly Gainas gave the signal; swords at once rose in every hand, and one man, bolder than the rest, rushed upon that figure standing in the center. With a loud cry, "Stilicho strikes thee!" he drove his sword through the side of this hated Prefect.

Quickly Rufinus fell, while each soldier ran to win his own share in the death. The victim's head was borne high on a pike into Constantinople; his right hand was cut off and carried through the city's streets with open palm, thrust forward to receive offerings from passers-by, who gladly laid them there in mockery. "From door to door," Saint Jerome was to write the following year, "the severed right hand of Rufinus begged alms, to the shame of his ever-hungry greed."

Stilicho had gained his revenge; Philostorgius names him as the man responsible for the slaying of Rufinus, and Eutropius followed Rufinus as master in Constantinople.

We return to the Goths left in Greece while Rufinus still lived, while Stilicho was marching for Italy and Gainas for Constantinople. Now the road was open once again for Gothic plundering and raid, still, it would seem, furthered by the treachery of Rufinus. Alaric and his men marched from Thessaly for the defile of Thermopylae, through which they were freely allowed to pass by its guardians, the proconsul Antiochus and the warden Gerontius; Rufinus had carefully chosen and appointed each. On the Gothic army went, carrying death and ruin to those it met, into Boeotia, where—so Zosimus states—its soldiers failed to destroy Thebes, partly because of its well-buttressed walls, partly because Alaric was in a hurry to capture Athens. He was hoping to win this prize by occupying the port of Piraeus and thus cutting off supplies of food.

Yet he was not destined to succeed; before long he was to enter the city, to receive gifts from its people, to feast with its leading men, to exchange oaths of peace with them. Zosimus attributes this vital change of intent to a vision of the Warrior Goddess Athene, marching in armor on the city's wall, ready for assault in its defence; and, also, of Achilles, standing before its ramparts, a very hero, as Homer had described him when in his wrath he rushed to avenge the death of Patroclus.

So runs the legend. But, at any rate, Alaric left Athens unharmed by his men, and went on to seize Megara, to pass easily across the Isthmus, to make himself master of Corinth, Argos and Sparta. From 395 until 397 he and his Goths carried on their savage campaign of conquest. In words of bitter grief, sent to his friend Heliodorus, Saint Jerome wrote of the tragedy of Greece and the Roman Empire, beset by barbarians:

> "The Roman world is falling down, and yet our neck, held high, is not bowed. What, think you, in what state of mind are now the men of Corinth, Athens, Sparta, Arcadia, of all Greece, over whom the barbarians now hold control?"
>
> Saint Jerome, *Epistulae*, LX, c. 16.

Meanwhile Stilicho was fighting to defend the West against barbarians in Gaul and in Germany; at last in 397 he was free to gather a fleet and sail to aid Greece in her crisis. Then, nevertheless, he allowed her enemies to take cover amid the ravines and caves of Mount Pholoe in Elis, northwest in the Peloponnesus. From there these Gothic raiders sought retreat in Epirus of northern Greece; finally they made peace with the Empire of the East. In 397 Eutropius, now acting for Arcadius, in his fear of further assault offered Alaric inducement toward firm alliance. He appointed him Master of Soldiers in Illyricum, an act which thoroughly disgusted Claudian of the West; for it made the East ruler of that land:

> The destroyer of the Greeks, he who of late ravaged Epirus unavenged, rules in Illyricum; now walls he once betrayed in friendly guise he enters, to declare his laws to men whose wives he rapes, whose sons he massacred.
>
> *In Eutropium* II, 214ff.

Yet not only Alaric but also Stilicho troubled the mind of Eutropius as a possible enemy. Might not Stilicho march for Constantinople? It would be wise to judge him thus; Eutropius obtained from Arcadius and the Senate of the East a decree naming Stilicho an "enemy of the Empire."

Illyricum remained a matter of disputed claim, but one of diminishing importance in politics. There were other troubles to face. Not until 437 was a definitely formal settlement made, when the West handed over its claim of possession to the Empire of the East.

2

Two years had now gone by since Eudoxia by her marriage had been raised to an Imperial throne. It is time to think of her as consort of Arcadius, as Empress amid the surge of events in Constantinople, as one drawn into its life, civil and social, gay and luxurious, Christian and pagan; to think of her, especially, as friend and as enemy of John Chrysostom.

She was a young woman of qualities good and bad, which warred with one another constantly in her mind. Bold and impetuous, she could yield to fear induced by superstition; independent in action, she was often influenced by those who talked with her, now hastening to do well, now as quickly rushing to hurt and injure. Barbarian by birth, she never for a moment forgot that she was Empress. Honors were her delight; so was luxury; splendor in dress, in jewelry, in receptions and banquets at the Court. For these she lived day by day. Sensitive to the attitude of those around her, she met any rudeness, any neglect, real or imagined, with anger and swift penalty. Her husband readily submitted to her charm; soon his was the name and hers the will, the ambition which governed his court, his cathedral, and his city; and in this fact we find much of the misfortune of her brief Imperial reign.

In September 397, Nectarius, bishop of Constantinople, died, old and frail, leaving no decisive acts to mark his memory. Since the see now ranked only below that of Rome itself, election of his successor was a matter of great importance. Consecration of that successor would be the duty and privilege of one Theophilus, as bishop (Patriarch) of Alexandria, and Theophilus for some time had held in mind his own candidate for office: Isidore, a priest of his, to whom very eagerly he wanted to show favor; largely, it was said, for his own interests. Theophilus, as we shall see, was no saint. Isidore was not elected for Constantinople, and it was Eutropius, the Imperial Chamberlain, who caused his rejection.

Eutropius, like Rufinus, was described with stinging hatred in two books of verse by Claudian. There he appears as a foul old man, his skin lying loose in wrinkles, his cheeks furrowed by age, his head bald in patches, his body wasted and shrunken. The description was true. But he held office and he held power; ever since the fall of Rufinus he had become the most influential minister in the Eastern Court. He watched now the canvassing, the intrigues set afoot by those who fought for election of this man or that as Patriarch of Constantinople. He knew that false words were spoken, bribes were offered, while at the same time anxious petitions were being made to the Emperor that he appoint a pastor loyal both to Church and State.

As Imperial envoy Eutropius had traveled far, to Eastern countries and cities; in Antioch, as he knew, there was a priest, John Chrysostom, of whom many were talking in wonder. He preached, they said, as no other man of his time; he worked among his people without cease; they loved him as a true Father in God. With them, as one of them, he had lived through those terrifying weeks of suspense at Antioch, waiting for the Emperor's judgment to fall upon them after their destruction of the statues. Yet in all severity he had denounced their sin (P.G. XLIX, 34):

"For seven days I have kept silence, as did the friends of Job; let me today open my mouth to lament this, the tragedy of us all. Who has cast upon us the evil eye, beloved? Who has been moved to malice against us? Whence came a change so great? Nothing was once held in higher respect than our city; nothing now more pitiful. Its people, so orderly, so tranquil—I would liken them to a horse that gives quick and ready answer to its rider's hand—suddenly now have run away, out of control, to do more evil than I may rightly tell. I grieve and I mourn; not for the dread threatening which may well strike us, but for the utter madness of that which you have done. Even though the Emperor should not be angry, should not punish or chastise, how, tell me, how are we to bear the shame of the things which have been done?"

And at last he had rejoiced with them in the letter of pardon from Theodosius (P.G. XLIX, 119):

"Blessed be God that we are here together! No longer fleeing from perils from without, eager to hear this news of today, we hurry here! No longer in anguish, trembling with fear and foreboding, we gather, safe and secure, shaking off our terror!"

So, Eutropius decided, John was to be his candidate, and he set to work with his usual cunning. First of all, he must defeat Theophilus, the bishop, in his support of Isidore. Many prominent men in Constantinople were in favor of John, and, knowing Theophilus and his opposition to John, they were putting on paper accusations against this bishop of Alexandria, whose character, as we have remarked, was distinctly open to attack. These they handed round to persons of importance in the city, among them to the Imperial Chamberlain. Eutropius saw his opportunity; he handed the papers to Theophilus himself, with the direct question: Which would he choose, to consecrate John for Constantinople or to face trial on these written charges? Theophilus, greatly alarmed by this onset, did not hesitate; with his own hands he would consecrate John.

This settled, Eutropius had to get their priest away from his people in Antioch without arousing another riot there. It would be extremely difficult, if not impossible, he was sure, for John to leave if his going should be made known, if they heard that they were to yield him to Constantinople. All was arranged in that city; clergy and people had approved John's election; the Emperor had confirmed it; his consent had been forwarded to Asterius, Count of the East, who lived in Antioch. At once, as soon as he received instruction, Asterius summoned John to his house; the Count, so his messenger said, wished to see him on a matter of great importance. John arrived; promptly, carrying no baggage except the little which his friends could provide, he was placed in a carriage and sent in all secrecy on his way to Constantinople. There Theophilus celebrated for him the ritual of consecration, and on February 26, 398, saw him enthroned as Patriarch. But through all the years that John was bishop of Constantinople Theophilus was his enemy.

John Chrysostom, so called from his "golden mouth," his fame as preacher, had been born of noble parentage in Antioch, and as a young man had given his energy to studies philosophic and rhetorical. Then had come a day when he realized "how toilsome and how unrighteous was life for those who spent it in the courts of law" (so Socrates wrote in the fifth century). John wanted quiet. Together with friends of his he had abandoned "a profession which looked only for gain in this world." He had turned to theology as a pupil of Meletius, Patriarch of Antioch; he had received Christian baptism and had attended the classes of the learned Diodorus, priest of the same city. During this time of study he was ordained lector, thus receiving the first office leading to the priesthood.

Eventually, however, this had not satisfied him, and he had gone off to try monastic discipline in the mountains near Antioch.

Again he had read much in theology and sacred history; in search of even deeper solitude he had lived two years in a cave, spending his nights in prayer and study, existing so far as possible without food, sleep, or warmth. This, of course, had brought complete breakdown, and he had returned to Antioch, to recover his health, to be ordained as deacon, and in 386, it would seem, as priest by Flavian, the good and devoted Patriarch of Antioch. He had remained there about twelve years, working devotedly for its citizens, holding firmly his custom of self-denial and simplicity, writing book after book and trying to live according to the thought of his *On the Priesthood* (P.G. xlviii, 680f.):

"He who prays to God for the whole city, and why do I say city? nay, rather for all on earth, pleading that God be merciful to the sins of all, not only of the living but also of those departed hence, what kind of a man, I ask you, must he be? . . .

"As one to whom the whole world is entrusted, as a Father of all, so the priest comes to God, asking that all the wars of the world be quenched, that tumults die down, that peace and prosperity abide, that swiftly the evils which beset us all, in public, in private, be done away. . . . And when he calls upon the Holy Spirit, when he offers the dread Sacrifice and holds in his hands the Lord of all, where, in what order shall we place him? What purity, what sense of his Office, shall we ask of him?"

Now he preached in his cathedral and he walked the streets of Constantinople, courteous to the noble and the wealthy, full of kindness and sympathy for those troubled by sickness, by poverty, by sin. Crowds every Sunday and feast day listened in wonder to the words which probed their inmost knowledge of themselves. Especially the lower classes, the simple and the poor, felt that here was one who understood denial and difficulty.

Among the enthusiastic was Eudoxia. As the Emperor Arcadius held his Imperial working in regard to matters of the Church, so did the Empress, both on her own account and through her influence over him. Eudoxia was religious by nature, and if not through her father, Bauto, the barbarian Frank, at least in the family of Marsa she had been taught the Catholic faith.

She therefore zealously supported John. It was the custom of Arian believers to gather by night on the eves of Sundays and other feasts at the gates of the city; there they would form two choirs and for hours stand singing hymns, choir answering choir verse by verse; the hymns, so Socrates writes, "were composed to suit Arian heretics." At dawn they would march, still singing, through the streets of Constantinople, then go out from its gates to an open place in which they would hold their service of prayer. Now and again they interrupted their sacred song to mock the orthodox Catholics: "Where," they would cry, "Where are they who hold that the One Power is three?"

John as bishop began to fear lest simple souls among his flock might be led astray into error of belief; for their sake he organized Catholic processions, also marching by night, with song declaring their creed. To further this work the Empress gave a gift of wax candles embedded in crosses of silver; kindled and carried by acolytes, these illuminated the march. She also ordered one of her attendants, Briso, skilled in singing, to arrange and instruct the choirs. This bold counter-step by John led to Arian jealousy, and finally to riot. One night Briso was hit in the face by a stone; even worse, several people from either side were killed. In his wrath Arcadius as Emperor forbade Arians to sing hymns in public.

Still more excitement had been aroused when the Empress herself was seen marching at the head of a multitude of John's congregation, carrying in her hands relics of martyrs which were being transferred from the Cathedral to the Church of St. Thomas the Apostle. Nine miles through hours of day and night she walked, for the church was on the outskirts of Constantinople, in Drypia. The bishop was delighted. From the pulpit of St. Thomas he spoke with characteristic candor (P.G. LXIII, 468):

"What can I say? Of what shall I speak? Of the power of the martyrs? Of the ardor of the city? Of the zeal of the Empress? Of the presence here of our rulers? Or of the shaming of the devil? Of the defeating of demons? . . .

"Women protected at home by their husbands, softer than melting wax, have left the shelter of their homes, to make this long pilgrimage on foot, vying in eagerness with the strongest men; and not only young women, but old women, too! Neither the delicacy which is their nature nor the luxury of their living nor the enormous crowd of tonight have kept them away. The Emperor and Empress themselves are here, forsaking chariots, attendants, body-guards, to mingle with all and sundry of their people. But why speak of women and princes? She herself, she who wears the diadem and is clothed in purple, not for a moment along all the long road would she be parted from the relics she bore! As a handmaid she has followed the holy martyrs, her hands around the casket and its veil. Trampling under foot all her human pride of majesty, in the midst of so vast a gathering of sightseers she has appeared, that woman on whom not one of the eunuchs that run to

and fro in the Imperial Palace may for a moment rest their eyes!"
(P.G. LXIII, 468f.).

John Chrysostom had been Patriarch of Constantinople for a
year, and Eudoxia had been Empress for nearly four, when tragedy
which was closely connected with both of them drew near Constantinople. It began with Eutropius; it ended with Gainas and it
did its evil work in the years 399–400.

From 396 onward Eutropius had been gaining power in Constantinople and with it hostility, even abhorrence, from its citizens.
They held him no man; his appearance was repulsive and his doings
were worse. Zosimus declares that the very thought of any man
nearer in power to the Emperor than himself was intolerable to
Eutropius, the Imperial Chamberlain; in fact he worked to remove any one from his path who held high authority or prominent
position. Among these was one Timasius who had long been commander in the army and had fought in many battles with marked
success. Eutropius heard constantly of his great and growing fame
and decided to work his ruin. In Laodicea, Syria, Timasius had
met by chance a man named Bargas. He was only a hawker of
sausages in the market, but he was amusing, ready with his
tongue, and a very pleasant companion. So Timasius took him away
from sausages, gave him a post in the army, and brought him to
Constantinople. He had no idea, of course, that Bargas had been
forbidden to enter its gates, as a criminal, one who had committed
dire offences against the law.

Bargas, indeed, was a shifty character, and Eutropius soon
discovered it to his satisfaction. Here was the tool with which to
get rid of Timasius. By dint of cunning suggestion of reward he
managed to persuade Bargas to bring forward and place before the
magistrates of Constantinople a charge of high treason, completely
false, against Timasius. Timasius was brought to trial, and the
Emperor himself presided over its proceedings; but he would not
pronounce judgment. All in the court maintained that it was disgraceful for a peddler of sausages, and a dishonest one at that, to
be the means of convicting an honored and famous general of the
Empire. Nevertheless Timasius was convicted, and condemned to
exile in a desert and barren land; no one ever set eyes upon him
again. Eutropius had won his case; but his mind was not yet at
peace. He must now remove from his path Bargas, who had also
received command in the army. One day, knowing well that
Bargas was away from home, Eutropius sent men whom he could
safely trust to talk secretly with his wife. She had no love for her
husband, and therefore she was easily persuaded to declare him

guilty of many grave crimes. At once, directly he heard that this had been done, Eutropius brought him to trial; he was condemned, and he received punishment held meet for him by those who feared Eutropius, Imperial Chamberlain.

Another trial engineered by this same jealous Chamberlain was that of Abundantius, a native of Scythia in Thrace. Honor had also come to him, including appointments as military general and consul-elect. Eutropius talked in private with the Emperor; the Emperor ordered him brought into Court; the unhappy victim was found guilty by his judges and sent to far-off Phoenicia. There he spent the remaining years of his life. No wonder that Zosimus could say: "Eutropius, drunken with wealth, believing in himself as his imagination pictured him, one lifted beyond the clouds, kept in his service men of almost every race, men who looked curiously into whatever was on foot, who learned each man's standing and fortune; and everything they learned made Eutropius even richer than before."

Nor was Stilicho exempt from his envy. According to Zosimus, in 397–398 Eutropius was secretly encouraging Gildo, a rebel against the government of Roman Africa, which was held by the West. Through Gildo's rebellion Roman Africa passed from the West to possession by the East, and a sharp division followed between Italy and Constantinople. Stilicho, as master of the West, was filled with anxiety; ships no longer came from Africa to Italy, laden with corn; there was hunger and threat of famine. Claudian wrote in anguished verse:

> This, amid many wailing calamities of Italy, ages of war, did Fabius and brave Marcellus do for me, Italy, that Gildo might gather wealth? To drink pure poison we forced fierce Syphax; savage Jugurtha we dragged, broken by Metellus, into Marius' power—And shall Gildo hold Numidia?
>
> *De Bello Gildonico,* I, 87ff.

But the rebellion was finally defeated by Stilicho, working through Mascezel, Gildo's own brother; on the last day of July, 398, Gildo died by violence, either executed by his pursuers, or strangled by his own hand in despair. Claudian's verse turned from misery to joy: the "south," by which he meant Africa, was now restored to the Empire of the West, and the two Imperial brothers, Honorius and Arcadius, were once again united in harmony and peace.

In the same year Stilicho became father-in-law of Honorius, and the resentment of Eutropius, Imperial Chamberlain, grew hotter. The year, however, brought him not only envy but also success, and twofold. He himself went forth as soldier to reinforce the campaign against the Huns who were troubling the Empire; in 398, as Claudian wrote in scorn, he "returned as victor": words literally true. Second, he was elected consul for 399; an event which horrified Rome and was received with mockery in Constantinople. It brought from Claudian some memorable lines:

> All omens have yielded to a eunuch consul; shame to earth and heaven! Robed, city by city, a proud old woman, he dishonors this year's fame.
>
> *In Eutropium,* I, 8ff.

And now begins the story of his fall. A soldier named Tribigild, of Gothic barbarian origin, a native of Scythia in the diocese of Thrace, had won high praise as ally of the Romans in their wars; he had turned to them as Gainas had turned, seeking promotion. Early in 399 through this hope he had called at the house of Eutropius in Constantinople to congratulate him on his consulship. His words were most respectful, but to his surprise he had been coldly received, even with contempt. His pride had been bitterly offended.

Shortly afterward he was commanding an army in Phrygia, Asia Minor, under order to defend for the Empire cities attacked by barbarians. There his discontent burst into action. The situation was favorable; his soldiers were, like himself, barbarian Goths, and they had encamped among Gothic settlers, allowed by Theodosius the Great to make their homes in Phrygia. Now, in 399, he gave the word: one and all might rise in revolt against the Empire of the East. He succeeded. Far and wide destruction spread, as raids increased in violence. Eutropius, appalled at the news, did all in his power to bring the rebellion to an end without open force. Quickly he offered Tribigild that promotion, that endowment, which at Constantinople he had refused to give. With no success; at last, acting as ever for the Emperor Arcadius, he ordered two generals to Asia Minor for its defence against Tribigild and his rage. They were Gainas, the Goth whom we have seen leading soldiers of the East on their way to murder Rufinus, and one Leo, a man of no skill or character who owed his military rank to Eutropius, his patron and friend.

Gainas held both influence and efficiency; but he, like Tribigild, hated Eutropius, bitterly jealous of his power over the Emperor. Secretly he shared also Tribigild's rebellious mind. So, once within Phrygia, he allowed plundering and devastation to continue; now and then he sent the rebels support from his own troops.

At the same time he forwarded reports concerning Tribigild to Arcadius at Constantinople, pretending all loyalty to the Roman Empire.

From Phrygia, now ravaged and ruined, Tribigild marched south into Pisidia and on to Pamphylia, gathering fresh recruits; there at last he met serious resistance. One Valentine, a man of spirit and some knowledge of military tactics, called upon his fellow-citizens in the town of Selge, farmers and men of all trades and occupations, to go out with him against these traitors who were destroying Roman lands. They came, and he led them into ambush, awaiting, high on a hill, their first sight of the Gothic rebels as they marched along a path far below. Word had come that Tribigild and his force were to march that way; the path was only a winding trail, known as "the snail." Directly they appeared and came into position, Valentine and his company hurled boulders and huge stones upon their heads. Many were killed at once; others plunged to their death, hurtling downward to drown in the swamps lying below.

Tribigild himself escaped, only to meet peril equally acute. Men from other parts of Pamphylia, following the bold example of Valentine, caught him and many others in a trap; they found themselves between two rivers, Melas and Eurymedon, unable to cross either. In his despair Tribigild somehow contrived to send a call for aid to Gainas.

It was received and answered; Tribigild was rescued. Yet not without fierce fighting, in which Leo, who had also come to Tribigild's support, was killed. Tribigild himself survived for a while, and then death removed him also from the scene.

Gainas, however, lived to bring trouble upon the Empire. His jealous hatred of Eutropius had reached its height. Had not this miserable eunuch been named by the Emperor Arcadius as consul? The fall of Eutropius was entirely necessary, he held, for the welfare of the East.

Therefore, as one desiring its good fortune, while Tribigild still lived, he sent word to Constantinople. Tribigild was indeed guilty of revolt, he acknowledged, again picturing himself as conscientiously loyal. Nothing, he warned Arcadius, would bring Tribigild into due obedience but the deposing of Eutropius by Imperial edict; this unworthy Chamberlain therefore must meet his doom, richly deserved.

The Emperor received this report and believed it sincere; he knew nothing of secret treachery, of rebellion, in the carefully concealed acts of Gainas. Whether, alone and unsupported, it would have reached its end in the fall of Eutropius we cannot say; but it obtained assistance in the Court of Constantinople from an unexpected source, the Empress Eudoxia.

Here, once again, the fault lay with Eutropius himself. One day in a fit of temper during an audience the Imperial Chamberlain, who had himself brought Eudoxia to her throne, foolishly and very rudely reminded her Imperial Majesty of that fact: "I, who brought you here, will very soon throw you out!" Eudoxia at once burst into rage. Catching up in her arms the two babies she had by this time borne to Arcadius, she rushed to his Imperial Chamber and poured out to him a tale of deadly insult offered her. Faced with this, amid a stream of tears from her and loud wailing from the infants, the Emperor capitulated. An order went out from his hand for the stripping from Eutropius of every office and every honor which he held. It was August, 399.

Naturally Eutropius was terrified. In fear for his very life he fled for refuge to the Cathedral of Saint Sophia. There was irony in this impulse; he himself, "the first eunuch ever appointed consul by the Emperor, in his desire that no accused man should be saved from punishment, had persuaded Arcadius to enact a law that all who rushed to seek sanctuary in the hope of evading punishment should promptly be dragged forth." So wrote Socrates.

The next Sunday, while the wretched Eutropius was still crouching under the altar of the Cathedral, John Chrysostom, bishop of Constantinople, held silent with fear a congregation which filled his Cathedral; he spoke from its high pulpit that all might hear every word he said. Some of those who listened blamed the preacher for the hard words which came from him; most of them had little or no pity for Eutropius.

John, indeed, was most anxious to save the life of the unhappy man cowering before him, to give help in any way possible. Yet he could but speak the truth. He knew the sins and vices of Eutropius; he knew how common in Constantinople these same sins and vices were. It was not for him to pass this tragedy over lightly, without due warning to all whom he must guide and guard.

With these words then, he began (P.G. LII, 391, 393f.):

"Always, in very truth, but now especially, it is the moment to say: 'Vanity of vanities, all things are vanity.' Where now is that brilliant robe of the consulship? Where those flaming torches? Where is the clapping of hands, where the dances, the banquets and festal gatherings? Where the wreaths of victory, the widespread hanging curtains? Where the roar of the city, those shouts of 'Hail, Eutropius!' in the chariot race, the stream of congratulation from those who went to see that sight?

"All, all are gone. A sudden storm of wind has torn down the leaves, has shown the tree naked to our eyes, left shaken from its roots . . . Where now are those falsely dyed friends? Where the parties and the feasts? Where the swarm of parasites, the unwatered wine served throughout the day, the multiple craft of cooks, the courtiers who tried with all their might to please this lordly statesman?"

Later on, the bishop changed his tone.

"I say these things, not to cast his trouble in his teeth, not to bring insult upon him, but to soften your hearts, to bring you to pity him; to judge his present misery punishment enough. There are many of our people so inhuman that they think evil of us who have allowed him sanctuary here . . . Truly one ought to give glory to God that through utter necessity and need He has brought this man to know the power and the mercy of the Church!"

But Gainas was urging the Emperor to put Eutropius to death. Soldiers of the Imperial service came to drag him from the Cathedral; they swore that if he came quietly, Constantinople would not see him die. He yielded, reassured, and he was taken to the island of Cyprus. Before long, so it was said, accusation once more rose against him, that he had insulted Majesty of the Crown by wearing insignia proper and lawful for none but the Emperor. His guards removed him to Chalcedon, a town in Asia Minor on the Thracian Bosporus, opposite Constantinople. Brought before a court of judges, presided over by Aurelian, the Praetorian Prefect, he was condemned and swiftly beheaded on the block of execution. There were various versions of the charges which caused his death; no doubt his crime was stated as treason. But his captors consoled their consciences in regard to that promise of life which they had given him; Chalcedon was not Constantinople.

It was autumn in 399. Eudoxia enjoyed her triumph; on the ninth of January, 400, she was formally crowned Augusta, Empress in her own right, and her portrait was sent throughout the Empire of the East: a rare honor.

Gainas meanwhile had steadily increased in power, in ambition to succeed Eutropius, even to wrest from the Emperor himself what he willed. His camp, strong and wide in its barbarian force, was settled near Chalcedon, and fear was in the hearts of the people of Constantinople. Would Gainas bring his army across that narrow stretch of water? What might happen, not only to Constan-

tinople, but to the towns of the Empire of the East in Asia Minor
and along the coast of the Black Sea?

It was still late in 399 when Arcadius, after asking advice from
his counselors, decided that the only thing he could do was to
grant Gainas whatever he might demand. A meeting was arranged
for this purpose in the Church of Saint Euphemia, Martyr, just
outside Chalcedon. Arcadius was docile, and Gainas, his rebel
soldier, was ruthless; no shadow of secrecy now covered his mind.
He was completely frank in demanding that the Emperor hand over
to him as captives three men of high standing, all friends of the
Empress: Aurelian, who had not only been consul but was now
Praetorian Prefect in the East, an honor which Gainas had ardently
desired; Saturninus, whose wife Castricia was constantly at Court;
and one John, from whom, according to Zosimus, the Emperor had
no secrets and in whom the Empress felt an interest which was
more than friendly.

Arcadius, then, faced with the choice of yea or nay, took the
easier step of consent. Constantinople was horrified. Surely these
men, so needed by all, would lose their lives? The Empress could
not rest day or night through anger and anxiety; of course Gainas
would remove them from his path to power. At last a deputation of
citizens approached the bishop, John Chrysostom. Would he himself go to the military camp of Gainas and do all he could to save
the three, now prisoners?

John went; we have a narrative, said to be in his own words,
which tells us of his work. He is represented here as addressing the
people of Constantinople after his journey to Chalcedon (P.G.
LII, 413ff.):

'At long last I am again here with you, beloved. My absence
has not been due to indifference or lack of courage. It has been
caused by keeping down tumults; by calming the surging waves of
rebellion, subduing the stormy tempest; by pulling men, shipwrecked and sinking, into the peace of harbor. And why? Because
I am one and the same Father for all, and I must care both for
those who stand upright and those who have fallen. . . .

"For this reason I was absent from you for a time, exhorting,
praying, entreating those in power that this calamity pass away.
And when this sullen anger ended, again I came back to you, you
who are in safety, sailing in deep calm. I went to them to banish
the storm; I have returned to you that there may be no storm. . . .

"For all things now are full of clamor and confusion; nothing
but rocks and dangerous crags, dark depths of sea. All is fear and
peril, suspicion, quivering terror and anguish. No man trusts his

fellow; each is afraid of his neighbor. Swiftly the crisis comes upon us. . . ."

The bishop had wrung from Gainas a promise that Aurelian, Saturninus, and John should not be executed as criminals; they were, however, to be sent into exile. The Empress Eudoxia felt little comfort; many, including Castricia, shared her mind. They had hoped for greater things from this journey of John Chrysostom. Had he done all that he could, they wondered? Had not the Emperor assured Gainas in their meeting that the office of Master of Military Services was his as long as he should desire it? And exile, for statesmen and friends, had been received in return!

Nor was Gainas content. True, he had promised Arcadius that he would keep peace with him, but that he had never meant to do. He must act at once and surprise Constantinople. So he crossed the Bosporus with his great army of Goths; he entered and occupied the city in the spring of 400.

There he as promptly set to work. First, he would make Arcadius and his counselors show him respect. It was not fitting that he, granted by the Emperor rank as Military Commander, should be forced as an Arian heretic to go outside the walls of the city for worship in church! Not one of the churches in Constantinople at this time was allowed to Arian believers. Now he made formal demand to the Emperor that a Catholic church in the city be given for their use.

Arcadius answered that he would consider the request. He then summoned his bishop to an audience.

John obeyed the call and in private gave Arcadius vigorous advice, as Theodoret tells:

"Make no such concession, Your Majesty," he said; "do not order that what is holy be given to dogs. Never will I be guilty of casting out those who teach and sing the Divine Word of God; never will I deliver His temple into the hands of them that blaspheme. Do not fear that barbarian; call us both, Gainas and me, and listen quietly to what is said. I will curb his tongue!"

At the audience John brought forward the law issued by Theodosius the Great: he had forbidden Arian worship in public within the walls of the city. The law was still standing, John insisted. Arcadius had to yield, and wrath drove Gainas from request to violence.

Now he decided to make open attack. Throughout the city there was rumor of coming trouble. Did not a comet, a sure herald of disaster, show its long tail of baleful light in the hours of darkness? Word came one day that Gainas and his Goths had raided the banks of Constantinople, hoping to seize much money. Happily those in charge had heard of his intention by secret message; they had hidden their wealth. Shortly afterward an attempt was made at night to set fire to the Palace; this also failed. And now it was the turn of the Goths to be afraid; the soldiers sent to attack the Palace returned with dreadful news. On their way in the darkness of night they had caught a vision of a multitude of men, seemingly warriors immensely tall. Most certainly it must be an army, entering the city to defend its people! "Nonsense," said Gainas; "I know well how few soldiers the Emperor has here in Constantinople. Nearly all his force has been sent to protect from our strength those cities of Asia!"

But when the next night Gainas heard the same story he went out himself, to see with his own eyes this vast host of armed warriors. It alarmed him almost as much as it had his men; he concluded that Arcadius had recalled from Asia his scattered troops for the guarding of Constantinople.

Socrates and Sozomen both tell of this vision of fear, caught by Gainas; Socrates explains it as a host of angels sent by Divine providence for the protection of the city.

By this time summer had arrived; it was July 400. Gainas had been in occupation six months and had won nothing. What was the good of staying? He decided to leave, at any rate for a while, and declared himself possessed by an evil spirit, in grave need of prayer. In reality he was conscious of failure, and failure prophesied defeat; he went to seek security in a church of St. John the Baptist, situated in the Hebdomon, a harbor on the coast seven miles from Constantinople. A church for him, as for Eutropius, meant sanctuary. When he left, his army divided; some men also started on their way out, others stayed where they had been stationed, inside the walls.

Those who had decided to go carried with them their swords and spears carefully hidden in earthenware jars and chairs made for women. They hoped to get through the gates safely; the guards would suppose that the jars contained provisions for the journey. But the guards were cautious. They discovered the weapons and forbade their export. In sudden anger the Gothic soldiers fell upon them. In the fight guards were killed; citizens joined the struggle; the struggle became a riot which spread throughout Constantinople, as both Goths, and Imperial men of arms and civilians, all weary of this long occupation, fought to win, once for all time. The Emperor declared Gainas a public enemy; the barbarians in the city were, he ordered, to be killed at sight. Many Goths were left lying dead in the streets, slain by the fury of Roman inhabitants; those who escaped fled for shelter to "the Church of Goths" where Gothic converts from Arianism held their services of worship. But by this time nothing could stop the rage of their enemies, so long held by their power. They leaped forward to lock and bar the doors of the church, so that none of those within could escape; they then threw flaming wood and waste upon its roof. All shut up within were burned to death.

Gainas heard of this as he clung to sanctuary, and swiftly he prepared to leave, hoping to reach Asia and his Gothic supporters there. Through Thrace he somehow made his way, joined here and there by soldiers who acknowledged his command. At last they came to the Chersonesus, and the Hellespont lay before them. If only they could cross that water, Gothic rebellion against the Empire could be renewed in Asia, they fervently believed. But how to get across? They improvised rough rafts by lashing timbers together and embarked. In vain; the rafts had no means of control, no steering gear; a violent storm rose and they drifted, tossed in all directions. Moreover, Arcadius by this time had sent an army after them, commanded by one Fravitta, also a barbarian by origin, but zealously loyal to Rome. He was well provided with ships which pursued the rafts and sank them as they swayed, drowning their terrified crews.

Gainas again was fortunate; he managed to reach Asia. But there his own fate met him. He fell in with a horde of wild Huns. Their chieftain, Uldin, decided promptly that here was a chance to slay the enemy of Arcadius and win his goodwill. He bade his barbarians fight with all force; Gainas saw his few followers fall and soon he himself lay dead. It was December 400, and Uldin sent his head, carefully processed in salt, as a Christmas gift to the Emperor in Constantinople.

Fravitta had not pursued the fugitive Gainas. Victory was his, and he saw no reason for further persecution. Eunapius of Sardis in his *History* gave fervent praise to this young general; like Eunapius himself, Fravitta was a pagan, devoted to his ancient gods. Eunapius also declared him as honest as he was religious: "he held the man, who said one thing and hid another in his mind, an enemy as evil as the gates of hell."

Full of joy, then, Fravitta came back to Constantinople. He did not know that most of its citizens scorned him as disloyal and treacherous; he had allowed escape, they were saying, to Gainas as one Goth, one barbarian, to another, for the sake of the race they held in common. The Emperor Arcadius, however, honored Fravitta by award of the consulship for 401; in that same year he was put to death as a traitor. Feeling against German barbarians was running high in the Imperial capital.

We return in 401 to the Empress Eudoxia, who had steadily been increasing her power and influence. Three daughters had now been born to her: in June 397, Flaccilla, who seems to have died at an early age; Pulcheria, in January 399; Arcadia, in April 400. Now in 401 she was expecting another child and anxiously hoping for a son. On April the tenth, 401, the birth of an heir to the Crown was announced with great rejoicing, and Eudoxia in her own joy marked the occasion by a signal impulse of generosity.

At the time two prelates were visiting Constantinople, both from Palestine: Porphyrius, bishop of Gaza, in the south, and his metropolitan, John, Archbishop of Caesarea, a port on the coast, well known to history. Palestine was under Byzantine rule, and his Archbishop had brought Porphyrius to the Empire's capital city with eager hope of aid; the bishop of Gaza was in great trouble. He was a devoted Father in God, but his city was full of heathen who were constantly molesting, hindering, and generally making life miserable for the few Christians it held. These had no church of their own and no money with which to build one.

So Porphyrius came with John of Caesarea to the Emperor and Empress to tell his need. Arcadius listened in silence; then for once gave his own decision, in the negative. The pagans of Gaza paid high taxes to the Imperial treasury; a favor to the Christians, especially the raising of a Christian church, might indeed offend them; they scorned those who scorned their faith. Eudoxia, however, felt differently; the Imperial Court, she decided, could not refuse to help these harassed people of her own calling in religion. The matter was left undecided; the Emperor refused to take it up again.

If the *Life of Porphyrius* by his deacon, Marcus, tells the truth, Eudoxia won her will in all peace by a bit of jesting, carried out by her instructions on the day of her son's baptism in the Cathedral at Constantinople. A day or two before the ceremony was to take place she told the two bishops, Porphyrius and John, to draw up a petition describing in detail the necessity of funds for the building of a Christian church in Gaza and to bring it with them to the Cathedral. As distinguished visitors they would of course be given a prominent place in the procession.

The little boy was duly baptized in the name of Theodosius, his grandfather. While this procession of prelates, Emperor, and nobles of the Court, magnificent in vestments, robes and military decorations, white, purple, and gold, was proceeding down the aisle on its way out, those of the crowded congregation who stood near suddenly saw Porphyrius of Gaza move forward toward the baby, carried high in the arms of a most important minister of the Palace. Bending over the child, Porphyrius called aloud, as Eudoxia had instructed him: "We have a petition for Your Piety!" meaning Theodosius Junior. With this he put the paper into the hand of the child's bearer, who received it, looked at it for a moment, and, as he, too, had been told to do, put his hand under the baby's head, made it nod as if in assent, and himself cried to all the people there: "His Magnificence commands that this petition be granted!"

Arcadius could not but laugh. It was a happy day for him and he yielded agreement. The Empress was delighted with her success, and Bishop Porphyrius left for home laden with far more treasure than he actually needed for his Christians.

Early in 401 John Chrysostom had been called to Ephesus on the coast of Asia Minor, an important see of the Empire, to superintend election of a bishop for its clergy and people. Much that was wrong was going on there and in other parts of Imperial Asia: sins against the Church; simony, holy office gained by bribes, dishonesty of various sort, negligence, lethargy in the face of heathen and heretics, all had spread far and wide. John was away from Constantinople some four or five months; during this time he felt compelled in duty to depose six bishops in Asia from their sees.

Naturally when he returned home he left behind him seeds of bitter anger and hatred which were to live on and bear harvest in later years. He returned, moreover, to trouble in his own city. This rose from two sources, general and individual.

Long before he left for Ephesus in 401 he had been keenly aware that feeling in regard to his sermons, preached every Sunday in his Cathedral, was sharply divided. The simple people loved his words, as they had always done since 398; the rich and aristocratic, those who gave its gay and luxurious character to society in Constantinople, had by 401 turned from admiration of his eloquence to resentment of his feelings and action. John as bishop was essentially the same man who had lived as hermit in the mountains, as priest in Antioch. Self-denial, not indulgence; austerity, not ostentation; culture of the soul and mind, not of the body: these formed his own practice, and these appeared in his preaching.

Some of his monks and clergy knew that he spoke directly to them when he bade his hearers be content in their own homes and manner of living, not to feast as parasites at rich men's tables. He who follows a trail of savory smoke, he told them, soon finds himself in the fire of intoxication. Their extravagance in public matters he also roundly rebuked; far too much money, he said, was spent in the Church for unnecessary purposes, for comfort, for display; they should give all they possibly could to further the building of hospitals and hostels for the sick and poor. Against public shows and spectacles in the Circus of Constantinople, rough, boisterous, lewd and obscene, he spoke to all vehemently, especially when his flock had gathered there on a day set apart for vigil and prayer. Among the monks who were angry at his censure there was one Isaac; he was a leader of those who called their bishop John a tyrant and said evil things against him to humbler folk. Men thought John uncharitable and morose because he was never seen at banquets and other social meetings; his friends in defence declared that his long abstinence in the mountains and the illness which followed it had limited in the strictest way the food which he could take.

But none took keener offence at his words of rebuke than the women of his congregation; and indeed his words were bold and strong as he looked at the wealthy audience before him, dressed in the height of fashion:

"It is not so hard when you don't see beautiful young women as it is to control yourself when you look at them. He who does not see the comely sight will be free from yearning. So when you see a lovely girl and you feel trouble coming on, don't look any more! 'But how, you say, can I do this?' Well, you can, if you realize that you are looking at phlegm and blood and perishable flesh. Then again you argue: 'The flower of that sight is radiant!' And I agree with you, that nothing is more radiant than flowers on earth; yet they, too, rot and waste away!" (P.G. LXIII, 658f.).

On clothes

"If, then, I tell you that rich men and women are really the more naked the more clothes they have on them, do not hate me for it. . . . How do I mean this? Well, when those silken mantles and precious stones disappear and are lost, then all of these millionaires will be seen dressed only in the robes of their virtues or their sins. And when the poor are clothed in great glory, then the rich, naked and unseemly, will be carried off to due penalty in prison" (P.G. LX, 196f.).

On luxuries of the table

"First, let me speak against women. There is nothing more disgraceful than a woman given to delicacies, nothing more distasteful than a woman given to drink. . . . But if she would be ashamed at such conduct, if she keeps silence, if she has learned how to blush and to speak properly, to fast instead of feasting, then her beauty is twice as great. . . .

"I lay down no rule for fasting, for no one here would listen. But I forbid an overdose of pleasure, I cut out luxury, for your own good. . . . What next? Well, if you want to live delightfully, then give to the poor; invite the Christ as your guest, and after your dinner you will still have delight" (P.G. LX, 207).

On weddings

"Let us not then dishonor marriages with devilish pomp and ceremony. . . . If you will drive away the devil from your marriage feasts, if you will banish those songs reeking of sex, those effeminate melodies, those disorderly dances, those obscene words, with roar of noise, floods of laughter and all the rest of the filthy customs of today, then you will draw to your feast the holy servants of Christ, and Christ with His Mother will come to your wedding. . . .

"I know how annoying and troublesome I seem to some people when I put forward these words against the customs which you have held so long. That doesn't worry me one whit! I don't need your favor, but I do need to be of use to you. . . . Custom is no excuse for sin" (P.G. LI, 210).

On women as illustrated by Eve

"Listen carefully to me. The woman says: 'The serpent deceived me.' Adam does not say: 'The woman deceived me,' but: 'She gave to me and I ate.' To be deceived by a human being of your own kind is not the same as being deceived by a reptile subject to your power. The former case is deception actual and real. . . . Again, it was not said of Adam that he declared 'the tree good for food,' but of the woman; that she ate the food and gave it to her husband.

"Therefore he did not sin, as one overcome by appetite; he was only persuaded by the woman. The woman taught him once for all, and upset everything. It is for this reason that Paul says: 'Let her not teach.'

"What, then, about other women, if this was Eve's doing? Yes, indeed; they are all weak and frivolous. . . . For we are told here, not that Eve alone suffered from deception, but that 'Woman' was deceived. The word 'Woman' is not to be applied to one, but to every woman. All feminine nature has thus fallen into error. . . .

"Then, is there any hope at all for women? Yes, says Paul. Well, what? Why, through the children borne by them. . . . God, you women, has given you this starting-point for salvation: the rearing of children. Not through herself alone will a woman be saved, but through others" (P.G.LXII, 545).

"What does blessed Paul say? 'Let a woman learn in silence.' What does this mean? He says: 'Let not a woman raise her voice in church.' In his Epistle to the Corinthians he wrote: 'It is a shocking thing that a woman should address the congregation.' Why this? Because the law has placed women in subjection. In another place he says: 'If women want to learn anything, let them ask their husbands at home' (I Corinthians, XIV, 35).

"In his time women through this teaching remained silent. Now, however, when women gather together there rises great uproar, loud screaming, much argument, and nowhere with as great noise as here. One can see them all talking away vehemently; as never talk rises in the forum of our city or in its Baths" (P.G. LXII, 543).

Over these words, and many more of their kind, the aristocratic ladies of Constantinople seethed with indignation, especially those who were close friends of the Emperor. There were Marsa and Castricia; the one, widow of Promotus, a noted general, and the other, wife of Saturninus, of equal rank in the army, were both constantly in the Palace, telling Eudoxia what they had heard. There was also Eugraphia, the center and focus of this rebellion, in whose house, of noble architecture and exquisite furnishing, angry men of wealth, clergy of the Church, and women of social standing gathered to talk and to plan.

As time went on the Patriarch John Chrysostom, without a thought of harming or hurting anyone, in his honest and simple desire to do his duty as father of his people, made other enemies, one after another. Naturally the resentment mentioned above made a favorable atmosphere for this; visitors to Constantinople heard of the talk always simmering in secret.

Among those who stirred it were three bishops. In his Dialogue on the *Life of Saint John Chrysostom,* Palladius, bishop of Helenopolis in Bithynia, tells that Acacius, since 378 bishop of Beroea in Syria, about 401 came on a visit to Constantinople and found no comfortable lodging in the city. This annoyed him greatly, and he remarked to his companions that John, its Patriarch, had shown him no hospitality, and that "he himself would cook a dish for John!" The story may not be true, but Acacius for some cause in later days was to serve the Patriarch hostility enough.

The second was Antiochus, bishop of Ptolemais in Phoenicia. He was renowned for his eloquence and his knowledge of rhetoric. He, too, came to Constantinople, to gather there many pupils and make much money. Happy in his winnings he returned home to Syria; but he took with him also many rumors and much comment concerning Constantinople's bishop.

Not long afterward Severian, bishop of Gabala, a city in Syria, heard of the success of this fellow-prelate and decided that a visit to the capital city would suit him well. He, also, was experienced in public speaking. Why not follow the example of Antiochus and enrich himself in that wealthy place? He came, and was hospitably received by John, a welcome which he repaid by extravagant compliments and ready assent to everything which John said. As he did the same for everyone of high station whom he met, Severian became very popular. He was entertained by the leading men of the city and their wives; often he was called to Court; the Emperor and, especially, the Empress, enjoyed his visits.

He was still in Constantinople, giving lectures to crowded audiences, when in the late winter of 400–401 John Chrysostom was obliged to start for Ephesus. Before he left, he entrusted the care of his Cathedral and his diocese in joint responsibility to Severian, who was to preach in his place, and to Serapion, archdeacon of the see, who was to administer all necessary business.

As we have seen, John encountered much trouble in Ephesus and others parts of Asia. His return was delayed, and he was absent from Constantinople more than three months; we may well believe that it was Severian who baptized the infant Theodosius. When at last the Patriarch came home, from many of his people he heard how wonderful this bishop of Gabala was, in his sermons, in his conversation, in his courtesy.

But Serapion, the archdeacon, had a very different tale to tell. As one belonging to the diocese of John, he had considered that in the Patriarch's absence he had the prior right of administration. Severian might preach as much as he liked, but Serapion was going to govern. Severian as bishop had thought otherwise. Bitter quarrel had grown up between them; Serapion had refused to pay Severian the respect due his office—so at least Severian declared—and the bishop was full of resentment. At the same time Serapion declared that Severian was heretic in his talk.

In this difficulty John thought that the best he could do was to thank this bishop of Gabala for all he had done in Constantinople, and done so well, and to suggest with all tact and humanity that it must be time for him to return to his see; his people must be longing to hear him preach again. After all, Serapion was archdeacon of the diocese and Severian was only a visitor, absent from his own work.

Severian at once suspected that he was being dismissed un-
wanted; he departed, but in wrath. Then Eudoxia the Empress
heard he had gone, and she flew into a temper. Quickly she called
John to her presence and blamed him severely; Severian was a
special friend of hers; John had treated him very rudely; she had
already despatched her most trusty and able attendant to catch him
on his way and bring him back.

Severian came back, rejoicing and triumphant; for a while
there was distinct coolness between him and the Patriarch. John was
human; he had tried to settle dispute as wisely as he could. It was
Eudoxia, we are told, who brought about reconciliation. One day,
in the Church of the Holy Apostles at Constantinople, she appealed
to John, asking that he renew friendship with Severian. Promptly
he visited the bishop of Gabala to offer explanation, and Severian
accepted it, in words, at least. Both declared the matter closed and
both spoke pleasant words, each concerning the other, in addresses
to congregations at the Cathedral. It was hard for John, but he
meant what he said; Severian of Gabala never was to forget what
he held as insult.

No one, however, was to prove hostile to this Patriarch of Constantinople as fiercely and unchangeably as Theophilus, Patriarch
of Alexandria, who so unwillingly had consecrated him bishop instead of his own priest and candidate, Isidore.

In this story of enmity we find a prominent place given to
monks who lived and prayed amid the desert land of Nitria in
Egypt. Their story tells of bitter persecution, of stern and cruel
working by Theophilus, and two reasons are given for this. One
is that the friendship of Theophilus for Isidore had in time turned
to intense dislike, that Isidore had sought refuge with these monks
in Nitria and had been received with warm hospitality. The other is
concerned with the doctrine taught by Origen of the third century,
a theologian known by name and work to all students in the Church.

Some of the Nitrian monks had visited Alexandria and naturally had discussed with its Patriarch the writings of Origen. Theophilus had of course read them; part he praised, much of their argument he rejected. In this the monks had ventured boldly to disagree.
Therefore they had not felt happy in talking with this learned
Patriarch; and when he had invited them to stay on in Alexandria
they had made it very clear that they preferred their desert cells.

So Theophilus had turned against them, his visitors, and their
brethren in Nitria. In 400 he had gathered at Alexandria a synod
in which he had gained condemnation both of the doctrine of
Origen and of its acceptance by these monks. He had not even

allowed them to appear for their defence. Three of their leaders he had excommunicated; he had obtained from civil authority a decree for the expulsion of Nitrian monks from Egypt; he had attacked and plundered their monasteries in the desert. Upon this many of them had fled to Palestine. Then Theophilus had written to its bishops to forbid giving of welcome or refuge in that land.

And therefore, probably in 401, some fifty of these Nitrian monks arrived in Constantinople to ask protection and support from its Emperor and from its Patriarch, John Chrysostom. At the head of this band of fugitives were four men, known to us from their stature and kinship as "The Four Tall Brothers."

John gave them kindly welcome, thinking that their trouble would be settled without delay; they were to say nothing about it, he told them, until he had written to his fellow-bishop, Theophilus. In the meantime he found for them lodging proper for their calling and arranged for them service of food and other necessities. In regard to matters spiritual, he asked advice from certain priests of Alexandria who happened to be staying in Constantinople. Did they know these monks? he asked. "We do know them," they answered promptly, "and they have suffered dire assault. But, Lord Bishop, with your permission we would advise you not to grant them fellowship of communion in your Church, lest you offend Theophilus. In all other ways be gracious to them; that is right for you in your office as bishop."

John followed this counsel, and the Nitrian monks declared to him that they were ready to cast anathema upon all false doctrine. He wrote to Theophilus, pleading with him as a fellow-bishop that he make peace with them; the Patriarch of Alexandria sent a flat refusal. Upon this the brethren from Egypt gave John a long written account of all that Theophilus had done, from Isidore down to their flight from Palestine. Again John wrote to the Patriarch: "These men are desperate; they even accuse you in writing. Do write and tell me what seems fitting and proper to do; they will not listen to me, and I have asked them to leave Constantinople." Now Theophilus wrote back in anger: "I suppose that you are not ignorant of the decree found among the Canons of Nicaea, forbidding a bishop to judge a dispute outside his own territory. But if you are ignorant, then learn it and stop writing accusations against us. For if I had to be judged, the judgment would properly come from bishops of Egypt, not from you, at a distance of seventy-five days journey from here!"

At this, John gave up, and decided to leave the question of these exiles and their fate alone. But they neither abandoned their course nor departed; they felt that in Constantinople, the capital city, lay their only hope. So they wrote out their story of persecution once again, and in great detail, declaring with all firmness their innocence of heresy. In Constantinople's Church of Saint John the Baptist, Martyr, they approached the Empress Eudoxia and presented to her this document of protest, addressed to her and to the Emperor. At the same time they implored her that Theophilus, whether he willed it or not, be summoned to Constantinople to face judgment in a synod presided over by John Chrysostom. Eudoxia promised that both Theophilus and all those who had joined him in these charges should be brought to account in an assembly of bishops.

Theophilus was duly summoned by Imperial script; but he did not arrive. Instead, he persuaded Epiphanius, bishop of Constantia in Cyprus, a prelate with a reputation for honorable character, to go to the capital and prepare the way for his arrival, should he ever decide to come. He knew that Epiphanius abhorred the doctrinal views of Origen; it had been through a suggestion made by him, Theophilus himself, that this bishop of Constantia had already called a Council for their condemnation in Cyprus.

Now, then, Theophilus carefully instructed him concerning his procedure at Constantinople. Epiphanius arrived there at the beginning of 403. He started his work by refusing the hospitality which John at once offered him in his own episcopal Palace; he went to stay in a private house. Next he called together bishops and other clergy then visiting Constantinople and read to them in solemn assembly a written denunciation of Origen's writings. It did not receive the assent for which he had hoped; many of those present refused to give it their signature when he passed it round.

Third, he absolutely refused to enter the Cathedral while its Patriarch was officiating, unless John first drove out the Nitrian monks from the city and with his own hand wrote his own condemnation of books written by Origen. To this John quietly answered that the whole matter of Origen must await the meeting of a General Council in Constantinople. Nor did he lose his episcopal temper when Epiphanius presumed, against canon law, to carry out ordinations in the churches of the city, outside his own ecclesiastical domain.

At last, however, when Epiphanius, who was old, it is fair to say, simple in mind, and foolishly delighted to be called to aid the Patriarch of Alexandria, decided to levy ban of excommunication against Dioscorus, the most distinguished of the Four Tall Brothers, and to pronounce censure against him himself, Patriarch of Constantinople, as one who was supporting the Nitrian heretics, John felt obliged to call him to order. He sent Serapion, his archdeacon, to Epiphanius with a message. Serapion found the bishop of Constantia in church, vested in pontifical array and about to begin his pronouncement. The archdeacon intervened just in time. "I come from the Patriarch," he said, before the bishop and his congregation, "and these are his words to you. Many things you are doing, Epiphanius, that are contrary to the rules of the Church. You have dared to carry out ritual of ordination in churches that are under my charge, without consulting me; on your own authority, you have celebrated Mass in my churches; you refused to come to a church of mine when I invited you, and now you are doing all these acts illegally in my episcopal see. Take care, Epiphanius! It may be that the people of Constantinople will rise in anger against you, and for your peril!"

Epiphanius, in a mingling of anger and fear, promptly took ship for his home in Cyprus. On the way he died, May 12, 403.

The bishop of Constantia had ceased to make trouble in the city. But because of him John once again had offended the Empress Eudoxia, who liked Epiphanius very well for his affable and respectful bearing. During his stay in Constantinople the Imperial heir to the throne, little Theodosius, had suddenly been taken ill; in great distress his mother had sent a message to the bishop, asking for his prayers. She was therefore indignant when she heard that he had left the city under shadow of rebuke and fear; frail in health, too, so frail that he had died on shipboard. This was the second time that a friend of hers, a friend of the Empress herself, had been driven away by John, and the fate of Epiphanius had been even more tragic than the shame brought upon Severian of Gabala.

Soon after Epiphanius had sailed from Constantinople, its Patriarch John, preaching in his Cathedral one Sunday, burst out into a torrent of words against women in general, and, so it seemed to some who were present, against one woman in particular: words so scathing and bitter that all were struck by wonder and surprise. Often they had heard him inveigh against the follies of the feminine sex, but never with scorn and wrath as on this morning. Naturally, as they streamed away from the doors, everyone was asking: What caused it? *Who* caused it?

We do not know. Socrates, the Byzantine historian, wrote: "After the departure of Epiphanius some people told that he had been moved to act against John by the Empress Eudoxia. And, as John was hot of temper and ready of tongue, he had at once in his preaching cast vituperation upon all women as a sex. But it was commonly thought that he had the Empress in mind when he spoke."

Next, among accusations put forward at a later time against John, it was stated that in one of his sermons he had called the Empress "a Jezebel." Moreover, the deacon Marcus in his *Life of Porphyrius* related another incident: a woman once said to John, so Marcus told, that the Empress Eudoxia had robbed her of land which her Imperial mind coveted. These two statements, placed together, recall to us the Jezebel who caused the death of Naboth the Jezreelite and gained possession of his vineyard (I Kings, c. 21). The truth, however, of neither statement is proved, and there is no certain evidence at all that John was thinking of Eudoxia in that sermon of his.

Nevertheless women friends of the Empress were not slow to suggest, even to declare, that the Patriach was hurling his words at her; they were happy to take revenge upon him in this easy way. He had, of course, mentioned no name; but Marsa, Castricia, and Eugraphia were all quite sure that he was insulting the Empress, and boldly they told her so. Their malicious work kindled into living flame the resentment which had long been smouldering within her. And the flame lived on, sinking only to rise in new vigor; from this time, the summer of 403, Eudoxia was the enemy of John Chrysostom of Constantinople, however much for the moment she had believed and declared herself his friend.

The way, therefore, was being paved for that other enemy of John, Theophilus of Alexandria. Theophilus was never to forgive John his hospitality to the Nitrian monks, those "heretics" who had dared to ask from Imperial authority that he, the Patriarch of Alexandria, be summoned to Constantinople for trial and judgment by a Council over which John Chrysostom was to preside.

There should be a synod, certainly; and its members should see, not himself but John, accused of offence against the Church. With all energy Theophilus set to work. He called prelates, whom he knew as hostile to John, to gather speedily in Chalcedon of Bithynia, on the Hellespont, opposite Constantinople; there he himself would meet them. Willingly and in great number they came; their leaders were Acacius of Beroea, Antiochus of Ptolemais, Severian of Gabala, and bishops of Asia whom John had deposed in 401. Also many others came at the call of the Emperor, who was pushed on to action by his wife.

The bishop of Chalcedon at the time was Cyrinus of Egypt, and he was noted for his dislike of John; the company assembled there enjoyed greatly his words of contempt: "impious, arrogant, utterly obstinate." Through an accident which left him lame he had to remain at Chalcedon when his fellow-prelates took ship for Constantinople. All except Theophilus; he decided to arrive alone and receive full honor in state. He was disappointed. No one of its clergy was at the harbor to welcome him when he arrived at the capital; they all knew that he had come for action against their Patriarch, and prudence, if not loyalty, kept them away. Only sailors from Alexandria who had brought ships laden with corn hailed him as one from their own land.

The synod was held in the autumn of 403; not in Constantinople but near Chalcedon, in a country mansion and on a wide estate shaded by oak-trees; hence it is known as "The Synod of the Oak." Here, as Socrates put it, "many absurd and ridiculous accusations were proffered against John, but mention of the books of Origen was not included." It was here that he was described as guilty of "high treason" by naming the Empress "a Jezebel" in his Cathedral.

John himself did not appear, nor did he obey four calls from the assembly, bidding him come to answer his accusers. He sent word that he did not intend to face trial by a Council of his enemies; that if he was to be judged, it must be by a General Council of the Church. They, the bishops who were putting him on trial, might summon him again and again; nothing would come of it. Finally, after a list of his sins had been read, surprising both in length and in content, the synod voted to depose him from his see of Constantinople. The decision was based, not primarily upon offences declared at the meeting, but upon his refusal to obey repeated orders to appear for trial. That insult, its members decided, was crime sufficient.

With its proceedings Pope Innocent I totally disagreed. He rejected its judgment and declared that another Synod should be assembled, of authorities from both East and West.

Meanwhile John remained unseen in his Cathedral. Toward evening on the last day of the trial, word of the verdict reached Constantinople from Chalcedon; it was received with wild shouts of rebellion by his people. All through the night they stood in crowded mass around the church, calling to him that it was unjust; his cause must be brought before a greater assembly, one with higher authority. The Emperor, again urged by Eudoxia, issued an Imperial order, commanding that the Patriarch be at once banished from the city, taken under guard into exile. Two days passed while citizens kept watch and the Emperor hesitated; on the third, secretly, in fear of arousing further riot, John gave himself up to the soldiers who waited outside. With them he crossed the Bosporus, to stay for the present in Bithynia.

Once it was heard that he really had gone, the uproar in Constantinople could be heard for miles around. All joined in the tumult; even those who had complained against their bishop now loudly declared this penalty unjust. Many raised jeers and yells of scorn against the Emperor, even more than those who shouted their angry contempt for the bishops at the Synod of the Oak. But it was Theophilus at whom the mob continually hurled their cries of "Shame!"

Through the hours Eudoxia listened to the noise, in fear that a rush would be made against the Imperial Palace, close to the Cathedral. A day passed, and suddenly in the Imperial bedroom there was "a shattering," "a breaking-up." So Palladius in his *Dialogue* (e.g.) described it; but he did not tell what happened and we do not know. Various theories have been offered: Was it word of the death of her firstborn, her daughter Flaccilla? Nothing is known concerning her except the date of her birth. Was it, as Theodoret declared, an earthquake which rocked the house during the night? Or was it a miscarriage which came upon her? Her last child, Marina, had been born in February 403, and it was now late in the year.

At any rate it drove her to action; she implored her husband to allow the Patriarch to return; the wrath of God was upon her. He yielded to her frantic entreaty, and at once she sent Briso, the eunuch whom among all her attendants she trusted most, to overtake John upon his way. To her messenger, we read, she gave a letter for the Patriarch: "She was entirely innocent of the plots against him; she revered him in honor as a bishop of the Church, as one who had baptized her children."

The Patriarch did not hurry back. Theodoret tells that Imperial legates were sent to beg him to return with all speed; the city was in peril. He did not come. A second, and then a third deputation was despatched; "the Bosporus was crowded with the multitude of messengers!" Theophilus by this time had fled for safety to Alexandria; he had heard that the mob in Constantinople was hunting for him, to throw him into the sea.

Presently a number of bishops gathered in the city to declare that John's see had been unjustly taken from him; then, after three days of absence, he again entered Constantinople, ablaze with torches, where he was met by his people, singing songs of joy especially composed for the occasion, carrying lighted tapers in their hands. They escorted him to the Cathedral, and from its pulpit he spoke, sending forth the first words which came to his mind:

"What shall I say, or what words shall I find? Blessed be God.! This I said when I went forth, this now again I declare; nay, all the time I was away I never ceased to say it! . . . Blessed be God who allowed me to go; blessed again be God who called me to return; blessed be God who allowed the storm; blessed be God who broke up the storm and gave us peace. Blessed was God when I was separated from you, and when I recovered you. . . . I was separated from you in body, but by no means in mind.

"And see how much the wiles of enemies have done! . . . They have gained for me six hundred friends. Before I went, my own people loved me, now even the Jews honor me. . . . Today there are games in the Circus, and not a soul is there. All have streamed like a torrent into the Cathedral. For verily your gathering is a torrent, and the floods are your voices which rise to heaven and tell your love for Father John!" (P.G. LII, 439f.).

Later on he spoke again, and now we find generous words for the Empress:

"Suddenly on the first day, when night had fallen, she, that most religious lady, sent me a letter with these words (I *have* to tell you her words): 'Please, Your Holiness, do not think that I knew what had happened. I am not guilty of shedding your blood! Wicked and abandoned men built up this contriving, this scheme of plot! Truly God is the witness of my tears, God to whom I offer sacrifice. . . . I remember that my children were baptized by your hands.' . . .

"Then she implored the Emperor, clasping his knees; 'We have destroyed the priest,' she cried, 'but let us bring him back again. There is no hope for our monarchy if we do not. I simply cannot be a party to these things that have been done!'

"So she spoke, weeping and calling upon God. . . . Then late yesterday evening she sent me a message: 'My prayer has been answered, I asked aright. I have gained a crown far more glorious than my Imperial diadem. I have recovered the priest, I have restored the head to the body, the helmsman to the ship, the shepherd to his flock, the bridegroom to his chamber!' "

They were the words of one who had been terrified, and terror had brought a change of heart. Some of them at least seemed true to her, spoken in her relief from the thought of penalty to come.

But Theophilus, as Sozomen declares, was not content, and active assault soon arose from his followers, supported by men from Egypt, against the people of Constantinople, still utterly deter-mined to defend their Patriarch. In this quarrel many were wounded and some were killed; finally in their fear Severian and other bishops hostile to John fled back to their own countries.

After their departure things for a while settled down in calm for Empire and Church at Constantinople. Then a last and final act was played in this tragic course of events; with Acacius, John Chrysostom, and the Empress Eudoxia taking the chief parts.

Its scene showed the dedication, in November of this same year, 403, of a silver statue of Eudoxia, mounted on a column of deep red porphyry and placed on a high platform in front of the Senate House of Constantinople. Her figure was beautifully moulded, partly covered by the graceful folds of a mantle. In honor of the Empress a holiday was proclaimed; dances, mimes and shows entertained the crowds which filled the public square. Much that was indecent was pictured and much that was obscene was heard; the merrymaking was strongly flavored with ancient pagan symbols and rites.

Shortly afterward Constantinople saw and heard its Patriarch in his pulpit, denouncing this return to heathen cult; this kind of celebration, he said, was a disgrace to the Church, especially on a Sunday and just outside the Cathedral of Holy Wisdom, Saint Sophia. John let loose his anger unrestrained, especially against those who had ordered and allowed the nauseous licence of that day of joy.

Probably Eudoxia heard the sermon; if not, she received its words with full emphasis from those who did. Forgotten at once were the fury, the terror, the relief of a time now some months past. It was her statue which was being honored; the Patriarch was reviling the honor and condemning her. With quick energy she told Arcadius that another synod must be called to wipe out her shame, to judge this affront from the Archbishop of Constantinople to her Imperial crown.

Nor was this all which she had to hear. Whether deliberately or not, within a few days the Archbishop began another address in his Cathedral with a sentence which fell upon pricked-up ears: "Again Herodias is raging; again she is disquieted; again she longs to receive the head of John upon a charger!"

Doubtless the sermon was given in honor of some Feast of Saint John the Baptist; the rather dramatic opening words would be exactly in the style of the preacher. Perhaps John, as he said them, did have himself in mind. To Eudoxia they were a direct insult.

To the enemies of John they provided fresh fuel for proceedings. Bishops gathered again in Constantinople to accuse him; the chief charge now was that after being formally deposed, on his own initiative he had resumed office and administration as bishop. Shortly before Christmas Day, 403, the Emperor sent word that he would not attend Mass in the Cathedral on that day, or at any time until the Patriarch was declared innocent of wrongdoing. John himself was content that inquiry be made concerning his alleged guilt.

For several months debate and questioning continued, until it was spring of 404. Then Antiochus of Ptolemais, with others who held John an illegal possessor of his see, sought private audience with the Emperor. "Easter is at hand," they said; "cast him out!" They knew that on Easter Eve there would be a great gathering of people in the Cathedral; it was the traditional day for the baptizing of the catechumens who had long been under instruction. Another riot might well arise. The Emperor did not dare to refuse; he shared their fear, and by messenger he told John to leave Constantinople. The answer came in all tranquillity: "I have received this Church from God for the salvation of its people; I cannot forsake it. If it be your will (for the city belongs to you), then drive me out by force; then I can have your authority for deserting my command!"

Reluctantly, but encouraged by the strong will of Eudoxia, Arcadius issued an Imperial decree, ordering John to hold himself deposed from his bishop's seat. No attempt, however, was made to deny him his episcopal Palace at this time; "for they feared some visitation of Divine anger and they wished if it struck them to restore him at once to his church and thus make their peace with God." Eudoxia evidently had not forgotten her terror at the "shattering" which had come upon her when John had first been expelled.

The Great Sabbath, Saturday, the vigil of Easter 404, arrived and Arcadius was seriously worried. What would happen when the Patriarch was not present to bless the neophytes, the newly born of the Church?

He summoned Acacius and Antiochus to the Palace once more and told them that he expected trouble. Why not restore John before it was too late? They replied quickly, in words few but clear: "Your Majesty, allow the deposing of John to be upon our heads!"

At the last moment forty bishops, supporters of John, approached the Emperor and the Empress, on Good Friday in the Church of the Martyrs. One of them spoke for all; "Paschaltide is upon us! For the sake of those who now are to be reborn into the Church, restore the bishop to his Cathedral!" Both Arcadius and Eudoxia remained silent. Then Paul, bishop of Krateia in Greece, boldly addressed the one he knew to be of firmer will: "Eudoxia," he said, "fear God! Have pity on your children; do not violate the sacred and solemn Feast of Christ by the shedding of blood!"

Again there was no answer, and all the forty left the church, to spend the rest of the day, some in utter depression, some in bewilderment at the things coming upon the Church.

We have two descriptions of the scenes in Constantinople on the night of the Easter vigil. Both come from the *Dialogue* of Palladius with Theodore: the one lies in a letter of John Chrysostom himself to Pope Innocent I, and the other in the general narrative of events (Palladius, *Dialogus* cc. 2 and 9).

The Cathedral was filled with people; within its Baptistery the clergymen were administering the baptismal rite; outside that chapel stood an endless line of those who awaited this; further away was the crowd of those already baptized, surrounded by their relatives and friends.

Suddenly in through the great doors rushed a force of soldiers, sent by John's enemies to assault and to drive all from the Church into the darkness of the night. Amid the confusion and uproar which followed, women screaming in panic, children crying, priests and deacons struck and beaten, the Cathedral was cleared; above the noise was heard a call that service would be continued in the Baths of Constantine. There those who had courage assembled in such order as was possible.

Soon in this secular place the ritual was being once more carried on; priests were saying the holy words, people were being baptized. This was too much for Antiochus, Severian, and Acacius, who were still in Constantinople, to watch and to allow. They hurried to the civil authorities: Would they at once clear the Baths of Constantine? "But it is night," said the magistrate, "and the crowd is enormous; we don't want to stir up trouble." Prompt answer came from those with Acacius: "There is not a soul in any of the churches; we are afraid that if the Emperor goes into the Cathedral and finds no one there, he will think that the people have refused to go because of their loyalty to John, and put the blame on us." This brought a strong protest from the officer of the law, who warned them of what would happen if he acted. Finally, however, he called an armed soldier, one Lucius, and ordered him to go and as quietly as possible to summon the crowd to leave the Baths. Lucius went, issued the command, and received no answer; he returned to tell that

"the crowd is determined to stay, and it can't be removed by force,
it is far too great." Promises and "golden words" sent him on his
way to try once more. It was now about three in the morning. With
drawn swords the soldiers fell upon the clergy who were baptizing,
upon those being baptized. They poured out the holy water and
spattered the font with blood; they ran right and left, wounding
both clergy and laity. Women awaiting baptism fled half-naked
with their husbands, terrified lest instant death or a fate worse
than death should strike them. The sacred vessels were seized as
plunder; many, priests and deacons, were arrested and carried off
to prison; those of high rank and office were driven out of the city.
Placards were put up everywhere, threatening dire penalty for
those who would not deny friendship with the Patriarch John.

Next morning, when the Emperor was out walking for exercise,
he came to a meadow of untilled land, white with a multitude of
men and women still in their baptismal robes; there were some
three thousand of them sitting there. In his surprise he turned to
his escort of soldiers. "What gathering is this?" he asked. The
answer was quickly thought up; all knew well that these were the
newly baptized, keeping Easter in the open, since churches were
forbidden them. But his guards did not tell Arcadius this; they
were no friends of John. Hoping to see further persecution they
merely said: "Heretics, Sir, carrying on their worship."

They soon had their desire. Clergy, laymen, and wives of distinguished citizens, were seized; from the women veils were torn, ear-
rings snatched. The captives were thrown into cells; and thus prisons
became churches in which hymns were sung and the Holy Mysteries
were celebrated. Scourges, torture on the rack, hideous oaths,
strove hard to condemn John, who—so wrote Palladius—"was until
the day of his death the enemy of sin in the Devil."

More than six weeks John still remained in his Archbishop's
house, and only a few saw him. His supporters were now known as
"Joannites," marked men; the simple folk who loved their Patriarch
kept guard around the Cathedral, watching in turn, night and day.

Theophilus remained in Alexandria. But Acacius, Antiochus,
and Severian were constantly complaining that the laws of the
Church had been broken. Was not John still in his episcopal
Palace? Never would the people of Constantinople quiet down,
they said, as long as he was in the city.

At last, shortly after Pentecost, the three bishops, together
with Cyrinus of Chalcedon, requested another meeting with Arcadius. "You, Your Majesty," they now declared, "in our eyes hold
all subject to yourself; you may do what you will to do. Do not,

therefore, try to appear more lenient than priests, more holy than bishops. Openly we have said to you: 'Upon our heads be the deposing of John.' Do not, then, ruin us all that you may spare one man!'"

The Emperor in face of these words and these men had no courage to hesitate longer. But even now he would not assume responsibility for what he did. He sent his secretary, Patricius, to John with this message of command: "Acacius, Antiochus, Severian and Cyrinus have taken your condemnation upon their own heads. Therefore commend yourself to God and depart from the Church of Constantinople!"

The Patriarch said farewell to his friends among bishops and other clergy. Then to the Baptistery of his Cathedral he called the women who long had worked with him: Olympias, the deaconess who had done him daily service, even preparing his frugal meals; Pentadia and Procla, also deaconesses; and Silvina, a widow of sincere and honest heart. As they stood around him he gave them his last words: "Come, my daughters, listen to me. The things that concern me have their end; I have finished my course and it may be that you will see my face no more. This is what I ask of you, that no one of you be driven away from your longstanding goodwill toward the Church of Constantinople; whosoever against his will may be brought here for election as bishop, do not try intrigue, but, with the consent of all, bow your heads as though to John himself. The Church cannot be without its bishop. So may God grant you His mercy; and remember me in your prayers."

Then he went out on his way, and, so Palladius wrote, "with him went out the Angel of the Church, in dread of the loneliness which evil principalities and powers had brought to pass."

That night the Cathedral of Saint Sophia caught fire; men said that its flame rose first from the seat in which John had sat as bishop. Soon, fanned by a rush of wind, it spread far and wide through the interior to the outer walls, even as far as the Senate House, to work its ruin there. Its cause was never known; each party, for and against John, attributed it to the other.

Many, indeed, were troubled in Constantinople after John's departure; the city was again a scene of turbulence and distress. Public assemblies were neglected; men no longer gathered in crowds at the forum or the Baths; some even left the city, to seek happiness far from its intrigue and injustice. Another man was elected its Patriarch and bishop: Arsacius, brother of that Nectarius who had preceded John. He was over eighty years old, quiet and mild, of no strong influence: "a man," Palladius declared, "more dumb than a fish, less fit for business than a frog." He died the next year. More striking—so the adherents of John told—was the tragedy that fell upon Cyrinus of Chalcedon, one of John's most bitter enemies. Incurable disease, eating away his body, struck him, as punishment, men said, for the lies he had told against his fellow-bishop.

Among those who suffered for their loyalty to John was one Eutropius, who was called by the Prefect of Constantinople to give evidence and steadily declared that he knew nothing. Various torture failed to drag out a word; so did imprisonment, and soon Eutropius died from shock and pain. Another friend of John, Olympias the deaconess, boldly faced the Prefect as he sat in Court. "Why did you set fire to the Cathedral?" he asked her. "That is not my custom in life," she retorted; "I have spent my income, which has been ample, in restoring the churches of God!" "I know your way of life quite well," said the Prefect. "Very well, then," answered Olympias. "In that case please act as my accuser, and let another be my judge." She was fined a heavy sum and gladly left Constantinople for Cyzicus in Asia Minor.

Meanwhile John had been taken to Cucusus in Armenia, and from there to Arabissus, some forty-five miles distant. Continually he wrote letters to his friends; his letters to Olympias, of special interest, we may still read. Continually he hoped for his return home, and Pope Innocent I worked hard for him. Their hope was never fulfilled. Order came in 407 from the Emperor Arcadius that John should be transferred as prisoner to Pityus on the shore of the Black Sea. He was on his way, in pouring rain, or in the intense heat of the sun, driven on by the soldiers of his escort, allowed little rest and no comfort, when he broke down and died, on Holy Cross Day, September 14, 407.

The Empress Eudoxia had departed this life three years before. She had lived to see the hatred and the persecution that had raged in Constantinople after the banishment of its Patriarch; she had heard of his suffering in Cucusus, from sickness, from cold, from raids of pirates, from loneliness, from lack of sleep, from lack of decent and civilized living.

Her conscience must have hurt her sorely. On the last day of September 404, Constantinople was visted by a terrific storm of hail, with stones, it was said, as large as pebbles. Many citizens believed that it was an act of God. Soon afterward trouble visited the Imperial Palace; Eudoxia herself died, on the sixth day of October, probably in no state of calm and through a miscarriage.

History will always connect her name with the fate of this Archbishop of Constantinople; not because she was an evil woman, but because she had always held herself, her fortune, and her dignity, of higher standing than the conscience which warned her. Of barbarian blood, she had something of its wild nature; she lived by impulse, not by standard. Theophilus, Acacius, Antiochus, Severian and Epiphanius were the active agents who drove John into exile; it was Eudoxia who incurred the greater guilt; who as Empress, as wife holding power of persuasion over the man who ordered action of Church and of State, in her resentment chose deliberately not to interfere, not to arrest the evil working of revenge.

CHAPTER THREE

Synesius and Hypatia

From Constantinople in the Empire of the East we now make our way, through the seas of Marmora, of the Aegean and the Mediterranean, to its Province or Diocese of Egypt in Africa. On the northwestern shore lay the region of the Pentapolis, the Five Towns, also known as Cyrenaica, from the earliest of these towns, Cyrene in Libya.

Cyrene holds in its founding a legend made famous by Herodotus and by Pindar. In Book IV of his *Histories* Herodotus tells that one Grinus from the isle of Thíra, now known as Santorini, one of the group of the Cyclades in the Aegean, went to Delphi to inquire of its oracle concerning his voice, troubled by stammering. The priestess of the oracle gave no answer to his question, but bade him go forth from Thíra to found a settlement for its people in Libya.

Nothing, however, was done, and the people of Thíra fell upon hard times. Once again counsel was sought from Delphi, and once again the people of Thíra were told to make their future dwelling in Libya.

This time they did leave their homes, about 630 B.C., to wander from place to place; finally they settled at Cyrene. There he who had first been told to go to Libya became their king, under the royal name of Battus; for long he and his descendants, the Battiadae, held the crown of rule in Cyrenaica, the land of Cyrene and its surrounding districts. Some two hundred years later Cyrenaica became a republic; then, under the Ptolemies, it was included in their kingdom of Egypt, and its city of Cyrene gained renown as a center not only of commerce, but of culture, of intellectual working and artistic wonder.

Eventually it passed, about A.D. 96, into the Roman Empire; in the fourth century of our era we find it a province of the Empire of the East, governed by the Imperial Prefect of Egypt.

Its character was to suffer change as the years went by. In this fourth century it still possessed wealth; it still held dwellings that looked out on gardens and fields, trees and flowers, fertile harvests of grain; it still held men who read for the love of reading, who toiled for the love of country. Here, sometime between 370 and 375, was born Synesius, of whom Byzantine historians were to write: "If any other man was learned, so in his time was he"; "By the renown of his name let him light up our history."

His family, aristocratic and well endowed, with pride traced its lineage to the ancient kingly rule over Sparta, whence, they declared, had come their ancestors across the seas to Cyrenaica. They were still of pagan faith and ritual; this, together with history, literature, and some philosophic background, we may imagine young Synesius learning from his father and friends at home. In one of his letters, written about 401 (No. 57) he was to tell: "From my childhood I have been sure that there exists for me a certain Divine blessing: leisure and that comfort in life which, as some one has said, belongs to those inspired by God. It consists in the nurture of the intellect, in the uniting with God of him who possesses a mind and reaps its fruit. In the things that are natural or belong to boys, or to lads or to youths, I had the smallest share. And when I grew to manhood not a whit did I change in my love, as a boy, of quiet tranquillity. I spent the days of my life as one who keeps one long, holy feast day, eager at all times to hold my spirit gracious, undisturbed by waves of passion and storm."

Synesius at this moment was not thinking of his keen enjoyment of sport; nor could he foresee the tumult of years to come.

In his early twenties, about 394, he left Cyrene for Alexandria and its famous school of learning, at that time crowded by students who were flocking to lectures on Platonic, and especially Neo-Platonic, philosophy given by a woman, Hypatia.

Hypatia, daughter of Theon, professor at the University of Alexandria in Egypt, had been her father's pupil in mathematics and astronomy; she was far to surpass him both in research and in fame. With wide knowledge, an original mind, ardent enthusiasm, and skill in teaching, she combined the charm of beauty and friendliness, and thus appealed to all who followed her words. Suidas in his *Lexicon* tells of a youth who fell desperately in love with her, as no doubt did many others. But Hypatia was wholly dedicated to her work. With kindly heart she sought the young man's good; she would have nothing of his passion. For Synesius she opened a path which was to lead him to heights of which he had never dreamed; until the day of his death she was his friend, his inspiration, the critic to whose judgment he submitted his work.

Some two years he stayed in Alexandria, sharing with many, men young and old, the joy of this new experience. To one of them, Herculian, he wrote (Letter 136): "You and I, we ourselves both saw and heard the true and real teacher of the mysteries of philosophy. . . . And when I look back upon our fellowship there, our sharing in that philosophy to which in constant labor we bowed our heads, my reason tells me that I owe our good fortune to the will of God. . . . It came about through no previous thought of mine, quite suddenly, as an entire surprise; I trace its happening to God as Leader. We will pray Him to bring to full purpose the work He has begun; may He give it us to follow philosophy, you and me, with each other! And if not thus, well, at any rate to follow philosophy!"

From Alexandria he went to Athens, drawn by its ancient renown as seat of classic learning. But it gave him little comfort. To his brother Euoptius he poured out his keen disappointment, even wrath (Letter 135): "May that miserable skipper who brought me here find a miserable end! Athens now has nothing noble within it, just the mere names of famous places! And just as the skin of an animal slaughtered in sacrifice marks only what was once alive, so philosophy has now been banished from Athens; the only thing left for one who goes there is to admire the Academy and the Lyceum buildings; also, by Zeus, that variegated colonnade, now no longer varied, from which the philosophy of Chrysippus won its name!"

In 396 Synesius was again at home in Cyrene, and there he stayed, winning respect and goodwill from its citizens through his labors in the public cause. The town had fallen upon evil days. Taxes had risen to the point of impossible payment; swarms of locusts had stripped fields and gardens of their harvest; raids of native barbarians in Africa had carried off plunder again and again; disease had visited home after home, killing old and young alike.

At last, in 399, a petition from its people implored the authorities to send Synesius as envoy to plead for its misery with the Emperor Arcadius in Constantinople. Synesius, all declared, was the right man to send; he was honest, firm in loyalty, possessed of courage; he knew well how to speak before the Imperial Court. Consent after some hesitation was given, and the representative of Cyrene arrived this same year at the capital city of the Empire in the East.

There Synesius was to stay nearly three years, from 399 until 402, and hard years they were, for him and for all in Constantinople. Twice he told of his unhappiness; once in his treatise, *On Dreams:*

"Would that it had not been my fate to see three accursed years in my life!"; and again in one of his *Hymns* (No. 3, ll. 431 ff.):

> "Where for three years long
> I dwelt in the highway
> Near the House of Empire,
> Royal hall of our land;
> There labor I bore,
> I bore pain of soul,
> With many a tear."

One day during this time—we do not know exactly when, but probably he had to await his turn—he delivered before the Emperor and His Court a speech which has come down to us under the name "Concerning the Imperial Rule"—*De Regno,* as it is generally called, although we still have its Greek original. Extremely frank, it shows resolution from beginning to end. Already its preface told Arcadius what to expect:

"Let not my words be judged boorish and rude by you. Let them not be put to silence before they have gone their brief way, just because they are not servants of persuasion, pleasant playfellows for youth. No! They are here to teach, to chastise in strict reality, to meet you in grievous manner. May you be strong to bear their fellowship, when your ears are not wholly filled with the praises which you have been accustomed to hear!"

Next Synesius told why he had come:

"Cyrene sends me to you to crown your head with gold, your spirit with philosophy: Cyrene, a Greek city, of name ancient and honorable, once famed in unending song of wise men, now poor and downcast: a great ruin, in need of its Emperor, if he will do for it something worthy of its ancient history."

Synesius offered with all ceremony the gold crown, gift of Cyrene, and then began his address. Here is some picture of its bold and lengthy periods:

"The duty of an Emperor is this: after due thought he must choose the right, reject the wrong path. Much Imperial action carried out hitherto among us by no means merits this praise.

"It is true that under Arcadius fame and wealth of Empire are exceedingly great. Its army is strong to conquer; but it lacks leadership. Men of countless cities reverence the Emperor; yet most of them have never seen him, and can never hope for this.

"What is, whence has come, the praise lavished upon our Empire under the rule of Arcadius? I can tell you. Praise such as this has risen from external matters; real and true prosperity is born of the inner nature of man's spirit. A ruler worthy of the name must endure all toil, must shun all comfort, must deny himself rest, must shoulder a multitude of cares. For his people he must work to gain what is good; he must labor without end to keep them from harm, to bring them peace and security, safety from evil, day and night. The ruler who has no will to feed his flocks but is himself fed fat by them—him I call no shepherd of his sheep, but a tyrant king!

"Do you, then, Arcadius, examine your life in this light. You are young, and you need the guidance of philosophy, of religion, of God.

"So, first of all, let me tell you that human nature is made up of many faculties: of more elements, more diversities, than a hydra has heads. The mind of a true man, whether he is monarch or mere citizen, must hold in subjection, in a peace which is divine, all these different elements within himself. In other words, a monarch must be monarch of his own self; no slave to pleasure, to pain, to any passion of nature which he shares in common with the brute beasts.

"What, then, must be his duty to those outside, to his own self, if he is to rule aright?

"He will meet with all friendship and fellowship the nobles and officers of his Court, while scorning to flatter them with untruth. Outside his Palace, by generous kindness he will win the hearts of his soldiers, who may be held his friends of the second class. He will call them out for review upon the field, in formal array of men, of armor, of horses. Once there, he will himself ride with his cavalry; he will run with those on foot; he will march, clad in armor, with his armed soldiers; he will bear his shield among his shield-bearers. His aim will always be to make them true comrades, fellow-fighters with himself; never will he descend to foolish jest or needless censure. So they, too, will be his friends; not of him but for him, will they be afraid. No motley herd of soldiers will he have before his eyes; but a company of individuals. Each of them he will know by name; to each he will give praise and honor due. And each therefore will give his utmost to his Emperor, to his State.

"A true Emperor will thus understand his implements and skillfully use them; just as a good shoe-maker creates his shoes, using his familiar tools aright.

"Again, no true Emperor will live for his showing forth in majesty. He will not allow himself to lose respect by constant parade; he will not make a custom of appearing publicly in gorgeous splendor, decked out in purple and gold, sparkling with jewels sought from far and near, proud as a peacock. This, I must admit, has been the custom in Constantinople. To you, Arcadius, in all frankness I must say that you do not hold yourself as a true, a really royal monarch, unless you display your majesty in the very leather of your shoes!

"Return to the discipline, the simplicity of olden time! Show yourself, not a mere figurehead of royalty, but a ruler who in very fact holds fast his Empire before the eyes of God and man!

"March out with your soldiers. But, I tell you, see to it that they are of your own land, of your own cities, of your own race and people! Call no barbarians to defend you; call those who will protect their own fields. Let our own men defend their Empire; let our own women see to our household cares! Men and women, but not of foreign, not of German blood!

"I pray you, before things come to that which even now is threatening us, see to it that the Roman spirit be restored, that Roman men win victory little by little through their own skill and strength. Cast out barbarians from all ranks of our army; cast out barbarians from office as magistrates, from honor as senators! Truly I do believe that Justice herself, Giver of counsel, that God, Lord of War, hide themselves for very shame whenever a man clad in barbaric skins leads Roman soldiers in Roman uniform to battle; whenever a barbarian, stripping himself of his sheepskin, takes his seat in civilian dress among Roman magistrates in Court, next to the consul, in front of those who have rightful claim. And then and there he proceeds to decide matters of State! Indeed I marvel at many things done now-a-days by us in our folly, but at none more than this!

"The barbarians wander out from their native land, only to be driven away from the lands of others. Now they are coming to us, begging for homes: a wild and ignorant race, men who repay kindness with crime. Your father, Arcadius, conquered them; but also he pitied them, and for his pity he paid the price. He granted their prayer and they settled in our Empire; he received them into our army, into our State; to these pestilential creatures, Arcadius, he gave Roman land. And so to this day they mock and insult us.

"With courage let us rise against them! By our command let them either till our earth for us or hasten in flight back whence they came! There let them declare to all who dwell across the

Danube that no longer in the Roman people will they find that hospitality which once they knew. Our Emperor is a youth of noble blood!"

We do not know how the Emperor Arcadius received this bold address; but Synesius did receive welcome aid for Cyrene.

Many men of high rank and note he met in Constantinople: Eutropius, Aurelian, Caesarius, Gainas, John Chrysostom, its Patriarch; so deeply did he concern himself with events of this time that even before he left this capital of the Eastern Empire he was at work on a picture of its history, framed in fiction. He called it *On Providence,* or *The Egyptians.* The first of these titles points to the Divine call which controls the cause of history; the second gives the scene in which he placed his work.

This was Egypt, and therefore while his "novel" reflected Constantinople's history, it did not reflect its Catholic religion in the years 399–402. The city of Thebes in Egypt stands here for Constantinople; the two chief characters in his story represent two persons, we may believe, of this time. One he has named Osiris, after the ancient pagan deity; the other appears as Typhos, the Greek word for "a furious whirlwind."

Authorities agree in seeing "Osiris" as Aurelian, whom we have already met. History knows him as son of Taurus, consul of the East in 361. In 383 Aurelian gained notice as builder of Saint Stephen's Church in Constantinople; in 393 he was City Prefect there. From 399 to 400 he was Praetorian Prefect of the East; it was he who presided over the court of law which sentenced Eutropius to death. In 400 he was consul. Between him and Synesius a warm friendship gradually grew, marked in letters which Synesius wrote to him:

"If there are any souls of cities—and there are: guardians, divine, sent from heaven—you may be sure that they all give thanks to you and that they remember the blessings which as chief magistrate you brought to all peoples" (Letter 31); "I hold that your God-inspired spirit was sent down from on high to be a blessing shared by all men" (Letter 38). It was Aurelian who gave to Synesius courage to speak his words to the Emperor.

The second figure in *The Egyptians,* Typhos, has been the subject of much controversy. Seeck would identify him with Caesarius, the elder brother of Aurelian. Caesarius was Master of Offices in the Empire of the East from 387 until 389; Praetorian Prefect, 396–398, sharing office with one Eutychian; consul in 397; again Praetorian Prefect 400–401. Mommsen vigorously opposes this identification. Bury supports it in his edition of Edward Gibbon; so does Wilhelm von Christ; other writers either see Gainas in this picture of Typhos or declare the problem unsolved.

The Egyptians, then, is a tale of ancient Egypt, pagan in religion, governed by a king whose two sons, Osiris and Typhos, differ entirely in character and in policy. Osiris is honest, endeavoring to do all that is good and highminded in the kingdom of Egypt; Typhos is corrupt, given to idleness, lust, and evil ambition. Osiris longs for knowledge; Typhos scorns study. Osiris works hard; Typhos laughs, spends his days in self-indulgence, caring for no one but himself.

These pictures painted, Synesius turns to events in his fictionalized history. At an early age Osiris gained military command, followed by Praetorian office and leadership of the Senate in Thebes. Typhos was appointed head of the royal Treasury, but only brought it disgrace; soon he was dismissed. Given another post, he forced again shameful repute upon his fellow-citizens. Often he burst into rage or anger against one or another; often he showed delight in the suffering, the loss which his negligence had caused. Much of his time was wasted in sleep.

Their father, king and high priest of Egypt, found joy in his younger, bitter disappointment in his elder son. His departure from this world, he knew, was drawing near; soon the bliss of absorption in the Infinite would be his. Which of his sons would succeed him as king?

This most important matter was regularly settled by formal election. So now proclamation of the day of election was made by heralds. The day arrived; priests and native-born soldiers of Egypt assembled for voting, as required by law. Others, of lower rank and dignity, were free to assemble or to be absent, as they willed; they might look on, but they were not allowed to vote. Swineherds and foreign-born soldiers had not even this privilege. Unfortunately for Typhos, swineherds and aliens, a rough and disorderly crowd, formed the greater portion of his adherents, fiercely eager to grasp what they held their right.

The multitude present on this day stood on two hills, divided by the river Nile; those who were to vote, on the one held sacred, those who took no part in the election, on the other. Soldiers of Egypt voted by show of hands, carefully counted; among the company of priests were three orders of rank. Highest were the prophets, interpreters of Divine oracles; next came those who presided over sacred feasts; the third division had charge of temples. All these priests voted by means of stone counters; the counter held by each prophet equaled in value the raising of a hundred hands by Egyptian soldiers; that of a priest of the second rank equaled twenty hands, that of one of the third rank equaled ten.

The name of Typhos, as the elder brother, was called aloud; counters were put forward, hands were raised. The same ritual followed for Osiris. Should the vote be equal, the king would make a decision between the two candidates.

Osiris stood calmly waiting the result; Typhos behaved as one insane, excited beyond control, leaping into the Nile amid the laughter of the crowd, promising money to those who gave him their votes.

The election fell to Osiris, and was received not only by ringing shouts of applause, but by signs from the gods of Elysium that all was well, and by thunder of wrath from the demons of hell and the supporters of Typhos. Now the old king, father of Osiris, departed this life in peace.

Osiris as king fulfilled his promise. For his people he once more worked ceaselessly, day and night, seeking for them wise government, culture in education, means for their comfort. Gladly he conferred honors well deserved; for those so devoted to learning and research that they had no time to earn their daily bread, he drew supplies from public funds; those who longed for leisure in contemplation of philosophy he freed from all public office; with all charity he labored to win and convert those of evil, shameful character.

On the other hand, Typhos nearly made an end of himself in his despair at failure. He would not eat, sleep, or forget. Constantly on every side he heard praise of King Osiris, his younger brother, heard how wise, how modest, how just, how merciful, and, as a final sting, how handsome he was!

Typhos was a married man, and his wife aided him constantly on his way to ruin. She loved the things of this world: dress, jewels, the theatre, public functions of all kinds. Her ambition was unbounded, and she was always throwing up against him his failure to win the royal crown. By this time her husband had reached late middle age; in spite of his bitter taunts, he adored this selfish, vain woman.

If she could not be queen of Egypt, she determined to excel every other woman of Thebes in luxury, in revels, in feastings at her house, in radiance of face and figure. No expense was spared, and having thus prepared her way, she made bold advances to prominent men, catching and holding them by her tactics, by the skill she undoubtedly possessed.

On the contrary, the wife of Osiris appears in this story as a model of virtue and modesty; she did not even venture to show herself outside her home!

At last Typhos was rescued from despair by the woman he had married; she was weary of seeing him so downcast. Moreover, his misery spoiled her brilliance in society. So now both husband and wife began to make merry. Banquets, wine and riotous revel filled their house and estate, indoors and outdoors alike; swimming pools were hollowed out in the gardens, with islands on which by night danced men and women, nude and noisy.

Finally revelry passed to revolution, again by the cunning of this wife of Typhos to whom Synesius gave no name. Her husband, of course, supported her in the first secret steps; so, Synesius declared, did the pagan demons of hell.

Her plotting was well timed. Recent disaster had fallen upon the commander of the Egyptian army. Very possibly in this commander Synesius was picturing Gainas, also a barbarian general, who in 400, when Synesius was in Constantinople, held not only Aurelian (the Osiris of Synesius) but also Constantinople (the Thebes of Synesius) imprisoned by his power.

With his men this commander had been sent by Osiris to subdue enemies of the Egyptian kingdom; part of his army had deserted him and several towns of Egypt had been ruined by assault. It left him in bitter discontent, and he poured out all this bitterness to his wife, a woman also of barbarian blood, simple in mind, of no imagination, entirely the opposite of the ambitious wife of Typhos.

Now this ambitious lady saw her chance to make her name memorable for all time. She hurried off to visit that poor woman, so simple, so depressed by her husband's defeat; and she followed up this first visit by constant calls, day and night. "I am worried about you," said this wife of Typhos to the wife of the barbarian commander, an ignorant soul; "terrible trouble is coming upon us, coming if Osiris as king gets his way. For Osiris is suspecting treachery; he believes that Typhos is plotting evil with barbarians, against him and his crown. Your husband, your children, and you yourself are all of barbarian race; Osiris is going to rid himself of you all, by ruin and by death."

The unhappy listener to these words was quickly terrified; whereupon the wife of Typhos proceeded to administer comfort. "I will take care of you," she said to her victim; "I have a wonderful plan, bold and sure, which will deliver us all from the tyranny of Osiris as lord. Now listen: if you barbarians unite with the followers of Typhos, we shall all be happy, both Egyptians and barbarians, under Typhos as king. No harm will be done to you, no movement against your barbarian people. All Egypt will be yours, as it were, to feast upon. Now do persuade the Commander, your husband, to join us in this!"

The barbarian wife took courage; the barbarians rose in revolt to support Typhos; Typhos became king and Osiris was held captive. The newly crowned rebel king even demanded death for his dethroned brother; but the same barbarians who had placed Typhos on the throne of Egypt refused him this. They were content to think of Osiris as one in retirement; they even gave him provision for his need.

Under Typhos as king, trouble, grievous and manifold, came upon Egypt. Taxation again rose, distributed in illegal and unjust measure; offices of State were sold at a price for the benefit of the Crown. Soon everywhere voices cried in complaint and lament; even, so Synesius wrote, the gods themselves in their pity made ready to punish the source of this distress.

For now the barbarians under Typhos and his commanding general (Gainas?) were occupying the capital of Egypt as a fortified camp. It is here that especially Synesius reflects his experience in Constantinople of 400 under the control of Gainas the Goth. Here his story of *The Egyptians* tells of dread visions of the night, terrifying the Commander of the barbarian army and his soldiers. Panic fell upon these fighters, once so bold; now in living fear of some force at work within the walls of the city, they were eager to flee far away. Entire power over its people had been given to barbarian soldiers by Typhos; now they hurried to escape. Taking their wives and children with them, seizing whatever among their possessions they held most precious, they rushed for the gates of this haunted town.

Its citizens, unarmed and therefore helpless until this moment, saw this sight of fleeing soldiers and felt a new fear. What did this sudden rush for the gates mean? Danger to all, without doubt. So they hastened to shut their doors, to hide within their homes; the report went round that a fire had been set, that in a few moments flames would envelop the city. Some decided to kill themselves rather than be burned alive; others thought only of escape by boat; barbarians held the gates.

Then, according to the story of Synesius—and his story may well be true at this point—an unexpected incident changed their minds. A little old woman was sitting to beg alms from those who passed through the gates to the world outside. Every morning at the first break of dawn she was there, for her daily bread meant more to her than did her sleep. To those who flung her a coin she foretold happy fortune, promising the goodwill of the gods.

Suddenly the outward rush of the barbarian army met her eyes. Of course, she thought, as they fled, they would seize everything they saw. Was she to lose her store of pennies? Quickly she turned upside down her little dish for coins and cried in anger against those who had been fed and housed by her city, and were now running away without thought of the citizens who remained. "Ungrateful wretches!" she shouted, and threw herself for protection to the ground. One of the barbarians, enraged by this taunt, turned aside to strike her down with his sword, and just in time was himself killed by another of his countrymen. So great and so quickly did the race for flight turn into disordered tumult.

Here, Synesius writes, the pagan gods of Thebes gave hope to its citizens. They greatly outnumbered those barbarian soldiers who had seized their city and were now deserting it. Now through this desertion men of the city hoped for freedom, gaining courage as their enemies fled. Frantically, rushing into the midst of the confused struggle, passionately longing to regain freedom, so vehemently did they fight, that before long they brought terror to those Goths who for some six months had held them prisoners in their own capital. Now far from its gates the barbarians fled.

Its citizens in joy of release held in Thebes solemn debate under the leadership of their priests. Finally they decided that Typhos should no longer be king. His evil rule, his utter lack of wisdom, the treachery of his wife, were all declared, and he was sentenced to banishment, with promise of torture from demons in the realm of the dead, once he had reached the River of Wailing in hell. Osiris was recalled, to reign in Egypt with even greater glory as his years increased.

Such, briefly told, is the dark record given us by Synesius of his own days in Constantinople, described in an Egyptian scene.

In 402 Constantinople was struck by a severe earthquake, noted by the chronicler Marcellinus, and Synesius left in a hurry. To his friend Pylaemenes (Letter 61) he wrote that he had had no time to say goodbye, even to Aurelian, his patron; "Again and again God shook the earth and men threw themselves down in crowds to pray. For the ground was quivering beneath them. I thought the sea a safer refuge than the land, and so I hurried to the harbor."

Either on his way home to Cyrene or after he had once more settled there, Synesius again visited Alexandria. The visit was memorable, for it brought him marriage; as he tells (No. 105): "God Himself and the law and the sacred hand of Theophilus gave me a wife." Since Theophilus, Patriarch of Alexandria, was a sternly orthodox Catholic, this wife, of whom we are told nothing, not even her name, must have been a Christian. It would seem probable that Synesius was baptized by the Church at this time.

Nevertheless he continued to delight in Neo-Platonic philosophy. Contemplation of the Divine, the Divine Being, was ever his end, his desire in life, whether as Neo-Platonist or as Christian; constantly he sought rest from the problems and troubles of this world in the Eternal.

His letters tell us of these years at home in Cyrene, marked both by peace and by war. To Pylaemenes he wrote in joy (Letter 101; in P.G. LXVI, Letter 100):

"You want to know what I am doing? I am deep in philosophy, my good friend; and I have as fellow-worker no human being, only blessed solitude! . . . I do believe that the very stars of heaven look down upon me kindly, each time they see me alone in a great land, gazing at them with an eye that understands. So pray with me that we may continue in our present course, and, for yourself, that you leave the ill-fated market-place of the world, you who use your powers so badly! You, with your wealth of prosperity, I do wish that you would look, not outward but inward! To receive happiness in exchange for success is to barter copper for gold. I myself rejoice when men laugh at me because I remain a private citizen, alone among many, while my kinsmen work so hard to get offices of State!"

And again (Letter 103):

"I would say that philosophy is of greater service to the private citizen, to his home, to cities, than rhetoric or any branch of art or knowledge you can mention, seeing that it serves all of these."

Also, to his friend Herculian (Letter 145):

"You have forgotten that I am trying to be a philosopher, and I hold every honor of little worth if it is not based on philosophy."

There were other joys of peace for Synesius in his home at Cyrene. To his brother Euoptius he told of them (Letter 114):

"Here with us one can go under the shade of a tree, and if you get weary of that, you can move from one tree to another, even from one whole orchard to another! What a delight to cross the little stream which flows on its way! How pleasant to watch the breeze from the west lightly playing on the trees! Yes, and there are the birds, singing in concert, and flowers of all colors; there are hedges in the meadows, work of farmers, work of Nature herself. All around there is fragrance, essence distilled by wholesome land."

Lastly, there was friendship. Synesius loved his friends only less than the God to whom he looked for support of mind and soul. So it appears in a letter from him to Herculian (No. 139):

"Love has varied sources. Sometimes it rises from the earth, born of human nature alone; and this is a love detestable, quickly fading, scarcely to be recognized.

"But God can take love under His control and make of it what He will. As the divine words of Plato tell us, He can unite two friends by His power, making them one in love: a love which rises far above time and space. And that should be the source of our union as friends, unless we mean to put our training in philosophy to shame."

There was, however, another side to life in Cyrene after Synesius had returned from travel, a side threatening and dark. Barbarians from Libya descended on its province in 405, and afterward, again and again, driving its people to a resistance which was to end in despair.

Letter after letter told his brother of disaster: of threshing floors set on fire, of fields laid waste, even of women carried off to serve as slaves. . . (No. 125):

"But no one among us blazes up in wrath! We just sit at home, waiting for soldiers to come to our aid, and they are worth just a bundle of figs!

"Shall we ever stop chattering nonsense? When shall we really come to our senses and muster men who break up clods of earth and till the ground? When shall we march to meet the enemy, for the sake of our children, our wives, our land? And, if you like, for the sake of the very soldiers themselves!"

Later on, about 407, Synesius wrote to this same brother (No. 107):

"You are surely not serious in forbidding us to get ready our weapons, when the enemy is facing us, carrying off all our herds, murdering our people in crowds day by day, and not a soldier to be seen! Will you, then, refuse private citizens the right to bear arms? Will you forbid a man who tries to save himself, the right to die, even if the State is angry with him?"

Trouble came also from men in high office in Cyrenaica, causing Synesius deep anxiety and angry rebellion. There was Cerealis, governor of the province. Concerning him Synesius wrote to one Simplicius, whose company he had enjoyed at Constantinople (Letter 129):

"Quickly he has covered himself . . . and his office with shame—in a word, the Roman State. He is a man open to bribery, even in small matters; he thinks nothing of his reputation and character. He knows nothing about war, and he is a nuisance in time of peace, of which he will enjoy very little! It did not take him long to upset and confuse everything here. . . .

"Alas for our young men lost to us, for harvests hoped for in vain! We have strewn our lands with enemy flames. Many of us held riches, in flocks, in trains of camels, in herds of grazing horses; all are gone, all have been driven away, and I am drowned in grief."

The letter finally hurls a curse upon Cerealis, so terrified by raid and invasion that, governor though he was, he fled to ship-board as a safer place than that harassed land. Now from his refuge he sent his decrees to his people: his people who were standing face to face with barbarian hordes.

Years of peril, misery and panic brought Synesius high honor from his country. Everywhere he had been seen and heard, leading men to battle, guarding their homes and citadels, keeping up their courage. Far and wide, throughout the Pentapolis, throughout Egypt itself, he was known by the year 409 as a man of wise policy, of ardent enthusiasm and determined will, as upholder of loyalty to his fellow-citizens, to his province, to his Emperor.

And yet this far-flung admiration was to bring him intense anguish, and unending conflict within his mind.

The year 409 saw the death of the bishop of Ptolemais, whose see regularly conferred upon its holder rank and responsibility as Metropolitan of the Pentapolis (Cyrenaica) in which Ptolemais lay. At once throughout the province of Cyrenaica voices arose, claiming that Synesius be consecrated as his successor. At this time both clergy and laity had great influence in the election of bishops. Moreover, here was an excellent candidate. For a bishop, in these years of turmoil, skill in politics was most important; this Father in God must be ready to devise methods of physical as well as spiritual guarding of his charge, together with sagacity and boldness in meeting either enemy or friend.

The distress which this widespread call gave to Synesius of Cyrene is vividly pictured in the Letter 105 which he wrote this same year to his brother.

Gratitude for the honor was immediately followed by a sense of utter unworthiness. The burden of quest for true philosophy was little enough compared with that now facing him. Was he in receiving honor from man to sin against God? He looked at himself; a man stumbling in the effort to discover the Divine; a man delighting in human fellowship, in long hours of quiet study, in sport and pastime, in hunting with his dogs.

But a bishop must be in very essence a man of God, not merely a student of the Divine; as far removed from pastime and play as holiness in a human being of this world could be; a soul naked to the eyes of all in its purity. He must be a man ready for all kinds of work, a specialist in all realms of law, spiritual and political, able to meet and to vanquish enemies of the Church. His burden must not crush him, must not extinguish or even dim the Divine spark within his soul. Doubtless there were men who could attain and keep this ideal; he himself, as only he himself could know in all reality, was of this earth, earthy, weak, insensible to the prick of conscience. Must not a bishop be himself free from taint of sin, free in order that he may cleanse the polluted souls of his people?

"Therefore let all who will read this letter of mine—and they will be many—know these facts, and know also that, whatever happens, I desire to be innocent of sin in the eyes of God and men, especially of Theophilus, Patriarch of Alexandria.

"What special reasons, then, stand in the way of my consecration as bishop?

"First: The wife given me by Theophilus himself. Never will I consent either to be parted from her or to live with her in secret like an adulterer. And I shall long, I shall pray, that children be born to us, many and the best.

"Second: You know, my brother, that philosophy does not hold certain dogmas widely received. Never will I judge it right to hold the soul of later birth than the body. Nor will I say that the world and its various parts will perish. Moreover, I hold the current doctrine of the Resurrection as sacred and mystical, but I am far from accepting the views of most people in regard to it.

"If, then, I should be called to the office of bishop, I should refuse to make pretence of belief. Truth is of God, and in all things I want to be truly guiltless before Him.

"Third: From boyhood I have been reproached for my undue passion for arrows and horses. As a bishop I should be unhappy, because I love sport. How should I feel, seeing my beloved dogs stripped of their hunting, my bow eaten by rust?

"Yet, if God should bid me accept a bishop's charge, I must obey his will."

In the end, it was Theophilus himself who wrung consent from this tortured mind. Seven months Synesius stayed in Alexandria, doubting, debating, finally deciding; there in 410 Theophilus laid hands upon him in consecration. Why he did this we do not know. It may be that he foresaw in this lover of philosophy conversion to Christian faith in time to come. He did know that

Synesius would toil without cease in honest labor for his Christian people; perhaps the Patriarch trusted that Christian influence. Of the wife of Synesius we hear no more; it may be that of her own will, to save him from deep trouble, she went her own way and left him to work alone. The customs of the Church in these early centuries, if not the law—actually laid down for the West about 306 by the Council assembled at Elvira in Spain—expected celibacy from its clergy.

So now the life of study was at an end for this bishop of Ptolemais; it was now his duty to stimulate, to discipline, to instruct, to defend those under his spiritual charge. Externally he followed the path of orthodox Christianity; inwardly, as the years went by, he drew nearer and nearer to the Christian Church and her creed. Problems faced him constantly in his Church and in his world; within him the uncertainty, the question of his honest right to hold his see as bishop, worked torment for his spirit.

One Andronicus was govenor of the Pentapolis at this time; between him and Synesius there was continual strife. In 411 the bishop was writing his letter *Against Andronicus* (Letter 57):

"What undoing lies in wait for Andronicus, the murderer of his country? What punishment will be fitting for his malicious heart? To me, indeed, far more grievous than all the calamities with which an avenging God has visited our sins, does Andronicus now seem. In addition to the troubles which we all share in common, he is for me a personal and a special evil. Through him the Tempter is pursuing me, eager that I flee from the ministry of the altar!

"To this I came, and all fearful things awaited me. Yes, and the promoter of all, the demon of war, ever thirsting for troubles, was Andronicus, devoted to the wrecking of our city.

"All around me lies shame and sorrow. Suddenly suffering has come upon my soul, with a swarm of anxious thoughts; images and reflections in my mind of things done or to do, and God far away. So if the things done by Andronicus are assaults of demons, they have done all they willed to do. No longer the familiar joy I used to find in prayer; only its empty form! Here and there I am borne, in the midst of all kinds of business, torn apart by anger, grief, and every sort of feeling . . .

"Why attempt, then, to join together things separated by God? You think it right"—and here Synesius, as in all this address (later on, published as a record of his words), was speaking before an audience of his clergy and people—"not that we bishops should administer affairs, but that we should administer them badly?

What could be more stupid? Do you need a political patron? Go to the man in charge of the laws of your government! You have need of God? Go to the priest of your city!"

At last Synesius decided to issue a decree of excommunication against Andronicus (Letter 58; To the Bishops):

"Let no one think of him or call him Christian; let all judge him one who has sinned against God, who is cast out with all his house from the Church in every place. This I now declare, and not because he has dealt the heaviest blow to the Pentapolis, worse than earthquake, locust, pestilence, fire, or war, a blow coming directly upon what had been left to us by these." Here Synesius tells in detail of the fearful tortures inflicted by this governor upon many victims of his anger. He then proceeds to describe his darkest crime:

"First and alone among us he insulted the Christ by deed and word: when he posted his orders on the door of the church, those outrageous orders by which he prevented those lawlessly ill-treated by him from fleeing for refuge and for prayer to the holy altar as sanctuary."

Yet when Andronicus in his terror of the Church had promised amendment, we find this bishop mercifully trying to aid the man he had so bitterly condemned. But Andronicus never regained the office he once had held.

History in the Pentapolis repeated itself. Barbarians again invaded, and Synesius as Father in God took charge of its protection. Heretics spread their poisonous doctrine; he ordered them banished and condemned. Rebellion arose among his own Christian people; he acted with kindness and tact, sending to the Patriarch Theophilus a long account of the quarrel.

We come now to his last years, and they were sad. His wife, it would seem, was not with him; the three sons which she had borne him, the sons who were the delight of his days at home, died one after the other, leaving him alone in a desolate house, amid fields destroyed beyond recall, towns ruined by continual raid.

Here again his letters give the story of these later years:

To Theophilus (Letter 69):

"You care, you do care for the Pentapolis, and therefore you will read public letters. These records of mine are afraid to tell of other and greater evils which have come upon it; the mail-carrier will let you know.

"All is now over, all is swept away! The cities remain, that is, they still remain at the moment I am writing; what will happen tomorrow God alone knows."

To Euoptius, his brother (Letter 88):

"I am living, not in private, but in a region built by enemies, and I must lament the affliction of every one around me. Again and again during each month I have to rush forward to the ramparts, as though I were paid to work with soldiers in camp instead of offering prayers! Only one of my three sons now remains to me."

To his friend Proclus (Letter 70):

"This winter the one son who remained for my comforting was taken from me by death. It was fated that as long as I could be with you I was happy; that fortune turned against me when you were no longer there. Give me, I beg of you, some encouragement in hearing from you: you who are as a father to me."

And, above all, three letters to the Hypatia whom to the day of his death he honored, reverenced, and loved. They are dated in 413 (Letters 80, 10, 16):

"Now I am left destitute of all things, unless you can do something for me. For I count you with your virtues a good refuge from trouble. You always have power; may you keep it and use it for greatest good."

"I greet you, blessed lady, and through you your most happy friends; for long I have been accusing you, I who am not held worthy to receive your letters any more. You all, I know, neglect me, not because I have done wrong, but because I am unfortunate in many ways, as unfortunate as a man can be. . . .

"I have lost my sons, my friends, and the goodwill of every one; and, the deepest pain of all, I have lost you, a spirit most divine: You, whom alone I hoped would stay with me: You, as one who would rise above the scorn of fate and the waves of fortune."

Finally:

"I have dictated this letter, lying in bed, and may you be well and happy when it reaches you: You, my mother, my sister, the teacher of my mind: You, in all these ways my benefactor. Frailty of body has followed upon the sickness of my soul. Little by little the memory of the children who have gone from me is taking its toll. Life was worth while for Synesius as long as he knew nothing of its ills; when, as it were, a torrent, held hitherto in check, streamed upon him in all its force, life lost all its savor. Oh! Would that I might either cease to live, or cease thinking of the grave of my sons!

"For you, may good health be yours, and greet for me your happy friends, beginning with father Theotecmus and brother Athanasius, and then all the rest. If there is another after your own heart, I must be grateful to him for this; please welcome him for me as a very dear friend. If you care at all for my fortunes, you do well; if you care nothing, neither do I."

Here letters cease their course, and so we may well believe that in 413 Synesius died.

Among his larger productions an early one told of his hunting; this is now lost. In another, called *On Dreams,* he records that "Life to me means books and hunting, when I am not serving as ambassador," that is, when he was at home in Cyrene.

On Dreams tells of visions from Divine source received during sleep, pointing toward events of the future, as yet unknown, both concerning life on earth and the destiny of man's soul. In such revelation Synesius rejoiced: "Divination," he wrote, "is the greatest of all good things." Divination brings light: "Many things which have happened to us when awake and are difficult to understand, philosophy reveals to us, either wholly or in part, when we lie asleep. Even matters of small import are foretold." Thus inspiration had come to him himself in regard to hunting; he dreamed that on a certain day good luck would be his, and the promise was fulfilled. In matters political, as the visit to Constantinople and the facing of his address to the Emperor Arcadius, conjurors and fortune-tellers had been of no use at all, had prophesied nothing; yet dreams, inspired, as Synesius believed, by heaven, had given it him to face the ordeal with high courage.

He tells, then, that the human mind, released during sleep from a flood of ordinary trifles, is free to receive guiding from Divine omniscience, in which nothing can be false or charlatan: "This skill of Divination is open to me, and I want to give it to my children," he writes; "for it demands no long journeying abroad, to the oracle of Delphi or the shrine of Ammon; all I have to do is to wash clean my hands, to pray aright, and then to fall asleep."

He who thus receives knowledge cannot contradict with assurance the prophecy given him. Many are they who have this experience of learning what awaits them: "It dwells with those who stay at home; it is the companion of those who travel abroad; it goes with men on military service; it administers the State; it works with the farmers and the merchants. No tyrant can forbid our dreams, unless he drive sleep from his kingdom. He is a foolish man who orders what cannot be done, and he is impious who decrees laws contrary to nature and to Divine will. And therefore all must be eager for this joy of Divination; this learning through dreams: woman, man, the old, the young, the poor and the rich, the private citizen and the holder of office, the man of the city and the peasant, he who works with tools and he who delivers orations. Divination tells of good, coming in the future; it tells ahead, in good time, that coming pleasure may be longer; it tells of evil which threatens, that precaution and prevention may intervene."

This, and much more, Synesius declared, had been written for his world by him, during the course of one night.

Another treatise, which he named *Dion* after the philosopher Dion Chrysostom, who lived at the turn of the second to the first century B.C., may well have occupied him during his stay at Cyrene after his second return from Alexandria. He is here still pagan at heart, even though married to a Christian wife; they were awaiting the birth of a child. For this child, and he was longing for a son, he was picturing his own aim, his own view of a mind devoted to philosophy:

"A philosopher, I judge, must hold nothing of evil in his character, nothing rude or rough; he must be initiated in the mysteries of the Graces, and be thoroughly Greek: by which I mean that he must know how to mingle with his fellow-men; he must be familiar, too, with all books of notable repute. For nothing else seems to have been the beginning of philosophy but a curiosity to learn, a desire to know; and therefore even in little children a mind that loves fables shows promise of a philosophic life!"

As the Greek scholar, so Synesius also held that he who seeks to follow philosophy must be stimulated by pleasure:

"For God has made pleasure a sticking-pin for the mind; by this pin it fastens to itself and gains the body's attention. Such a pin is beauty of words."

Contemplation of the good, the true, the beautiful, was his delight; at this time, however, he was devoted to Greek teaching, ancient and medieval; here is nothing of Christian mysticism:

"I already have heard of barbarous men from the most aristocratic peoples, leading a life of contemplation, taking no part in political affairs, keeping themselves aloof from society, eager to free themselves from nature's claim. They have sacred hymns, holy symbols, and certain prescribed approaches to the Divine. But in reality all these things cut them off from the Divine, turn their minds to a lower place of rest. They live apart from one another, and they never see or hear anything of the artistic, gracious, or intellectual."

In his last years Synesius had changed; imperfect though it was, there is definite evidence in his writings of Christian faith and spirit. Once again we find this evidence in his letters. Amid the suffering of these years he wrote to one Cyril, a bishop banished from his see by his Patriarch, who was probably Theophilus of Alexandria (Letter 12):

"Go to your Mother, the Church, brother Cyril; from her you have not been cut off, only separated for a while as penance for your sins.

"And may even this prove not wholly bitter to you."

To another bishop, driven from office because he would not tolerate the doctrine held by Arian heretics (Letter 128):

"What you were, you have held fast; you have not rejected your faith. . . . When a man is cast out from those enrolled in impious service, he is not robbed of the throne of true religion! Those people" (the Arians) "in ancient days were at war with God, and enemy to the holy Fathers of the Church."

To one John, who, it was said, had entered monastic life within that Church (Letter 146):

"I think that you are happier than one's prayers could wish for you: you who have left us mortals who wander in dark night amid the meadows of Ate, wallowing in worldly cares; you who have retreated from these burdens while you are still here on earth, to lay hold upon a blessed life.

"And all this is true, unless your friend Ganus, in telling us about it, thought it his business to tell lies; goodwill is so marvellously skillful in hiding the truth!

"Well, at any rate, this Ganus declares that you are dedicated to the solitary life, that you come into the city for one purpose only: just to find books, books on theology."

In another letter (No. 126) Synesius writes that he himself is building a monastery.

There is also evidence in his letters and other work, here and there, of Christian doctrine accepted by him. The letter *Against Andronicus* (No. 57) declares: "It was needful that Christ be sacrificed that He might pay the price of sin for all."

But especially in his hymns can we see the rising tide of Christian belief. When these were written we are not sure, but opinion veers for date toward the last years of his life. We have nine hymns from his pen; in form, they show Greek meters, anacreontic and anapaestic trimeters; in thought, a mingling of Neo-Platonic and Christian tradition.

Thus again and again a Holy Trinity is revered as God. Yet it is not the Holy Trinity of Catholic faith, though there is indeed Unity here, the Three in One (Hymn 2):

> One source, one foundation
> In threefold radiance strives.
> For there is depth of the Father,
> There also His glorious Son,
> Mighty offspring of His heart,
> Wisdom, Creator of the world.
> There also the unifying Light
> Of the Holy Spirit flames.

The First Person of the Holy Trinity in this verse of Synesius is God the Father, Who by His will and design brought forth His Son. The Son is pure and perfect Wisdom, Creator and Upholder of this world of ours and of all within it. Not only human life—body, mind, and soul—but also all Nature sings His praise. It rises in concert from Night and from Day, from sky and from wind, from land and from water, snow and storm, herbs and grasses; from cattle, from birds, from the fish which swim in shoals amid the sea.

To Synesius, God the Son, Holy Wisdom, is the Third Person of the Holy Trinity. The Second Person is God, the Holy Spirit, "the midmost Unifying Principle, Center of procession from God the Father to God the Son."

Each Person of this Holy Trinity is equal; all together make Unity in one perfect bond.

To this Supreme Unity Synesius pours out his praise, his devotion, his need. He prays that he may be freed from the prison of this flesh for contemplation of the Divine in blessed liberty; that his days be free from sin, from disease of spirit or of body, from troubles that devour the mind; that neither wealth nor poverty bind him to this earth (Hymn 3):

> Grant me, O Father,
> Grant to Thy servant
> Now, in flight of learning
> To open wide my wings.

And, when at last he flees from his sinful body, may he leap upward to the halls of Heaven, to the Source whence flowed his soul (*ibid.*):

> A drop from tide celestial
> I fell upon this earth;
> To that tide restore me!

He prays for his country, Egypt; for his home, his family, his wife, his sons. Three times (Hymns 5, 7, and 8) he writes of Christ as Son of the Virgin. In the fifth he tells of "the Christ Incarnate, born of a Virgin; Christ the Creator, the Life of the Universe, the Savior of mankind":

> For Thee the sun-god runs his course,
> In ceaseless dawn of day;
> For Thee the bull-faced moon at night
> Drives darkness far away.
> For Thee are born the fruits of earth,
> For Thee the flocks are fed.
> From stream which none may dare to name,
> With quickening radiance spread,
> Thou givest life to ordered worlds,
> Life radiant, strong and whole.
> And from Thy heart came forth to man
> His light, his mind, his soul.

The seventh hymn tells of Jesus of Jerusalem, immortal God, Mighty Son of God, Wisdom without measure, born of a Virgin, receiving gifts of gold, frankincense, and myrrh from the Magi guided by a star. It tells of the Descent of the Incarnate Lord after death to Hades. The ninth also tells of this, and of His freeing souls imprisoned there in fetters of death and fear. To this Synesius adds the terror of heathen guards of Hades—Orcus and the ferocious Cerberus—at the sight of the Redeemer.

The last hymn, No. 10, is an appeal to the Lord Christ from Synesius in his need:

> Be mindful, O Christ,
> Son of God,
> Reigning on high,
> Of Thy servant
> With sinful heart,
> Who wrote these words.
> And grant to me
> Forgiveness of sin
> Deep in my heart,
> In my tarnished soul.
> May I behold You,
> Jesus the Savior,

Thy glory in Heaven.
And when I come
Songs will I sing
To You, Healer of souls,
Healer of bodies;
To the Great Father, too,
And the Spirit Divine.

Perhaps the Christian spirit of this bishop of Ptolemais is most clearly shown in the pathetic words of his *Catastasis,* "Discourse," which describes his mind and thought during barbarian assaults toward the end of his life. Here in translation is part of its last chapter (P.G. LXVI, 1571).

"Alas for Cyrene, whose public records trace descendants, down to myself, from Hercules! Do not think of me as antiquated, as out-of-date, when, among those who know, I lament those of noble birth, now no longer here! Alas for those Doric graves, amid which I shall never rest! Alas for Ptolemais, and for me, the last priest of its line!

"For me, too, dread fate is at hand. I can say no more; tears have overtaken and held my tongue. Of one thing alone do I think —that I must go, forsaking things holy, things sacred. I must leave by sea. Yet, when someone calls me to the ship, I shall beg for still a little time. First, to the Church of God I will go, and there I will walk around its altar; there I will water its precious pavement with my tears; I will not run away before I kiss that door, and that throne! There again and again—O! how many times?—I shall call upon God and change my mind! How often shall I clasp those latticed gates in my hands! . . .

"The time of assault, that fated time, draws near, that time which, they say, the winged messenger threatened, the leader of the enemy host. Truly that moment of peril will force priests to hasten to the courts of the Lord! And I myself, I shall stand firm in my own place, in the Church. I shall guard the vessels of holy water; I shall cling to the sacred pillars which uphold the Table safe and unharmed. There I shall sit still, while I live; there I shall lie when I am dead.

"For I am a priest of God, and perhaps it is for me to complete my service in offering Him my life."

In the sixth century Evagrius Scholasticus, a Christian lawyer who wrote in lively Greek an *Ecclesiastical History,* pictures in it Synesius as a man after his own heart and mind:

"Since I am trying hard to describe the times of Cyril, so

famous in history, as vividly as I can, come, let Synesius of Cyrene appear, to adorn our conversation with his own memories. This Synesius was indeed learned and skilled in all other things; but in philosophy he reached the summit of artistic honor. Why, among Christians he was held a marvel, Christians who judge what they see neither by partiality nor by antipathy. And so they persuaded him to submit to the saving new birth of baptism, to take upon himself the yoke of the priesthood, when he was not yet willing to believe the traditional doctrine of the Resurrection. For they thought, and with very good reason, that with his other virtues he would cherish also this, and they were not defrauded of their hope. What kind of man and how great a man he was, his letters, written after his consecration, letters, so elegant, so eloquent, so learned, bear witness; as also does his address made to the Emperor, and all the good works from his pen."

Hypatia was still lecturing at Alexandria in this year 413; we turn to Socrates for our knowledge of the two years which remained to her on this earth.

In 412 Theophilus, Patriarch of Alexandria, had died, and had been succeeded by his nephew Cyril, after a grim struggle between candidates. Of Cyril we shall learn later; here it will be enough to show that, like his uncle, he held determined stand for orthodoxy in the Catholic Church and was to carry on determined war against those who did not follow her faith.

Very soon, then, he was directing his wrath against the Novatianists in Alexandria; a sect which had gained its name from one Noyatian, a Roman priest of the third century of our era. Novatian is an interesting figure. He won deserved honor as theologian from his work *On the Trinity,* a treatise firmly Catholic. In later years, however, he was criticized by many in the Church, for two reasons. First, he declared that those who had sinned by denial of their faith in order to save their lives during the persecution of the Christian Church by the Emperor Decius (249–251) were not to be allowed absolution and communion of the altar. God, said Novatian, had indeed power to forgive such mortal sin as theirs; but He had not given this particular right to His priests in this world.

Second: When Novatian heard that Cornelius, bishop of Rome, was willing to grant reconciliation with the Church to these lapsed Christians, in anger he himself sought consecration as bishop, and as such he opposed Cornelius in Italy, appearing as rival and "anti-Pope."

Novatian himself died for his Christian faith during the persecution of Valerian, Emperor from 253 until 258. But his many followers, stern and grim, went further in error than he had done; they denied reception into the Church to any one guilty of any sin held mortal. Until the seventh century they were to stand against the Church; then their schism gradually disappeared.

In Alexandria Cyril as Patriarch "closed all their churches, after removing all sacred vessels and ornaments, and then deprived their bishop Theopemptus of all his rights and privileges."

Far more fierce was the campaign of Cyril against the Jews in Alexandria. Here again Socrates is our source. Above all men those of Alexandria were most easily incited to savage uprising and riot, especially on festive occasions. Such riots were apt to occur on the Sabbath day when Jews were at leisure, free to gather in the public theater and to enjoy dances given by experts in ballet.

On one of these Saturdays the crowd found another matter of interest present in the theater. Christian men were there in great number to hear Orestes, City Prefect of Alexandria, speak on vital questions of politics. The Jews heartily hated Christians, and the more heartily, on this occasion, since among the crowd were many supporters of the Patriarch Cyril, whom they especially detested as their enemy. One of the most loyal among Cyril's Christian supporters was Hierax, a teacher of children in Alexandria; he was well known for his delight in the Patriarch's speeches and sermons.

Directly the Jews caught sight of Hierax they shouted that he had come to raise riot in the theater. Orestes had long been held a bitter enemy to Cyril and his stern measures. Had he not openly declared that bishops were quick to pluck power from the hands of prefects, and that Cyril was opposed to him himself, as Prefect of Alexandria?

Amid the continuing uproar Orestes broke off his speech, ordered Hierax arrested, and put to torture then and there in full sight of Jews and Christians.

Christian men naturally hurried to tell their Patriarch of this treatment ordered by the Prefect. Cyril at once summoned leaders among the Jews to his presence; in strong language he warned them of trouble to come, did they not cease giving insult and grievous injury to Christian men.

To no purpose; threats increased the wrath of Jews and they resolved to act then and there. In secret conference they decided to open attack upon the Christians by night. All was carefully arranged; in order to distinguish Jewish enemy from Christian victim, each Jew was told to carry a circlet woven from palm fibre.

On the night agreed upon, the Jewish leaders sent men run-

ning through the city, crying "The Church of Alexander is on fire!"
Every Christian who heard the call ran to the rescue. Toward the
same church rushed the Jews, to rob and to murder every one who
did not hold out before him that circlet of palm.

Daybreak revealed a dreadful sight, of bodies lying dead and
unburied, of men wounded, robbed, and helpless. Every one knew
it was the work of the Jews. In utter fury Cyril marched at the head
of a host of his men to the Jewish synagogue; there he halted, and
commanded his followers to drive every Jew they could find out of
the gates of Alexandria, and to seize what he held, food or weapon
or money of copper or gold.

In equal rage the Prefect, Orestes, hurried messengers on their
way toward Constantinople to inform the Emperor, now Theodosius
the Second, of Cyril's vengeance against the Jewish inhabitants of
his city.

Then monks of Nitria, of whom we heard in connection with
Theophilus, Patriarch of Alexandria, came in haste and in hun-
dreds, from their mountain solitudes, eager to aid Cyril and protect
him from assault. Some fifty of them, running along in the city
street, came upon Orestes in his carriage. "Killer!", "Gentile!" they
shouted. The Prefect, sure that this insult had been prompted by
Cyril, called out: "I am a Christian, baptized at Constantinople by
its bishop, Atticus!" In answer, a monk, Ammonius, hurled a heavy
stone at Orestes; it struck him on the head and blood flowed quickly from the wound. At this point nearly all his officers ran to hide
in the crowd standing around, terrified by this assault, while men
of the city rushed forward to defend their Prefect.

Ammonius was caught where he stood, and taken to prison.
As soon as Orestes was well enough, he ordered the monk into his
presence, put him to torture, and continued the torture until his
prisoner died.

In very different terms these happenings were reported to
Theodosius at Constantinople. Cyril for his part sent word that
he held Ammonius, lying in state in the Cathedral of Alexandria,
worthy of a martyr's crown. Other report, however, judged that
Ammonius had suffered for his rash folly, and soon Cyril thought
it well to discontinue his praise.

Enmity continued between Patriarch and Prefect, even after
Cyril as Patriarch had made an overture toward reconciliation.
Of this Orestes would hear nothing, not even when Cyril on the
Book of the Holy Gospels gave assurance of sincerity.

It has been necessary to describe these events in order to prepare the way for the fate—and fate it was—of the philosopher

Hypatia. It was a happy thing for Synesius that he did not live until 415.

Tragedy indeed came to her through her skill and power of wise and cool deliberation, in dealing with problems not only of mental and physical science but of current politics. Men of high office in Alexandria frequently sought her counsel; Orestes, its Prefect, often talked with her.

And so rumor went around the city amid Christian men and women that it was the influence of this pagan counselor, the philosopher Hypatia, which was hindering reconciliation of Orestes with the Patriarch, Cyril.

Little by little, the wrath of the citizens at this thought burned into flame; soon the flame of anger burst into explosion. One day the sight of Hypatia, driving home serenely in her carriage from a lecture, drove those who had been seeking her into fury. They dragged her from her seat and carried her to "the Church of Caesar." There they stripped her of her clothes, beat her to death with potsherds, tore her limb from limb, and burned the fragments which had held that revered mind. It was the season of Lent, March 415.

In fairness to Cyril it should be said that, although many of those who murdered Hypatia were in his service as "infirmarians," men who gave of their own will their aid and support to the hospitals of Alexandria, men who also served him in causes less desirable, yet no evidence allows us to believe that the Patriarch of Alexandria was in any way directly responsible for this ghastly crime.

The poet Palladas, who lived in Alexandria during the fifth century, wrote for her in Greek verse a cry of awe and wonder:

> When I see thee, I worship thee, thee and thy words,
> Beholding the starry dwelling of the Maiden;
> For all thy life by thee is passed with God Himself!
> O holy Hypatia, O words of beauty's grace,
> Thou, the pure star of wise and true philosophy!

CHAPTER FOUR

Honorius and Galla Placidia

From the East we now pass to the Empire of the West. It was under the nominal rule of Honorius, brother of Arcadius and ten years old in 395, the year of his accession, but under the actual direction of Stilicho, appointed by Theodosius the Great as defender of Honorius during his minority.

If Arcadius was weak and indolent, Honorius was in general nothing but a figurehead: cowardly, indifferent, apathetic, save when driven to act by some strong emotion or by a desire to gain what for the moment he willed.

Theodosius I, the Great, had left another child, his youngest: a girl named Galla Placidia, offspring of his second marriage, with Galla. The exact date of her birth is not known, probably it was about 388; in that case she would have been some six years old when her mother died in 394. Her early years were spent in Milan and in Rome, under the care of Serena, wife of Stilicho; and of their daughters, Maria and Thermantia, who married her half-brother, the Emperor, one after the other: in 398, when Placidia, as she is generally called, was about ten, and in 408, when she was about twenty years old.

In character and in spirit she was entirely different from her half-brothers, born to Flaccilla, the first wife of Theodosius; it was Placidia who had inherited the courage, the energy, the quick zeal for political action, the determination, so marked in their father. As girl and young woman she listened eagerly to news of events, to the talk at Court, to the words of her brother Honorius and his ministers concerning success or failure, hope or fear, in the Empire of the West.

Twice had Stilicho, its Commander-in-Chief, allowed Alaric and his Goths to escape from him: once in 395 in Thessaly by order of Arcadius, a second time in 397 by his own will near Mount Phloe. He had hoped to bring success to the West, and therefore to himself, by alliance with this Gothic chieftain and his sturdy fighters; he had even, we may think, discussed this matter of alliance with Alaric himself.

But in 401 we find Alaric working for his own ends. There was then no thought of alliance with Stilicho in his mind. He was now king of the Visigoths, Goths of the West; he was going to invade Italy, to force concessions from its Emperor Honorius. It was the month of November; marching to Milan, where the Court was in residence, he laid siege to its ramparts. Claudian pictures the terror of Honorius, even thinking of escape to Gaul:

> Why think you of shameful flight, why of Gallic lands, why do you long, leaving Latium behind you, by the distant Saône to fortify your camp? Shall, forsooth, our city pass to Arctic tribesmen? Shall our kingdom settle on the Rhône, its body survive its head?
>
> *De Bello Gothico,* 296ff.

Stilicho was absent in Raetia, across the Alps north of Italy, where he was holding back from another invasion of Italy a barbarian force under Radagaisus. Early in 402 success set him free and he marched south to relieve Milan:

> O land of Italy, accept our friendship's bond, our hearts, which share alike with thee our common fate. Tarry awhile, protecting by thine arms those walls, till I return for signal to thy chosen host.
>
> *Ibid.* 310ff.

Baffled at Milan, Alaric had now to decide on his next move. He withdrew to Pollentia (Pollenza), near Turin, for preparation and debate with his soldiers. Claudian gives us here his conception of this council, a picture very probably true:

> One of the oldest men in this gathering rises to speak his mind:

> Often in vain I warned thee that in Macedon thou keep sworn pact, safe in its keeping to abide. But since hot flame of youth snatched thee to wander far, now then, at least, if any care thou hast for thine, escape these bounds, I beg, while foes are far away, while yet thou canst slip headlong from this Western land; lest, eager to rob anew, thou lose all once won, and as a wolf to shepherd, pay for past misdeeds within the fold.
>
> *De Bello Gothico,* 496ff.

In anger Alaric answers him:

If old age, helpless in mind, robbed of its sense, did not forgive thee, never while my life is strong, would Danube's stream
hear unavenged these words of shame! Shall I, who put to
flight so many Emperors, as the river Hebrus knows, suffer
thee to stand and talk of flight for me, when all Nature herself yields me obedience?

Ibid. 521ff.

On Easter Day, April 6, 402, the battle of Pollentia was fought
between the armies of Alaric and Stilicho, with disaster on each
side and no certain victory for either Goth or Roman. The Emperor
Honorius had had enough of alarm. He moved with all his Court
from Milan, so easily blockaded, to Ravenna: Ravenna was protected by outlying marshes.

The Goths left Italy, only to return under Alaric's command
for assault upon Verona. Once more Alaric safely withdrew from his
attempt, and once more nothing of importance was gained, even
though in 403 Honorius left security in Ravenna to celebrate a
"triumph" at Rome. No wonder that the Spanish priest Orosius,
writing early in this same fifth century his *Histories against the
Pagans,* declared: "I say nothing about Alaric the king, again and
again conquered with his Goths, again and again surrounded, always allowed to escape."

Stilicho, it would seem, could not make Alaric his personal
enemy; his thoughts were constantly fixed upon Eastern Illyricum.
With Alaric he made alliance; the Visigothic king promised to
await his call for aid in its capture.

Impatiently he waited while Stilicho made ready. But the opportunity for which Stilicho was longing had not yet arrived when in
405 he was faced by a sudden invasion of barbarians under Radagaisus, this time into northern Italy itself. At once, Stilicho knew
well, this must be crushed; in the words of Orosius, this Radagaisus
was "by far the most savage of all enemies, in years of old or years
of the present. In a sudden rush he flooded all Italy. They say that
his army held more than two hundred thousand Goths. He combined this incredible multitude with untamed courage and the fact
that he was a pagan of Scythian blood; as was the custom among
barbarian peoples of this kind, he had vowed to offer all the blood
of the Romans to his heathen gods."

Yet before the year 406 ended he was defeated, captured, and
put to death, and Stilicho, his conqueror, could at last determine
to call upon Alaric, his ally, for support. That Illyrian land he was

resolved to win, undeterred by the grim fact that in December of this same year a host of barbarians—Vandals, Suevians and Alans—were swarming from Germany across the Rhine to plunder Gaul.

In 407, as he was about to march forward, trouble again intervened. A letter to his Commander-in-Chief arrived from the Emperor Honorius himself. A usurper, this letter told, Constantine by name, had been hailed by his soldiers as "Emperor" in Britain; from Britain he had crossed to Gaul and there also had claimed the Imperial throne. Much of Gaul he had already occupied.

The relationship of Britain to Rome, its ruler, had been of varied kind during recent years. Claudian in 399 had represented Rome as offering words of gratitude to Honorius, the Emperor, for his protection of Britain (*Against Eutropius* I, 392ff.):

> What power I have with thee as Emperor, No distant things do teach; Saxons conquered, the sea kinder, Picts overcome, and Britain free from fear.

In 400 the same poet had described Britain herself as thanking Stilicho for her safety (*Consulship of Stilicho* II, 250ff.):

> "Me, too, dying through enemies near by," she said, "Stilicho protected, when the Scot all Ireland roused against me, and seas foamed with unfriendly oars."

In late 401 or early 402, however, Stilicho, before the battle of Pollentia against Alaric and his Visigoths, had had need of all the troops he could muster. He had been forced to call men from Britain, and Britain had lost part of her defence (*The Gothic War*, 416f.):

> That legion came to him, stationed in far Britain, soldiers who crushed the cruel Scot . . .

Fear had fallen upon the people thus deprived of soldiers; it was for them, they decided, to look after themselves, to appoint an Emperor of their own making, a leader who would protect them against the invaders, Picts, Scots, or Saxons, so ready to sail to Britain's shores.

In 406 they had elected one Marcus for their Imperial throne; before long in scorn and contempt they had put him to death. Early in 407 one Gratian had succeeded him; after four months he, too, was condemned to the axe.

Constantine, chosen as Britain's "Emperor" the same year, had nothing but his name, magic in past history, to give him election; he came from the ranks. Quickly, however, he had shown sagacity by leaving Britain for Gaul and thus in all likelihood escaping murder.

In this crisis, with a usurper of Imperial claim for both Britain and Gaul, Stilicho could do nothing but forget Illyricum and hasten to Ravenna for debate and discussion with ministers of its Court; Honorius himself was helpless.

Alaric, again left waiting by Stilicho, in 408 decided to make use of wasted time. He sent to Ravenna an indignant letter. In the service of Stilicho, he wrote, of the Emperor Honorius and of the Empire of the West, he had marched from Epirus in Greece to Noricum, a province northeast of Italy, that he might be near Illyricum. Was not the gaining of Eastern Illyricum a work for the profit of the West?

Letter in hand and Honorius by his side, Stilicho hurried to consult the Senate at Rome. Alaric, he reported, was demanding an immense sum, no less than four thousand pounds of gold, as compensation for his trouble and waste of time. Should payment be made? Or would war against Alaric be the better course?

The Senate was of the opinion that Alaric, in Noricum, was now an invader of Western land, and that war must drive him out. Stilicho opposed this motion and frankly gave his argument; that Alaric had been waiting to join him in transferring Illyrian land from the rule of Arcadius to that of Honorius; "and so we should have done had not the Emperor written to me concerning the trouble in Gaul."

The sum demanded was handed over to Alaric; not, Zosimus tells us, "by the Senate's own will, but through its fear of Stilicho." One senator, of rank and high position in Rome, spoke up when the vote gained approval: "This is no making of peace, but a pact of servitude!" And even he, directly the meeting was over, fled for refuge to a church near by, fearing penalty for his daring.

This settled, Honorius prepared to leave Rome at once for Ravenna and safety; he was in panic lest Alaric, now so near at hand, should march against Rome, besiege and capture it, along with himself, the Emperor, its head. This terror Stilicho tried long and vigorously to quench; he felt that Honorius owed his presence to his capital city. As a final argument he brought forward a report that mutiny had broken out among the soldiers in Ticinum, a city later known as Pavia, north of Ravenna. He talked in vain; the Emperor started on his way and reached Bologna.

There, also, trouble met him. It was now May in the year 408 and news came from Constantinople that his brother Arcadius had died. Moreover, soldiers in Bologna were rising in rebellion; the city was full of disorder. Stilicho must come at once, to quell this unrest and to consult with him concerning Constantinople and the succession in rule. The heir to the Imperial crown of the East, Theodosius the Second, born to Arcadius and Eudoxia in 401, was only seven years old. Honorius felt that it was his duty to go at once to Constantinople for the arranging of regency and settled government.

Stilicho came, crushed the riot, and disagreed with Honorius. By no means should the Emperor leave Italy while Constantine was usurping the throne in Gaul, even by this time holding his Court in the city of Arles. Were Honorius absent abroad, Alaric might decide to invade Italy. Who knew? Far better for Honorius to remain at home and endeavor to persuade Alaric to unite his barbarians with Roman legions in a march again Constantine! He himself, Stilicho, would go to Constantinople to represent the Emperor in appointing a regent.

Honorius, who always followed the suggestions of Stilicho, meekly wrote letters to Constantinople and to Alaric, then as fast as he could left Bologna for Ravenna. He was weary of matters of state. At Ravenna he was looking forward to building and stocking a magnificent poultry-yard, an occupation full of pleasure and peace.

Stilicho remained at Bologna; he had not the slightest intention of traveling to the East. Unfortunately for him in 408 Honorius, his Emperor, found other material for his mind at Ravenna besides his cocks and hens. In his Court there was a minister of some importance, one Olympius, with whom he was on friendly terms; often they talked together on matters of mutual interest. Olympius, born near the Black Sea, was Christian by profession, and Honorius liked to discuss with him matters connected with the Church, especially plans for legislation against heathen and heretics. The Emperor was strictly orthodox in his religious views, and Olympius knew it; he was very careful in what he said.

With him in attendance Honorius went on to stay at Ticinum, hoping by amicable and frank address to calm down its rebel garrison. As they journeyed Olympius skillfully brought their talk round to Stilicho, working gradually from praise to doubt and question, then finally to open criticism. Olympius hated the Commander-in-Chief with all his jealous heart and soul.

At last he felt that he might safely venture upon a crucial point, highly interesting to Honorius at the moment: "Why, Sire, do you think that Stilicho is so keen on going to Constantinople? I can tell you, and truly. He means to murder your nephew, Theodosius, and so to win for his own son, Eucherius, the Imperial throne of the East!" The Emperor was overcome with horror. Surely

Olympius would not have dared to say this to him unless it were true. Could it be true?

Olympius went further. Among the soldiers at Ticinum, excited by discontent, he constantly threw out hints, tales against Stilicho; watching, like a witch bent over her cauldron, his poisonous words inflame their minds, until rebellion rose to boiling wrath against this Commander and all who spoke for him.

And so one day in 408 this bubbling brew burst in fury to destroy those known or thought to be supporters of Stilicho. In quick succession they were cut down: the Praetorian Prefect and the Master of Soldiers in Gaul, who were in Ticinum at this time; the Praetorian Prefect of Italy, its Master of Horse, its Count of the Palace Guards, its President of the Treasury, its Count of the Imperial Patrimony. For long Honorius lay, shivering with fear, hidden in his Palace. Yet even he could not hear of wholesale massacre unmoved; when the uproar was at its height he threw aside his Imperial purple and in his tunic rushed out to startle the raving mob into a moment of quiet. Only a moment; even as he called aloud for peace one of his confidential counselors was killed, grasping the Emperor's feet and crying for his life.

At Bologna Stilicho waited, tense with anxiety. Was the Emperor alive or dead? What was he to do? He called an assembly of his soldiers, and they voted immediate march for battle against the revolt, whatever the Emperor's fate. Then word came that Honorius was safe, and Stilicho hesitated. Was it wise to lead out from Bologna these men, all of Germanic, barbarian race, to punish and to discipline the garrison at Ticinum, citizens of Roman nationality?

No, he decided, it was not; and he forbade the move. Deep resentment followed; all were angry, especially when Stilicho's reason became known. Sarus, a Gothic officer of great value, powerful both in muscle and in mind, sullenly retired to his tent. What would Honorius think if Stilicho did not appear at Ticinum?

Stilicho did not go near Ticinum; while his barbarians argued in their wrath he left for Ravenna. It was not difficult for Olympius to convince the Emperor that Stilicho was his enemy; to induce him to order by letter Stilicho's arrest in Ravenna.

The letter arrived and Stilicho heard of its command; at once he rushed for church and sanctuary. Next morning military officers entered the church, accompanied by the bishop of Ravenna; in his presence they declared on their solemn oath that Honorius had not ordered sentence of death, merely detaining under guard. Stilicho yielded to persuasion and left the church. He was hardly

outside when a second letter from the Emperor arrived, commanding his death as penalty for treason. At once he was led out to face
the executioner. Soldiers and servants in loyalty ran to rescue him;
with threats of dire penalty he waved them away and bent his
head beneath the axe, August 22, 408.

His son Eucherius met the same fate. Honorius sent two of
his men, Arsacius and Terentius, to pursue and kill him. They
allowed their victim in mockery to take brief refuge in a church
of Rome, then carried out the Emperor's order. Zosimus remarks
that if these two servants had not been hurrying to escape Alaric
and his Goths, the life of Eucherius would have been saved.

Olympius, now master of offices and first in favor with Honorius, gave lavish reward to those who had worked, willingly or not,
against Stilicho; and the utmost punishment to those suspected of
being his friends. The Emperor fully approved these acts. Stilicho's
executioner, Heraclian, was appointed Count of the Roman province of Africa; Arsacius and Terentius were given office as Imperial
chamberlains. Anyone suspected of knowing anything concerning
Stilicho and his acts was ordered to appear for grilling examination
in Court; if he could, or would, tell nothing, he was soundly beaten,
tortured, even to death. From those who had held office under
Stilicho huge fines were extorted, paid as taxes to the Imperial
Treasury. The Emperor himself dismissed from his Palace Thermantia, daughter of Stilicho, whom in this same year, 408, he had
made his second wife and Empress; she was deprived of all claim
to title and sent home to her mother, Serena.

But nothing said under trial or torture proved that Stilicho
was actual traitor in deed to Honorius. Nevertheless rumor of his
treachery ran around widely, and many believed it. The Gothic
writer Jordanes, who wrote in the sixth century his *Romana*, "History of Rome," found space in his scant narrative to declare:
"Stilicho's two daughters, one after another, were wedded to the
Emperor Honorius, and each of them died a virgin. Stilicho scorned
Honorius and coveted his throne; so he bribed with gifts of money
Alans, Suevi, and Vandals to rise against that throne. He longed
to make his son Eucherius Emperor; and Eucherius was a pagan,
contriving crafty snares to entrap Christian men."

Meanwhile Alaric the Visigoth was still in Noricum, awaiting
events and thinking that peace was preferable to continual war. To
Honorius he now sent envoys, offering, in return for a moderate sum
money from the government of Italy, to keep the peace, to support this promise by yielding hostages, and to withdraw his soldiers
from the Roman province of Noricum. Honorius took the offer

to his prime minister, Olympius, for due deliberation; Olympius rejected it. He had full power of administration, and he worked for no good end; but Honorius at once followed his advice.

Alaric, then, thrown into quick anger at the dismissal of his bid for peace, determined to retaliate by war. From Pannonia he summoned for his aid his brother-in-law Athaulf and marched for Rome. It was autumn in 408 when he encamped before its walls and entered upon blockade for all within.

His approach was watched with great fear by those who guarded the city: fear not only of the enemy outside, but of any who might give support to Alaric from within. Of all persons, suspicion soon fell upon Serena: widow of Stilicho, but also mother-in-law of Honorius himself. Had not Stilicho made Alaric his ally? Had not Serena again and again endeavored to influence the Emperor and his ministers?

Here the Emperor's half-sister, Galla Placidia, enters the story. She was now about twenty years old, and was living in Rome. Zosimus tells that she supported its Senate in condemning Serena to death. If Serena were removed, it was said, Alaric would depart from the city; she was a traitor and he was relying on her aid. These foolish rumors, dependent upon the fact that Serena had been wife of Stilicho and that she was vitally interested in politics, passed from gossip into stubborn assurance; Serena died by strangling at Rome's command.

Zosimus the pagan, our chief authority for these years, gives another version of her fate. She was entirely innocent of treachery against Rome, he was sure, but she had sinned against the Mother of the Gods. In 394, fourteen years before, when Theodosius the Great was marking his victory over Eugenius by driving out the pagan priests and priestesses and closing their temples, Serena merrily had decided to take a look at the empty shrine of Rhea. There the image of the goddess was still standing in human form, and around its neck sparkled a magnificent circlet of jewels. Quickly, believing that she was alone, Serena seized it for her own delight. Then suddenly from the silence rose a stream of insult, ending in a threat of violence: "May you and your husband and your children suffer worthy punishment!" It came from an old woman, a Vestal Virgin left in the temple of the Goddess.

Serena paid no attention, gave no answer. What harm could that withered creature do? Soon, however, night after night brought her a dream of fearful doom, of death about to fall on her. Doom did follow this vision, when her husband and her son were put to death, her daughter was shamed, and her own neck yielded to suspicion of treason on her part, if not to her guilt in the seizure of that necklace of Rhea, Mother of Zeus.

This, Zosimus continues, did not deter Alaric from attacking Rome in 408. He blockaded its gates; he occupied its harbor on the river Tiber, thus cutting off incoming supplies of food. Day after day citizens looked valiantly for aid from the Emperor at Ravenna; none came. Food still on hand within the city itself soon was being doled out in rations; first each family received one half of the usual amount, and then only one third. Hunger was followed by famine, and famine by death. Dead bodies lay everywhere within the walls; they could not be carried outside because of the blockade. Finally "the city became a tomb of the dead, and if lack of food had not destroyed its life, the stench rising from its corpses would have been quite sufficient."

So began the winter of 408. Two figures rise above its gloom and tragedy. Laeta, widow of the Emperor Gratian and therefore a kinswoman of Honorius, with her mother spent recklessly the resources left them by Theodosius the Great, in doing all that was possible for starving fellow-citizens.

Driven by despair but with a brave front, the Senate at Rome sent envoys to Alaric. Their people, the message told, were ready to make peace, provided that the conditions offered by him were not impossibly severe. If, however, it was his will to make war upon them, they still knew how to fight.

No one in the city was really sure whether Alaric himself or some other Goth was carrying on this siege. It seemed wise, therefore, to send with the envoys one who knew Alaric personally and understood his character. He was John, head of the clerical bureau in Rome, a man skilled in diplomacy who might well be of service. Perhaps it was he who, some fifteen years later, in 423, seized Imperial rule in Rome.

Diplomacy, however, was of little use in this meeting. The envoys soon found out that they were face to face with Alaric, a barbarian king. At their words "We are ready for battle," he replied, "Thick corn is easier to cut than thin!" and roared with laughter. When they asked him to name his terms he answered: "All the gold, all the silver, all the furnishings, all the barbarian slaves, owned by the city!"

It was mockery, and for a moment no one spoke. Then one of the messengers, braver than his companions, asked in derision: "Well, if you take all this, what will be left to us?" "Your lives," was the curt answer.

The Romans met this by a request for brief truce; the Senate would wish to discuss their answer.

Discussion, of course, led to nothing. Then one morning Pompeianus, Prefect of Rome, rose in the House to offer a suggestion. He had heard, he said, from men passing through the city that the people of Narni in Umbria, threatened by assault of barbarians, had offered prayer and sacrifice to the pagan gods of ancient time, beseeching their aid. Terrific peals of thunder and flashes of lightning had followed; the barbarians had fled, and with them all fear. "Could we do the same here in Rome?" Pompeianus asked.

The Senate, after some shaking of heads, voted to consider the proposal. To begin with, someone suggested that Pompeianus might examine the ancient Etruscan books of ritual. This proposal disturbed rather than comforted his Christian conscience, and he resolved to seek audience with the Pope, Innocent the First. Innocent, who well understood Rome's peril, decided that her safety was of vital importance; he authorized the Senate to use all the resources it held, even pagan ritual. But on one condition, and in this he was resolute: in secrecy, and only in secrecy, not in public.

The Prefect carried this instruction to officials at Rome, and they would hear nothing concerning secrecy; the Senate must openly declare what was to be done, and either on the Capitoline Hill or in the Forum, sacrifice must be offered in public view to the ancient gods of Rome or not be offered at all. Since no one of due office could be found to officiate on these terms, the suggestion was dropped and Rome turned again to debate.

Again legates were despatched to Alaric, praying for definite and possible terms of peace, and this time they were given. Rome, said the Visigothic king, might win peace from him at the price of five thousand pounds in gold, of thirty thousand in silver, with three thousand fleeces dyed scarlet, and pepper three thousand pounds in weight.

This report again caused consternation. The Treasury of Rome could not begin to yield such enormous tribute. After long and anxious argument one device alone seemed to offer any hope: to tax each citizen with all strictness, to wring from each man every coin he could afford to contribute. This was agreed upon, and the duty of assessing each man's tax was laid upon a magistrate named Palladius, with power to command. He worked out his scheme and collection was duly made from house to house; yet, in spite of drastic determination, the amount finally gathered fell woefully short of what was required.

Once more the Senate met; in zealous wrath Zosimus recorded its decision. As a last measure a vote was passed to strip from statues and images, still preserved, even honored in Rome, of the gods of pagan days all the precious metal and jewels which adorned them; also to melt down figures wrought in silver or gold.

The tribute, now at last sufficient, was conveyed to Alaric, and hostages were also offered him; in return the gates of Rome were thrown open and the Gothic army marched away, in December 408. But the long, hard siege had left disorder in the city; from its gates a multitude of slaves, sick of hardship, poured out to join the barbarians, who swept down against Roman citizens on their way to the harbor, seizing the provision they carried. It is to Alaric's credit that when he heard of these attacks he forbade them under threat of severe penalty.

The early days of 409 brought to the Emperor Honorius, still in retreat at Ravenna, envoys bearing a petition from Constantine, usurper since 407 of Imperial title in Gaul and Britain. Now he asked pardon for his act; it had been forced upon him, he declared, by his army. Honorius listened and meditated. His peace with Alaric, as he knew, was not assured, not even expected to last long; he did not want Italy to have two wars on her mind or on her payroll. More-over, Constantine was holding captive—so he had heard—two of the House of Theodosius the Great and therefore kinsmen of Honorius himself, the nobles Verenian and Didymus. It would be wise to be civil to this impostor. Honorius therefore made answer in gracious words, declared that Constantine should be co-Emperor, and even sent him as a gift an Imperial robe of purple. So Constantine be-came co-Emperor in the West.

It was all done in vain; the throats of those kinsmen had al-ready been cut.

The tenure of Constantine in Imperial rule, however, was of brief duration. Brief though it was, it had embraced Spain. This portion of his "empire" he eventually entrusted to the care of his son Constans, to whom, "once a monk, sad to say," declares Orosius, one of our authorities here, "he had given rank as Caesar." Un-fortunately Constans was allowed to take with him to Spain bar-barian soldiers in his army, a fatal error. *Hinc,* observes Orosius, borrowing from Virgil, *apud Hispaniam prima mali labes:* "Hence came for Spain the first stroke of evil." In former days the guarding of mountain passes over the Pyrenees, of paths from Gaul into Spain, had been committed to native Spaniards, who had vigorously kept watch. Now one Gerontius, with a band of soldiers enrolled in the Imperial service and known as "Honoriaci," used their eyes and their minds in raids for the plunder of its lands, so attractively fertile. So did others who from ransacked Gaul looked with longing envy toward that Spain in which, so they had heard, unnumbered riches were to be found. In the early autumn of 409 a multitude of barbarians, Vandals, with Suevians and Alans, were allowed by these guards, so negligent and probably so treacherous, so contemptuous of duty to the Empire, to march through the mountains from Gaul to Spain and, once across the border, to work their will in ruthless devastation.

The Vandals carried out this invasion under their king, at this time Gunderic; gradually under him from 409 onwards as one people in Spain they became settled and secure.

In Rome trouble had also early in 409 raised its head again and again. Terror remained even after Alaric's soldiers had marched from its walls in December 408. Hostages had been offered by the Emperor, but he had not delivered them. Instead he had summoned from Dalmatia six thousand men to guard this capital city; early in 409 they came, strong and confident, eager to support the defence. Their leader, Valens, had no greater joy than to face danger. All was useless; Alaric lay in wait to rush out, to kill and capture. Then once more Athaulf came to support his brother-in-law, Alaric. In a vain attempt to move Honorius into energetic working for peace did senators, magistrates, ministers, even Pope Innocent himself, hurry to Ravenna.

Also early in 409 rebellion had broken out in the Imperial Palace. The eunuchs who were in attendance had risen against a Master of Offices who oppressed individuals and did nothing for Rome in her misery. Before the throne of the Emperor himself they had declared Olympius the cause of all the troubles of these years. Faced by this eruption Honorius could do nothing but submit to their demand; Olympius had been deposed and had fled for refuge to Dalmatia.

With his removal from office at Court a new list of its ministers had appeared. Influence over the Emperor had now passed to Jovius, a man equal if not superior to Olympius in his ambition; he had been appointed Praetorian Prefect of Italy.

One of the names on this list merits a few words. He was Generid, Master of Soldiers in Dalmatia, Pannonia, Noricum, and Raetia; he was therefore of important standing.

He was also a pagan, and Zosimus, his fellow in devotion to the heathen gods of Rome, gives him an attractive character: a barbarian by birth, but one of virtue and valor, with a hatred of greed in any shape. When the Emperor issued an order forbidding the pagans, whom, as erring and mistaken, his orthodox mind despised. to appear at Court wearing the military insignia of Rome, whatever their rank in his army, Generid, Commander of a multitude of soldiers, stayed at home. Honorius sent him word to appear at once with his men; Generid replied courteously, giving the reason for his absence; he could not show disrespect to his rank. In anxious embarrassment the Emperor gave answer that as reward for high and honorable service Generid might appear in military dress; every one would understand this exception allowed him. "No," retorted Generid; "I will not accept an honor of which my soldiers are deprived by law!" The law was repealed; henceforth Christian and heathen fighters attended Court in full military honor.

Like Olympius, the new Praetorian Prefect wanted to be the one and only ruler in the Palace, dominating all from the Emperor downward. It was necessary, then, to get rid of all who might work for the return of Olympius, who as Master of offices had been first favorite with Honorius and, of course, well served at court.

Jovius decided that his best plan would be: first, to incite rebellion among the Imperial guards at Ravenna; then to accuse as its ringleaders the officers appointed by Olympius. His work was successful; soldiers, secretly instructed by him, demanded conference with Honorius for the satisfaction of their complaints. The Emperor fled to hide; inquiry was made and two men, both Masters of Soldiers, in rank awarded them by Olympius, were declared guilty. Their names were Turpilio and Vigilantius, and they had won high praise in the army. Honorius did not dare to condemn them to death; they were sentenced to exile and actually escorted by a strong force to their ship. Its captain carried a secret order from Jovius for their execution; as soon as they were on the high seas, the order was promptly obeyed.

Our next view of this Jovius, chief minister in Imperial favor, finds him with Rome's enemy, Alaric. Jovius had known Alaric well in the past; he had received hospitality as his friend. Would it not now be for his own glory to contrive some definite settlement of peace between Roman and Goth? He invited Alaric to meet him at Ariminum (Rimini), some thirty miles from Ravenna, and drew from him after long conference the terms on which he would consent to peace with Rome: an annual yielding by Rome both of money and of provisions for food, in settled amount; the grant of the provinces of Venetia, Noricum and Dalmatia, to himself, Alaric, and to his Gothic people, for the building of homes and communities.

These conditions as given by Alaric Jovius forwarded in a letter to the Emperor, adding that he felt it would be wise to offer Alaric also appointment as Master of Soldiers in the Roman army; this honor might induce him to lighten his terms.

Alaric was still staying as guest of Jovius when the Emperor's reply arrived. They were talking together in his tent when the messenger from the Palace delivered the letter; quickly Jovius opened it and read it aloud, sure of its acceptance of all that he had stated. It began very well. Honorius was willing to render the tribute required; Jovius as Praetorian Prefect must know, of course, what he was doing and what Rome was able to give. But the honor of Master of Soldiers he would never, *never* consent to confer upon Alaric, or upon any one of his barbarian race.

Alaric, well content with the first words of the letter, bristled with rage as he heard its end. He was always given to sudden impulses of anger, to acting without thought. Now he turned directly to send command to his soldiers: "We march in battle order straight to the siege of Rome!" The Goths in haste obeyed, while Jovius, anxious to free himself from blame, hurried back to Ravenna and the Emperor.

With skill and dexterity he brought Honorius to approve the situation. It was a wonderful chance now to win victory for all time over the Goths, he said, and the Emperor rejoiced to believe him. He actually swore a solemn oath never to make peace with Alaric until the Visigothic king stood before him, conquered and beaten. And Jovius played his hand further. By the head of the Emperor—the most forceful oath known in usage at the Imperial Court—he bound himself and all his officers, civil and military alike, to fight for the same end.

The prospect of battle drove Honorius into action. He summoned for his support ten thousand Huns, confederate allies of Rome; he ordered supplies of corn and cattle from Dalmatia for their provisioning. He sent out spies to find by what route Alaric planned to approach the city; he called upon every means of support he could think of in any place.

News of this unexpected enemy in action reached Alaric. His rage had calmed down. Might it not be better to keep on exacting, and receiving, tribute from Rome rather than reduce her to helpless starvation? Money and food were needed by his Goths. Why not try conciliation and tact rather than war and waste?

From the cities around his camp various bishops of the Church were collected, with the request that they bear this message from the King of the Goths to the Emperor of Rome: "Do not,

Sire, I beg of you as Emperor, do not allow that City of Rome which for more than a thousand years has ruled a great part of this earth to be destroyed by savage barbarians! Let not its massive towers, its multitude of buildings, be ruined and swallowed up in flames of assault! No! Let there be peace, and peace on terms exceedingly moderate! No need have I, Alaric, of rank or dignity; nor do I now seek those provinces which recently I demanded for the settlement of my people in homes and harvests. Noricum—Upper and Lower, at the furthest course of the Danube—Noricum will suffice us. Are not those lands of Noricum harassed by continual raids? Is it not true that they yield but scant tribute to Rome's treasury? They will satisfy us. Do not think, moreover, Lord Emperor, of granting us, the Visigoths, any larger supply of provision than you yourself judge fair and sufficient for our need. We will think no more of the gold which once we demanded. And let us hope that friendship and alliance in war may abide steadfast, in the years to come, between Goth and Roman; that together we may stand against the enemy, whosoever he may be who shall dare to take up arms for war against our united force!"

It all sounded very good, and everyone who heard its words marveled at their change in tone. Many in Rome and in Ravenna were longing for peace and security. But Jovius wanted a triumph; if Stilicho could meet Alaric in battle, so could he. It was entirely impossible, he said, and his followers saw fit to argue, that he, or any minister of the Imperial Court, should allow the acceptance of these terms, or any terms of peace, however moderate. Had they not, every one of them, bound themselves by the most solemn oath, on the life of the Sacred Emperor himself, never to make peace with Alaric?

Zosimus drily adds that if they had sworn by the Lord God worshiped among the Christians, perhaps they could have gained through the Divine Mercy pardon for violating their given word. But of course an oath as solemn as that sworn by the Emperor's head no one could dream of breaking!

Alaric the king had bowed his head in vain; once more he received rejection, and once more he burst into a passion of anger. And this time he did not relent. In the autumn of 409 he marched for the second blockading of Rome. Again he occupied Ostia, its port; again supplies of food were cut off from the city; again famine spread through its darkened streets.

Its citizens, however, had had enough of hunger, filth, and sickness. Better to yield to the Goths than die. They surrendered, caring no longer for sanction and consent from the Emperor at Ravenna; they promised to submit to whatever Alaric should will.

His will took a course which carried immense shock to Honorius, at a distance from Rome. Alaric promptly issued orders that Honorius was no longer to be revered and obeyed as Emperor; the Imperial throne of the West, its crown and its purple, were to be under rule of Attalus, Prefect of Rome.

Attalus was a friend of Alaric: Greek by birth, born in Asia Minor, brought up in the pagan tradition; now by persuasion from Alaric, an Arian Christian himself, he was baptized by an Arian bishop, Sigesar. The Catholic Church was to hold him heretic; pagan citizens hoped for a renewal of the ancient religion in Rome; Honorius, the orthodox Catholic, was more shocked by the prospect of an Arian Emperor in charge of Rome than by the thought of his own loss of authority.

The day after his coronation the new "Emperor" appeared before the Roman Senate to deliver a long harangue full of wonderful arrogance, including a promise of unlimited conquest to be won by his power. Some citizens hoped this might hold truth and that their present head might be different in character from Honorius. At any rate, the siege was over, and they could now eat their fill. But the aristocratic clan of the Anicii held this usurper and his words in baleful contempt.

Alaric stood firmly behind the man of his appointing, ready with both counsel and criticism. Of both Attalus had need. Danger threatened Rome from its province of northern Africa; Heraclian, Count of Africa, still held Honorius his Emperor; he would hear nothing of Attalus. Attalus, therefore, said Alaric, must send a strong army at once to subdue Heraclian, and he would do well to appoint as its leader one Druma, an experienced and energetic general.

But Attalus was taking no advice from anyone, even Alaric. Had not the soothsayers in Rome prophesied that he would occupy Africa without a struggle? He despatched a small force under Constans, a soldier of far less worth, but his friend. Then he marched against Honorius himself, still in Ravenna.

Greatly perturbed by news of this advance, Honorius endeavored to conciliate this rival while he was still at a distance. He sent off legates to offer Attalus power as co-Emperor; they would rule the West, he said, in happy partnership.

Another shock awaited him. Answer to this offer arrived not from Attalus, but from Jovius. Jovius had been, so Honorius confidently believed, not only his Praetorian Prefect but also his most loyal supporter. Now, Honorius learned, this Jovius, following as ever the changing wind, had transferred his allegiance to Attalus as "Emperor," and Attalus had rewarded him by appointment as his Praetorian Prefect of Italy. As such he now wrote to Honorius a letter of utter scorn in the name of the new holder of the throne. Attalus, said this letter, was going to strip Honorius of his very name, to mar and mutilate his person, and to send him off to some remote island, there to live alone and forgotten.

Honorius, lawful Emperor though he was, shivered in fear. As soon as he could think at all he decided to take ship immediately for Constantinople and the shelter of his nephew's Court. He had actually gathered a fleet in the harbor of Ravenna when, to the great surprise of all its people, four thousand soldiers arrived there from the East. Their coming had long been expected, long delayed. Now Honorius "as one aroused from drunken sleep," gave to them the business of protecting Ravenna's walls and decided to remain where he was, far from Rome.

Early in 410 it was known in that city that the expedition to Africa had been a failure. Constans had been killed; fresh troops had been sent; Attalus had even consented to appoint Druma as leader against Count Heraclian. Jovius, disgusted by the new Emperor's lack of success, had turned back to vow loyalty to Honorius; he was for ever accusing Attalus in these days as both incapable and even treacherous. Alaric did not listen; he still had hope for Attalus; so much hope that he went out on campaign against cities that refused to accept Attalus as Emperor. Yet Alaric was no Honorius, captivated by a friend. As time went on he was forced to admit that Attalus had no initiative, no skill as ruler; he was always suggesting foolish, useless plans.

Heraclian closed the ports of Africa. Corn no longer arrived in Rome, and hunger before long drove its people to do anything to anyone for food; a voice, it was said, was heard crying in the Circus: "A price upon human flesh!"

In the summer at Rimini with formal procedure Alaric deposed the "Emperor" he had enthroned, stripping from him the Imperial crown and purple. These were restored to Honorius by Alaric himself; Attalus, as one who had been his friend, was allowed to stay in the Gothic camp for secure guarding against those who hated and despised him.

Then Alaric, weary of war, went off to the outskirts of Ravenna, to treat of peace with Honorius: a step which was to have curious and terrible results. Alaric was at this moment in actual fact the enemy of Honorius; another man of Gothic race, the chieftain Sarus, had been strictly neutral in the war between Honorius and Alaric, taking the side of neither Roman nor Goth. But he was meditating friendship with Honorius, and his jealous mind was enraged at the thought of alliance between that Emperor and the Gothic Alaric. He rushed upon Alaric's camp and killed some of his men, shouting that he himself was going to defend Honorius and that Alaric had better keep away.

The thought of a treaty between Honorius and Sarus aroused furious resentment in Alaric; for the third time, now in August 410, he ordered his army to march upon Rome.

This third assault of Alaric upon Rome was far more serious than those of 408 and 409, though it was far more brief. For three days his Visigoths ransacked the city, burning, seizing, destroying. Alaric allowed this orgy of plunder. His men might carry off citizens as captives; they might rob houses and people, of jewels, of silver and gold, of robes and tapestries, of furniture and paintings. But, although the Catholic Church knew him as a heretic Arian, the Visigothic king held himself Christian in faith and practice; as such he gave special orders. Orosius gives us these commands of Alaric, issued before working havoc in Rome: "If any of its citizens should have fled for safety to holy places, and in especial to the churches of the Apostles Peter and Paul, his men were, first of all, to leave them alone, safe and unharmed; but also, secondly, so far as was possible, they were to stay and stop other Gothic soldiers, bent on bloodshed in these places for the sake of robbery."

Orosius then continues: "As the barbarians were rushing here and there through the city, one of them, strong of arm and a Christian, came upon an elderly nun in her convent. With all due respect he said to her: 'Please bring me the gold and silver held in this house.' 'Certainly,' she answered, 'if you will wait a moment. We hold in our keeping a quantity of treasure.' Piece by piece she brought all out, and, untrained as he was, he stood still, looking at them, amazed at their size, their weight, their beauty. But he did not know for what purpose they were there. Seeing his ignorance, the nun explained: 'These are the sacred vessels of Peter the Apostle. Take them if you dare; you will see what will happen. I am not able to defend them myself, and therefore I will not try to hold them.' The Goth, moved to awe by the fear of God and the faith of this woman, sent word to Alaric of this incident, and the king at once ordered all holy vessels already carried off to be returned to St. Peter's unharmed. Moreover, this nun, and all who declared themselves Christians, were to be escorted with the same protection. The convent was, it is said, a long distance from St. Peter's—half the distance of the city. And so, amid great wonder of all who saw the sight, men marched in procession, each bearing openly on his head a vessel of gold or silver, defended by drawn swords on all sides in reverent honor. Romans and Goths joined in singing a Christian hymn"; and Orosius adds that many pagans were walking with the Christians. Such, at least, is his story.

Nevertheless many were seized and held. Among them was the Princess Galla Placidia; she was living, not at Ravenna with her royal brother, but courageously at Rome, the center of action and importance. When or exactly where she was taken prisoner we do not know for certain. Most authorities, Greek and Latin, place her capture in this late summer of 410, during the third attack of Alaric. Zosimus, however, writes of her as already in the keeping of Alaric as a hostage when he deposed Attalus earlier in the year; she was treated, he adds, with all honor and courtesy.

It may not be amiss to note here a story told by Procopius of Caesarea in his *History of the War against the Vandals*, and also by Zonaras in his *Epitome Historiarum*. It concerns the Emperor and his thought of Rome in August 410. At Ravenna Honorius spent much time in his poultry-yard. There one day a servant who had charge of it came to him in great distress. "Rome," he said, "is no more, dead and gone." In astonishment the Emperor cried aloud: "Why, just a few minutes ago she was eating from my hands!" He had a prize hen called 'Rome,' and he looked most unhappy at this bad news. The servant explained that Rome's city had been ruined by Alaric. "Oh, my dear man," said Honorius, "I really thought you meant that Rome, my bird, had died!"

The tale very probably is fiction, thought up by a malicious mind.

In this year, 410, the Emperor of Rome wrote a letter to the people of Britain. They had deeply resented the fact that their "Emperor" Constantine had left them for Gaul, even though he had reserved soldiers for their defence. These soldiers, they had decided, were not sufficient in number to drive away invaders, and they had appealed to Honorius. If he would help them, they had declared, they would surely be loyal to the Empire for all days to come.

Honorius could do nothing for them; Alaric was at the gates of Rome. His answer to their petition merely recommended with all firmness that the people of Britain do all in their power to protect by their own efforts their land and those who dwelt within it.

The same year saw the death of Alaric; we read of this in the

Getica, "History of the Goths" by Jordanes, here drawing much material from Cassiodorus: "With the spoils of all Italy which he had seized, Alaric by way of Sicily was planning to cross to Africa, a land then at peace. But since man is not free to order his doings without the assent of God, that terrible strait of water between Italy and Sicily sank some of his ships and played havoc with many more. Through this mishap he was thrown out of his course and while he was wondering what to do, death suddenly fell upon him.

"Then his friends in great sorrow, for they loved him well, turned aside the river Busento from its channel near the city of Cosenza; then their long lines of prisoners dug out a grave in the center of this channel, now empty, buried Alaric there with much treasure, and turned the river back again into its proper course. Finally, lest ever at any time by any one the place of Alaric's burial should be discovered, all those who as prisoners had done the digging were at once killed. These ceremonies completed, kingship over the Goths was given to Athaulf, Alaric's brother-in-law."

Jordanes now describes this new ruler: "He was indeed a man outstanding both in mind and in body; not very tall, but beautifully moulded in figure and most attractive in face."

For some two years Athaulf and his followers remained in Italy; in 412 they crossed the Alps and entered Gaul. With him Athaulf took both Galla Placidia, a convenient hostage in the case of trouble from Rome, and Attalus, once its "Emperor."

Placidia was not only brave and vigorous; she was also a young woman of beauty and charm. Among the many who admired and sought her was a soldier, born in Illyricum, whose name, Constantius, is well known in Roman history; he had set his heart upon making her his wife. Under Theodosius the Great and Honorius he had fought well to win victory; in 411 he had led his army against the city of Arles in Gaul, held as headquarters by the usurper Constantine. From this peril Constantine had fled to a monastery, and there he had received ordination as priest. To induce him to return to Arles Constantius with solemn oath had given him a pledge of security; none should harm him. Relying on this Roman general's good faith, Constantine, "Emperor" and priest, had come back to Arles and, knowing that Constantius must conquer, had opened the city gates to him and his soldiers. Quickly the usurper was seized and sent off under strong guard by command of Constantius himself for judgment by the true and lawful Emperor in Italy. Long before he had crossed the mountains his fate was a certainty to all; Honorius had never forgotten that this Constantine had killed his kinsmen Verenian and Didymus. He died beneath the headsman's axe this same year, at a place thirty miles from Ravenna. Constantius also returned to Italy, but in triumph; he now held high hope of winning Placidia from the Goths, of receiving her from her brother as bride.

Placidia had never given him reason for hope. Bold, crafty and skillful he undoubtedly was, but he did not suit her aristocratic mind, neither in appearance nor in character. Olympiodorus, writing in this fifth century, described him as "peering out upon his world from his large eyes in somewhat gloomy and sullen mood. His head was flat; his neck was thick and broad. When he rode his horse he leaned forward, crouching on its neck; swiftly he glanced now to one side, now to the other, obviously wanting to look like a man worthy of a throne. At banquets and festive gatherings he was merry and sociable, entering into all that was going on, often trying hard to rival the mimes and actors in their jest and sport."

Constantine, tyrant in Gaul, had met execution in September 411. When in 412 Athaulf, Placidia, and Attalus arrived in that land, they found yet another usurper there; one Jovinus had been raised to "Imperial" rule. Attalus, seeking, as ever, to appear a man of importance, told Athaulf that he would do well to give Jovinus his support. Athaulf offered it, and it was roughly refused. This rejection by a usurper made Athaulf enemy of Jovinus for the remainder of his life.

Another who was seriously thinking of giving aid to Jovinus was the Goth Sarus. He had given up all thought of friendship with Rome and its Emperor Honorius; better far, he now decided, to join Jovinus in revolt.

In this decision he found tragedy. Athaulf, his fellow-Goth, could not bear to see Jovinus, who had scorned his own offer of assistance, supported by friendly alliance with Sarus, a chieftain of undoubted intelligence and power. In 413 he marched against Sarus with a large force. The attack was unexpected and Sarus had with him only a few men. With unbelievable courage and endurance he fought. To no purpose; he was captured, a sack was thrown over his head, and he was borne off to death.

With Sarus thus removed from support of Jovinus, why not next remove Jovinus himself from life? This act, Athaulf now thought, would surely please Honorius and his ministers; surely it would bring an end to the war still simmering, if not in active force, between Goth and Roman.

Again Athaulf succeeded; in this same year, 413, the head of Jovinus the usurper in Gaul, was triumphantly set high for all to see.

But Honorius required, in return for peace with the Visigoths, more than the murder of even a usurper of "Imperial" authority. He wanted, above all, the restoration and return of his sister, Galla Placidia, and in this he was, of course, fervently encouraged by her suitor, Constantius.

Moreover, Athaulf himself had added to his service of ridding the Emperor of Jovinus a demand for Placidia's restoration to Ravenna and Rome; also a demand for supplies of corn from Rome. His Goths were hungry.

Corn at this moment could not be supplied by Rome to any one, not even Goths; Count Heraclian of Africa, the country from which came Rome's supply, was now in 413 once more in revolt against the Empire of the West; once more he had refused to send provision to Italy; his ports were closed to the Romans.

Heraclian was indeed angry with Rome, so angry that he sailed with a large fleet for Italy to terrify Honorius by invasion. The terror fell back upon his own head. In Italy he landed, only to hurry back home in a single ship, unsupported by the fleet he now had lost. He arrived in Africa; at Carthage the Imperial government condemned him to instant execution as a man unworthy of life.

The deeds of Athaulf, however grim, must have moved Galla Placidia to admire her captor's courage. True, he had fought against Rome, he had captured in Gaul the Roman cities of Narbonne, Bordeaux, and Toulouse. He was pressing hard his demand for corn; yet he had lifted the burden of Jovinus and Sarus from the worried mind of Honorius the Emperor. Again, Athaulf, comely and proud in face, figure, and bearing, was entirely different in Placidia's eager eyes from Constantius, who broke his word in treachery and acted like a clown.

Far more delight, however, came to her as she talked with this king of the Visigoths. Athaulf in these days was telling her his thought on matters international; Placidia listened and in turn told her own. Orosius gives us a picture of their growing sympathy one with another: "I myself," he writes, "once met a man from Narbonne who had served well in the field under Theodosius. He was devoted to his religion, a man sensible and thoughtful, and he was talking with Jerome, that most blessed priest, at Bethlehem in Palestine. He said that he had been a close friend of Athaulf, at Narbonne, and that he had often heard on good authority what he, a man strong in mind and character, used to say about himself. In years past he had longed to blot out the very name of Rome, to call all territory hitherto governed by Rome an Empire of the Goths alone. He would make, and he would name, and the Gothic

Empire should be, to put it simply, what the Roman Empire was, and Athaulf himself would now become what Caesar Augustus once had been.

Long he had thought, had watched his Gothic people. And at last he knew, knew surely, that the Goths would never be brought to obey laws, because of their undisciplined and barbaric nature. Yet he was equally sure that an Empire must have laws; for a State without laws is no State at all.

He had therefore made up his mind to seek glory for himself in restoring anew and in bringing to greater splendor the name of Rome; and this he would do through the power of the Goths. He, the leader who had not been able to change Roman into Gothic, would be held by future ages as the man who had brought back the Roman Empire to its former renown. For this reason he desired no war; he had set his heart upon peace."

As they talked, as they built up their ideal for their two peoples, the captor and his captive fell in love with each other. To his vast displeasure Honorius heard that his enemy and his sister would soon be man and wife. Their marriage was celebrated with high ceremony at Narbonne in January 414.

The historian Olympiodorus has described its scene. In the entrance hall of a house owned by Ingenius, a leading citizen of Narbonne, sat the bride, a central figure, with her bridegroom beside her, both attired in Roman and royal style, as indeed was the whole furnishing of the hall. Many gifts were now offered to Placidia. Athaulf brought to her fifty handsome youths in silk robes, each carrying two large rounded plates: one filled with pieces of gold, the other with precious stones, priceless in value, the harvest of the plundering of Rome in 410 by the Goths.

Songs were chanted, games were played, and much revel of rejoicing delighted the guests, Roman and Goth alike. Attalus, once "Emperor" in Rome, proudly led the singing as choirmaster.

Soon Athaulf and Placidia, according to their plan, were working among Romans in Gaul with friendly endeavor for peace; Constantius, who was himself there, would have none of it. Doubtless Constantius was the wrong person to approach; but his refusal to listen gave deep disappointment. Especially to Athaulf; in his vexation he did a foolish thing. Once more he declared Attalus raised to power as "Emperor," a successor to Jovinus in Gaul.

The move was an entire failure. This we know from the verses of one Paulinus, born at Pella in Macedonia, but in these days living at Bordeaux. When over eighty years old he composed—

a toilsome business—a poem which he called *Eucharisticos:* a thanksgiving to the Lord of Heaven for His mercies to a man long and
severely tried and troubled.

Paulinus had lived through the continual raids of the barbarians who had ravaged Gaul ever since 406. His home as boy and
man was in Bordeaux; there he entered the service of Attalus, the
"Emperor" in Gaul, as "Count of his Private Bounty." No good did
this do him; he complained that this office had been forced upon
him by the pretender.

Then in 414, the year of his marriage, Athaulf resolved to leave
Gaul with his Goths, to settle in Spain; his soldiers had been repeatedly attacked by the Roman Constantius and his men. Before
he left he took his revenge; he ordered his Goths to harry and
plunder the southern part of Aquitaine and to work ruin in Bordeaux by fire. Paulinus lost his home and was forced to flee to
Bazas in Gascony.

All this he tells in somewhat barbarous Latin hexameters. But
his story holds much interesting detail; here in a rough translation
are lines 291 to 320:

> Yet, for me to the lot of which I here have told, was added yet
> another task, of greater toil, when, seeking vain comfort, the
> tyrant Attalus burdened me, though absent, with mark of honor
> vain, empty indeed: "Count of his private, own Largesses";
> he gave this to me, this, which he knew held no reward, when he
> himself had ceased to trust his royal rank, relying foolishly on
> Gothic aid alone, Goths whom as protectors he could not hope
> to hold, defenders of his present life, not of his throne, himself
> owning no private wealth, no men-at-arms. I therefore sided
> not with that weak Emperor, confessing that I chose rather a
> peace with Goths; which then by Goths themselves was eagerly
> desired, soon spreading to others, through money they received.
> Nor need one repent of this, since in our Empire we see now
> many who prosper through Gothic aid, many who once were
> suffering bitter distress. And I myself was one of those deprived
> of all, robbed of all property, survivor of my land. For when,
> ordered by King Athaulf, Goths left that land, Goths of our
> city, once welcomed by us in peace, on us, as though we were
> subdued victims of war, inflicting cruel injury, burned our
> whole town. And therefore, recognized as Count of that same
> king, whose associates they did not hold as their friends, me
> they stripped of all my goods, my mother with me, also; both

subject to one common fate of doom, believing that in this they spared us, caught in war, in that, unharmed, they let us freely go our way.

Eucharisticos, 291ff.

Athaulf and Placidia settled in Barcelona; there a son was born whom they named Theodosius after his grandfather. But their joy was brief; in 415 the baby died and was buried in a silver coffin at a church near the city walls.

Summer of this year brought Placidia even deeper mourning. One day, while staying at Tarraco in Spain, Athaulf went, as he continually went, to inspect the horses in his stables. One of his men, Dubius by name, was there waiting for him. He, too, was a Goth, and he had once been in the service of a Gothic chieftain, possibly Sarus, whom Athaulf had ruthlessly killed. Longing for revenge, he had now his chance; he rushed forward with his knife, to wound Athaulf so severely that in a little time he died. In his last hour he managed to say a few words in his brother's ear: "Send Placidia back to Honorius, and, if you can, see that the Goths make peace with Rome." His brother did not succeed him. The next king of the Goths was Singeric, brother of Sarus, and he had no love for Athaulf or his wife. Athaulf had had six children by a former marriage; they were now in the care of Sigesar, that Arian bishop of the Goths who had baptized Attalus at Alaric's desire. Every one of them Singeric seized and killed. He treated Placidia with rough brutality; as an insult to her dead husband he forced her to walk on foot twelve miles, before his horse as he rode. Seven days after his crowning he was himself removed by murder.

One Wallia, now hailed as king, was a happy contrast. In 416 he concluded an honorable peace with Honorius and restored his sister, Placidia, to her home in Italy. One of Wallia's royal ministers conducted her as far as the Pyrenees, and from that point Constantius with splendid courtesy saw her safely all the way to Ravenna. In return abundant freight of corn was sent from Italy to Gaul; Rome's supply had been renewed after Heraclian's death. Then, in the last months of 418, Constantius as representative of the Emperor confirmed peace between Rome and the Goths by giving to them and their king, Wallia, the province of Aquitaine Secunda between the rivers Loire and Garonne, with also some cities in provinces nearby. There, leaving Spain, Goths went to settle as allies—*foederati*—of the Romans; it was the same policy which Theodosius the Great had approved and carried out in Thrace. They made Toulouse their chief and capital city.

Long before this time, however, in 416, Constantius in Italy, face to face with Placidia in their own country, was renewing his suit for her hand; she was now some twenty-eight years old. Again he had no success; she still resisted him, and even her servants encouraged her to turn away. Seeck has suggested, as one reason for this refusal, her loyalty to the Catholic Church, which at this time frowned upon marriage for a widow. Ennslin has suggested her pride; was she not daughter and sister of Emperors, and by her marriage a queen? The chief obstacle in her mind, no doubt, was that she did not love Constantius and never would.

Yet finally her will, if not her heart, was conquered. On the first of January, 417, Honorius and Constantius together celebrated their entry upon the consulship of Rome's government, Honorius for the eleventh time, Constantius for the second. The ceremony was at its height when before a vast congregation the Emperor took his sister's hand and gave her to his fellow-consul. Marriage followed at once, solemnized with elaborate ritual.

As ever, tragedy followed close upon rejoicing. Now it was to fall upon Attalus, by this time "wearing the shadow of Imperial rule," as Orosius describes him. Left lonely and unprotected when the Goths had moved to Spain, he decided to leave Gaul by sea. His ship ran into trouble; he was captured, then delivered to Constantius, who in turn gave him over for judgment to Honorius the Emperor. The date of his capture was 416. In 417 the Emperor came from Ravenna to Rome; he wished to share with its citizens the joy of peace with the Goths, of the return and the marriage of his sister. He would enhance this joy, he thought, by delivering sentence in public to Attalus, the usurper.

Into the great square of Rome's center Honorius rode on the appointed day, carrying behind him in his chariot the false "Emperor," bound fast. Before a multitude of avid sightseers the true Emperor slowly ascended, one by one, the steps of the high tribunal set up in the midst of the square, sat down upon its throne, looked around him with much satisfaction, then summoned his prisoner to the lowest step. There Attalus lay, crouching in terror. For a few moments there was silence; then from the height above judgment fell upon him: the thumb and first finger were to be cut from his right hand, and he was to live for the rest of his life on the island of Lipara, off the north shore of Sicily. Honorius remembered that Attalus once had threatened him with the same fate of exile.

Marriage gave two children to Constantius and Placidia: first a daughter, Justa Grata Honoria, and then in July, 419, a son, Flavius Placidus Valentinianus. About eighteen months later, on

February 8, 421, Honorius raised his brother-in-law to union as co-Emperor with himself; thus Placidia also was now declared Empress by both her brother and her husband; at her own urgent demand her little son gained the title of "Most Noble," princely in rank. Since Honorius had no son, Placidia was eagerly hoping to see him some day enthroned as successor in the line of Emperors of the West.

This second marriage, nevertheless, was not in itself a happy one. We need not believe a story of Olympiodorus concerning Placidia. A certain Libanius, he told, famed for his power over man and nature, came from Asia to Ravenna and boasted that he could conquer barbarian enemies by his own magic spells, without any army at all; the Empress threatened to leave her husband unless at once he sent this heathen juggler to the death he deserved. It is a foolish tale, not in keeping with the character of Placidia: a devout daughter of the Church and a woman confident in her own influence at Court.

Constantius, that able Master of Soldiers, was no man to rule an Empire. Constantinople even refused him his title. Word of his elevation was sent there in formal order, to Theodosius the Second, now twenty years old and ruling in his own right of Emperor of the East; it met nothing but contempt. News of this scorn so upset Rome's co-Emperor that he fell ill, angry that he had ever accepted the honor given him by Honorius. Life, he was now finding out, was no longer what it once had been. The joy of strategy in military campaign was over. As Emperor he could not even come and go as he would; he could not jest and sport in the hall of feasting; he must observe etiquette and protocol. No wonder that he was sick; he even had dreams, dreadful dreams, foreboding evil. Olympiodorus tells that one night a voice rang in his ear: "The sixth month has gone; the seventh is begnning!" In the seventh month of his reign as co-Emperor he died of pleurisy, on September 2, 421. Olympiodorus adds a worse detail: that money, which had meant nothing to Constantius before his marriage with Placidia, as her husband was constantly in his mind. He became greedy and avaricious; and after his death men came in a stream from all sides to Ravenna, requiring satisfaction for sums of which—so they said—he had robbed them.

His widow did not mourn his loss very long; she had other troubles to dwell upon. The Court of the West was facing serious difficulty. We saw that barbarian fighters, Vandals and Alans, who in 406 had crossed the Rhine from Germany into Gaul, in 409 had invaded Spain under King Gunderic, that there they had plundered at their will. Finally they had settled in the South, in the Spanish province of Baetica.

In 422 Castinus, Master of Soldiers, who previously had fought the Franks in Gaul, was sent by Honorius to subdue these pirates; with him the government of the West ordered one Boniface to march for this Spanish campaign. Boniface was a soldier of high repute. Had he not done signal service for Rome in 413, when he had stayed the assault of Athaulf upon Marseilles, wounding him almost to death? And had not that city in its joy given him ringing applause? At this moment in 422 he was eagerly looking forward to a position of honor and responsibility, not in Spain, but in the rule of Roman Africa.

And now he was to serve under Castinus in Spain. It was a great disappointment; but doubtless he would have obeyed the order, had not Castinus received him at Ravenna with haughty and humiliating words. Boniface lost his temper. He refused to fight under Castinus; he hurried to the harbor of Porto, and there, disregarding Imperial authority, he took ship for Africa. The chronicler Prosper remarks at this point: "Now started many troubles and evil happenings for the Empire of the West."

Castinus, with a strong force of Visigoths for his support, set out for Spain to subdue those Vandal invaders of Roman lands. So vehemently did he lay siege to the walls of cities they had occupied that they were ready to yield and own themselves conquered, when suddenly the Visigothic auxiliaries of Castinus deserted him. Without them he could do nothing; he fled for refuge at Tarraco (Tarragona). It was an evil hour for Ravenna.

But worse was to fall upon the Empress Placidia in her own family at home. Her brother, the Emperor Honorius himself, now to her shame and disgust began to shower upon her marked and unseemly tokens of affection, even in public; courtiers and servants began to whisper scandal. Rumors of their gossip soon reached Placidia; in her wrath she so fiercely rebuked Honorius that quarrel broke out between them and quickly spread to partisans of each. Nobles of the Court upheld and defended the Emperor, in genuine or pretended loyalty; the barbarian soldiers who had served under Athaulf and Constantius and were now keeping guard for Placidia, readily flew to her side. Loud accusations were hurled against Honorius by her old nurse, Elpidia, and by Spadusa, her steward, the comptroller of her property. The whole Palace was soon in turmoil, from the Imperial chambers to the kitchens. At last Honorius ordered his sister to leave Ravenna for Rome; whispers were flying round that she was seeking aid against him from "enemies": whispers which probably meant that she was calling the Visigoths to her support. Rome was no home for her; in despair she sought refuge at Constantinople. One comfort she still had: a firm friend in Boniface, by this time, 423, Count of Africa. He sent her supplies of money for her journey with her two children, Honoria and Valentinian.

No good welcome greeted her at the Court of the East. Its Emperor, Theodosius II, and his sister Pulcheria, who was herself Augusta, Empress in her own right, had refused to acknowledge the Imperial titles of Constantius and Placidia in 421; now again, in 423, they had no intention of allowing them.

But events in the West were to force Theodosius to change his mind in this. Shortly after Placidia had left Ravenna, its Emperor Honorius, long sick with dropsy, died on August 15, 423. Valentinian, heir to the Western throne as son of the co-Emperor Constantius and Placidia, was but four years old; rule of the united Empire, East and West, fell to Theodosius at once. And at once he took care that his rule should continue in sure safety. Without delay he occupied by force Salona in Dalmatia, a needed precaution against invaders; he looked forward to governing from both Constantinople and Rome or Ravenna; he appointed Castinus consul for 424 in the West. Castinus, he well knew, was no friend of Placidia and had no desire to see her Regent in the West for her son Valentinian.

Then word came to Ravenna that Boniface, Count of Africa, was bitterly angry at this opposition to what he held the right of Valentinian and Placidia. Fear seized the minds of nobles in its Court. Roman Africa was still the source of Italy's supplies of grain; might not Boniface do as Heraclian had done in 413, cut off from Italy her provision of food? Deeply worried, they at last resolved that they would not be ruled by one in the East; they would have their own Emperor, present to act for their defence and direction, neither a woman nor a child. They elected one John, head of the Imperial bureau of clerks and secretaries. Great applause attended his coronation, as he stood, arrayed in Imperial purple, at Rome in December 423. Yet, for the superstitious, one portent marred the ceremony. A mysterious voice was heard, crying aloud: "He falls! He does not stand!" The crowd roared in answer: "He stands! He does not fall!"

Not only Castinus, but Aetius, another official of distinction in Ravenna, gave this usurper support.

It may be of interest to note here some thought of medieval historians concerning John, Aetius, and their opponent, Boniface.

In his *History of the Vandal War,* told in Greek by the sixth-century writer Procopius of Caesarea, this portrait, somewhat surprising, is given of John:

"Mild and gentle he was in character and yet of marked intelligence, well able to lay claim to valor. Five years, at any rate, he held his power, and ruled with moderation, nor lent his ears to slanderers. Not of his own will did he cause unjust death nor allow the carrying off of men's possessions. Nothing whatsoever could he do in regard to the barbarian peoples, since the Byzantine Court was his enemy."

We may remark at once that Procopius was entirely wrong in his statement of "five years."

Of Aetius and of Boniface the same Procopius declared:

"There were two commanders of the Romans, Aetius and Boniface; both were in the highest degree experienced through many wars, and inferior to none at that time. They differed, it is true, in their politics; but both had reached so high merit of character in all manly virtue that if any one were to name either of them as 'the last of the Romans,' he would not be wrong. Indeed, so it happened, all the excellence of Roman nature had fallen to these two men."

These are highflown words, and they must be judged by events.

Aetius had been born toward the end of the fourth century, at Durostorum (Silistria) on the Danube in Lower Moesia. He was son of Gaudentius, a general of skill and shrewd tactic in the Roman army, Count of Africa and Master of Cavalry, killed in Gaul by a rebel soldier. His wife, the mother of Aetius, came from a noble and wealthy house of Italy. We find their son under Honorius in early years, holding an official post among clerks of the Palace. Then he had been sent by the Roman West as hostage to Alaric; later on, as hostage to the Huns of Pannonia. With them he had grown into a firm and lasting friendship which was to aid his career greatly in days to come. Home again in Italy, he had married a daughter of Carpilio, once Count of Domestics in the West; their son Carpilio went in his turn to serve as hostage among the Huns.

Gregory of Tours, writing in the sixth century his *History of the Franks,* took from an older authority, Renatus Profuturus Frigeridus, a very bright picture of Aetius: "Of middle stature, strong and courageous, comely in form, knowing nothing of infirmity or other like burden, keen in mind, active of body, a most ready horseman, well skilled with arrow or pike, marvellous in battle."

It was the fact—that the nobles of the Imperial Court of the West had dared to elect a usurper at Ravenna—which turned Theodosius the Second from his purpose of ruling both East and West. He now decided to declare his child cousin, Valentinian, Emperor in the West, and to make his mother, Placidia, Regent there. True, she was a woman, and it would be hard for her to steer the course of politics amid men of differing views and ambitions, to face barbarians, constantly restless in rebellion and hungry for power. Yet she had learned much, in Ravenna, in Rome, in Gaul and in Spain; she knew the barbarian mind and her will was strong.

Directly after his crowning John sent off envoys to Constantinople, with the request that the Emperor Theodosius acknowledge him as Imperial ruler of the West. He also despatched a formidable army of soldiers against Boniface in Africa; he was not only eager to prove his power in Italy but also to receive African corn. Nevertheless it was a move which brought him danger in the inevitable weakening of the military force at his command. He therefore despatched Aetius, who was now Comptroller of the Palace, to those Huns of Pannonia with whom Aetius had long been on most friendly terms. Quickly Aetius was to bring back with him to Italy as great an army of fierce fighters as his persuasion could produce.

By this time the year 424 was well on its course. In Constantinople Theodosius the Second acted with boldness and decision. He met the envoys of John with utter scorn; it is even said that he threw them into prison. He declared Galla Placidia, who with her children was still at the Eastern Court, Empress in the West by just right; and for the second time, as prelude to further honor, the title of "Most Noble" was conferred upon her little son. Report tells that this child, Valentinian, was now, in his fifth year, betrothed to a daughter of Theodosius, an infant born in 422. Her name was Licinia Eudoxia.

Next, with all speed, Imperial troops of the East were called into active service under command of Ardaburius, Master of Soldiers, a general greatly admired for his deeds of valor in battle; his son, Aspar, was ordered to march with him in rank of captain for his support. Under their protection the Empress Placidia and her two children, Valentinian and his sister Honoria, now about six years old, began their journey back to Italy and to its recognition of the respect due a lawful throne.

At Thessalonica in Macedonia, Helion, Master of Offices in Constantinople, appointed by Theodosius to act as his representative, invested Valentinian with the royal title of "Caesar." It was now

October 424. On to Dalmatia the army from the East marched, to hold as conquerors for a while its city of Salona. There necessity divided their force in two, under separate leaders. Ardaburius took ship for Aquileia at the head of the Adriatic; Aspar, with Placidia and the children made for the same city by land.

Soon Ardaburius and his men were caught at sea by a raging storm which drove them off their course; after a long struggle with wind and waves they fell into the hands of sailors who in hope of gain carried the Commander-in-Chief straight to John at Ravenna. To John's immense joy; now, with Ardaburius safely his prisoner, surely Theodosius would acknowledge him, John, as Emperor of the West. He would not leave his good general Ardaburius to suffer harm, perhaps death, in Ravenna.

With this bright prospect before him—a prospect, indeed, entirely false—John felt that he could treat his captive very pleasantly. Ardaburius was given much freedom in the city to do as he would; he talked often with men whom John had appointed to office and command. Most of them, he soon discovered, were already turning to rebellion against their new ruler; little by little, with caution and cunning, Ardaburius fed fuel to the rising fire.

When he felt that the time had come, he sent word in secret to his son Aspar. Aspar had carried on bravely. He had brought his charges safe and sound to Aquileia; the city had yielded to quick assault by his troops; he was waiting for a message from his father, sure that by some means it would one day arrive.

It came: "The hour is at hand; march for Ravenna!" The march began. Placidia and her children were left under ample guard at Aquileia; Aspar, with an expert company of horsemen, took the road to Ravenna and the usurper John.

Soon, however, there was no road; they were lost in the marshes surrounding Ravenna. Even Aspar was helpless. How could one order soldiers on horseback to ride forward into a seemingly bottomless swamp, stretching far and wide?

Then a miracle happened; the historian Socrates tells its story. An "angel of God" appeared in the form of a shepherd, who knew the one and only track. Calmly he entered upon that green quaking mass of mud and slime, turned round and beckoned to all to follow. With quaking hearts they did; there was nothing else to do but risk their lives. And safely they crossed it, men and horses. We can well understand that Socrates believed it pure miracle. "No one," he wrote, "had ever been known to pass through before. Truly God for the first time in history made here the impassable passable for men!"

"When they had thus conquered the swamp, they found the gates of Ravenna open; they rode in, and captured the tyrant John." Those in his service willingly left him; eagerly they hurried to support Aspar.

Straight back to Aquileia John was taken, there to face the Empress, now Regent, who condemned him to a traitor's death. It was by this time May or June 425, and he had been "Emperor" about eighteen months. Then and there his right hand was cut off; mounted upon a donkey's back he was led around the racecourse at Aquileia, while its people shouted and yelled derision; death followed quickly.

His capture was hailed with great rejoicing at Constantinople. Socrates told that the Emperor Theodosius, now a young man of twenty-four, was in the Circus when the report came to him, looking upon the public games and the crowd enjoying them. At once he rose from his high seat to announce what had happened; then: "Let us now leave the pleasures of the Circus," he called aloud, "and go to church to thank the Lord whose right hand has crushed the enemy!" All marched in procession to the Cathedral, singing in chorus a hymn of gratitude.

"Three days after the death of John, Aetius arrived in Italy, bringing"—so Philostorgius declared—"an army of sixty thousand Huns for the support of this usurper." It was too late. Placidia, when she returned to Italy, in her joy gave no thought to revenge. She promptly forgave Aetius his disloyalty, conferred upon him the title of Count, and sent him off with her command to march against rebel barbarians in Gaul. As Seeck remarks, she did not trust him enough at this time to want his presence in Ravenna. She bade him at once to send homeward to Pannonia that mighty force of Huns; and this Aetius readily did, rewarding them in full for their aid. Hostages they left in Italy, as guarantee of future alliance with Placidia and her son. Castinus was sent into exile. How far he had aided John we do not really know; the chronicler Prosper dared to say that "without Castinus, so it seemed, John would not have presumed to seize the throne of the West."

It was time for Theodosius now to establish in law and justice that throne. He started from Constantinople, determined to carry out this duty himself; but at Thessalonica sickness fell upon him and he was forced to turn round for home. Once again Helion acted in his place; on the twenty-third of October, 425, he crowned at Rome the boy, six years old, cousin of Theodosius, and named him Valentinian the Third. Placidia the Empress was formally appointed Regent, destined to act until her son should be of age to rule in his own right.

CHAPTER FIVE

Pulcheria and Theodosius II

As we have seen, Arcadius, Emperor of the East in Constantinople, died on May 1, 408. Five children had been borne to him by his wife, the Empress Eudoxia: four girls and one boy, Theodosius the Second, whose birth in 401 we have also noted. His eldest sister, Flaccilla, born in 397, very probably died early, as we hear nothing concerning her. The other three were Pulcheria, now a little girl of nine, Arcadia, now eight, and Marina, the youngest, in her sixth year.

Toward the ending of his reign Arcadius—so we are told—worried deeply over the situation of his Empire in the East. What would befall it in these years of invasion and battle? He himself, he knew well, had done little enough. His son and heir, a mere infant, had been proclaimed co-Emperor with his father on January 10, 402; his mother had died in 404.

Tradition, unreliable but given us by several Byzantine historians, tells that in his fear Arcadius decided to find support for his son. Here is the story as given by Theophanes:

"Theodosius, a little boy, faced life alone, without protection; his father foresaw intrigue and plot to ensnare him. Therefore in his last will and testament Arcadius placed his son under the care of a king as guardian. Yezdegerd, King of Persia, in due course received this commission and generously fulfilled its charge; he protected the Empire in the East from assault by his own realm and by any other power. To Constantinople he sent his representative the eunuch Antiochus, a man of admirable character and high skill (so Theophanes describes him), with strict instructions to defend and direct young Theodosius during his minority. To the Roman Senate Yezdegerd wrote a warning: "Arcadius is dead. He has left his boy in my hands, and I have appointed one empowered and able to act for me. Let no one attempt evil against the child. If he does, I shall declare war afresh against the Roman Empire, a war without truce."

Antiochus came, and there was peace between Constantinople and Persia. Little Theodosius was taught and trained by him. Yet it may be that from this training in childhood sprang the forceful and disastrous influence which eunuch chamberlains at Court were to hold over this Emperor in years to come.

Controlling power over government in Constantinople was now in the hands of one Anthemius, Praetorian Prefect in the East, Patrician, and, with Stilicho, consul for the year 405. His ability in politics was marked; his thought and learning were sound. In 405 John Chrysostom wrote from his exile at Cucusus in Armenia to tell his pleasure in hearing that Anthemius, his friend, held office: "Indeed," he said, "so splendidly distinguished are you that I congratulate the magistrates and the Court of the East for your magnificence. They have not honored you; you have honored them. . . . Nor because of this appointing have I added to my love for you; nothing has been added to you which you did not already have. It is not the Prefect or the Consul whom we love. It is the master, the most civilized Anthemius, a man of great intelligence, possessed by love of knowledge and wisdom."

Others in the wide circle of those who admired Anthemius were the poet Theotimus, who made verses in his praise, and Synesius of Cyrene, whom we have seen in character and career. To Theotimus Synesius wrote, after in 410 he had himself been consecrated bishop of Cyrenaic Ptolemais: "I have not held you more blessed by your own friendship with that great man, Anthemius, than the great Anthemius is, through your thought concerning him. What is better for a man possessed of power than a friend of honest character, not colored by paint and dye?"

Anthemius, then, administered government in the East with eminent success. One of his notable achievements was his fortification of the city of Constantinople in 413 by prolonging its walls, its means of defence. On July 4, 414, his governing came to an end. That day saw Pulcheria, a girl of fifteen years and six months, proclaimed not only Augusta, Empress in her own right, but also Regent for her brother, then thirteen. Henceforward, as Galla Placidia later on in Rome and Ravenna, so at Constantinople a woman held the reins of control.

Pulcheria, indeed, was far stronger in determination than her aunt; for nearly forty years and in threefold manner she determined the tone and the custom of life in the Imperial Court and Palace. She directed the education of her brother, always subservient to her desire, even in regard to the choice of his bride of future days; she directed the foreign and the domestic policy of the East; in

Church and in State alike, it was Pulcheria who influenced council and Crown by her will.

Once declared Regent, she swiftly banished Antiochus from court. Intensely devoted to the Catholic religion, as the eldest and the only resolute member—so far as history tells—of the family left by Arcadius, she brought its power to bear on all. It is Sozomen who most vividly describes life in the palace under her leading. She had already taken a vow of virginity; she persuaded her sisters, Arcadia and Marina, to do the same; nothing but formal friendship with men was allowed. Vessels, offerings from herself and her brother, sparkling with gold and precious stones in the Cathedral of Constantinople, gave witness to their will to serve the Lord of Heaven; an inscription on the altar made this clear. Atticus, Patriarch of Constantinople, guided the Imperial family in matters spiritual; for the three sisters he wrote a special treatise, *On Faith and on the Virgin Life*.

As Socrates declares, the Palace was "almost a monastery." Fasting was strictly observed, especially on Wednesday and Friday; by day and by night brother and sisters gathered for prayer and for chanting of hymns; in hours free from political discussion and decision Pulcheria, Arcadia, and Marina busied themselves in weaving material and working from it garments for the poor: "Empresses in rank they were, born and brought up in Imperial state; but slothful idleness they held unworthy of their sacred vows, and far from their life they banished it."

The Regent, however, was not content to train her brother in holy religion alone. At fifteen he would take upon himself solemn responsibility as Emperor in fact; he must be prepared. As a little boy he had learned his lessons under the supervision of his father, Arcadius; his fellow-pupil, we are told, was Paulinus, son of the Count of Domestics in those years.

With all energy Pulcheria set to work. Herself a young woman of dignity in manner, of skill in learning, one who was well able to speak and to write both Greek and Latin, she did her best to pass on to her brother all she had, all she knew. She taught him how an Emperor must walk, and ride his horse, alone or in procession; how he should sit upon his throne; how wear his Imperial armor and robes; how speak with dignity. By no means must he yield to loud laughter; as the occasion demanded he must show himself, now mild and forbearing, now in formidable majesty; above all, he must listen patiently and with grace to all who sought from him aid or counsel.

Theodosius had patience, but little else to prepare him for his destiny. Once again the spirit of Theodosius the Great had been reborn, not in the heir, but in the female of his line. And therefore it was still under her influence that he was to live and reign, long after, perhaps in 416, she had yielded to him Imperial authority. To strategy of politics and war he preferred the fine arts of peace; he loved to ride his horse, to practice archery, to study stars in the sky, to paint, to mould in clay. He was by nature kind, affable, easily led; from the control of his sister he passed to domination by the ministers of his Court. He hated to be cruel; John of Antioch, Byzantine historian, wrote of him as Emperor: "In tolerance and charity he, so to speak, excelled all men. . . . If anyone were led away to capital punishment, fitly deserved, the appeal of the Emperor's kindly heart forbade the guilty one's death."

Not only was he foolishly kind; he was careless, and often he was to neglect his duty in the administration of his Empire. Nicephorus and other Byzantine writers have told a tale which marks this heedlessness. Pulcheria had in vain tried to bring him to diligent scrutiny of State documents placed before him for his signature; he would sign them unread. At last in despair she composed one which declared Eudocia, his wife, either sold into slavery by legal contract or made over in gift to live as bondswoman; the versions vary. Without one look at the deed before him, he confirmed it, and his sister soundly rebuked him for his folly.

Reading, theological and scientific, especially on matter of astronomy, he enjoyed to the full; philosophy he preferred to practice in amateur fashion rather than study its theories in books.

So much, then, for the characters of Pulcheria and her brother. Against all the praise of this young Empress and Regent there stand out the words of Eunapius of Sardis, a historian in the fourth and early years of the fifth century: "While Pulcheria reigned, peoples were put up for sale in public for those who wanted to buy rule over them. . . . Therefore he who longed to plunder the land around the Hellespont bought it as for his own; another bought Macedonia, another, Cyrene, each one sick with disease of corruption or with hatred of his enemies."

As Thomas Hodgkin has observed, however, these evils were not peculiar either to Pulcheria or to her time. Moreover, as has also been noted, Eunapius was a fierce upholder of his heathen faith and totally opposed to Pulcheria's Catholic religion.

In 421 Theodosius was twenty years old and Pulcheria had already long been holding in mind the question of his marriage; where was she to find a wife, an Empress, who would both delight and direct this feckless brother of hers? Theodosius, as was his habit, was leaving this problem to his sister. He had, nevertheless, his own ideas on the matter, as John Malalas tells in his entertaining picture: "I want you to find me a young girl, very, very comely, the most beautiful ever seen in Constantinople, of royal or patrician family. And if she isn't marvelously good-looking, I have no use for her, however worthy or royal or rich she may be. But whoever was her father, if she is a virgin and ever so good to look at, I take her!"

So his sister, with the aid of Paulinus, their friend, hunted high and low, and at last came upon a girl who seemed exactly right. Her name was Athenais, for she was Greek, born in Athens, daughter of Leontius, professor of rhetoric there and a man of wealth. Recently he had died, and it was found that in his will he had bequeathed nearly all his fortune to his sons, Valerian and Gesios. To his only daughter he had left but one hundred gold coins. "Her fortune will take care of her," he had written; "for she excels all women in the world."

Athenais did not see matters in this light; she implored her two brothers, both older than herself, to share their inheritance with her. They not only refused, but drove her from home, to find refuge and comfort in the house of her aunt, her mother's sister. The aunt took her to Constantinople, to another relative, an aunt on her father's side. Once safely lodged within the city, the two older women boldly ventured to put her fate in petition before the Empress Pulcheria herself. Then Athenais in her own person pleaded her need of support, and, as she spoke, Pulcheria felt that here was the very bride she had so long sought. Athenais was not only a girl of striking beauty and charm; she was, one could see, of unusual intelligence and knowledge. Her father, she told the Empress, had given all care to her education in Athens, especially in matters literary and artistic.

Soon for Pulcheria only one anxious question remained. Athenais had come from a city teeming with youth and dissipation; she had come to another of the same sort. Was she virtuous? Was she still a virgin? The question, put in some hesitation by the Empress, who heartily detested such a vulgar subject, brought from the girl a vigorous "Oh, yes! My father guarded me well."

Now all was settled in Pulcheria's mind, and she placed Athenais with both her aunts under the care of the Palace chamberlain.

Promptly the Empress then hurried to the Emperor with the wonderful news; full of excitement he begged her to arrange that, hidden behind a curtain, he might look upon this marvel. Both he and Paulinus were more than delighted with what they both saw and heard.

The two young people met, and all was well. In due time the marriage was arranged. First, since Athenais had been brought up in pagan creed and philosophy, she was baptized by the Patriarch Atticus and given a Christian name, Eudocia, a name of a kind familiar to the Imperial House of Constantinople; on June 7, 421, she became the wife of Theodosius the Second. Cedrenus in the *Historiarum Compendium,* has left us a picture of the bridegroom: "Theodosius was of middle height; his eyes, black and somewhat prominent, glanced sharply around; his nose was slender and straight, his hair the color of honey."

It was a happy day for all. The bride not only won all hearts by her courtesy and grace; she soon proved herself well able to hold her own in debate and discussion with her husband, and long they talked.

The only doubt now remaining had passed to worry those two brothers of hers; amazed at her good fortune, they feared a bad result for themselves. But Eudocia was now content; a third share of a family fortune was no longer of importance. She called both of them to Constantinople and promoted them to high rank; with the Emperor's cooperation she appointed Gesios Praetorian Prefect of Illyricum and Valerian Master of Offices.

In this same year, 421, Theodosius was at war against the Persians; its story gives detail of some interest. King Yezdegerd, friend of the Emperor Arcadius, had died in 420, and his successor meted out such cruel treatment to Christians, whose religion he abhorred, that Constantinople retaliated by battle. The Greek army, under the general Ardaburius, won victory from the Persians during August, 421, and then marched with many prisoners to defend Mesopotamia from their camp at Amida on its border.

The captured men had long been without food; they were starving. Socrates tells that, moved by their misery, Acacius, bishop of Amida, called his clergy together. "Our God," he said to them, "needs neither dishes nor cups. He neither eats nor drinks; for He has need of nothing. Our church holds heavy vessels, of gold and of silver, given us by the goodwill and generosity of those received into her communion. It is, then, only proper that by their yield of value we redeem these captives and relieve their need." The sacred vessels were melted down; Acacius was able to restore all the prisoners to health, to provide ransom for each, and to see them depart for their own land.

The following year saw further victory for Theodosius: Peace was made with Persia, and the Empress Eudocia celebrated this triumph by writing a poem in Greek hexameter verse. The same year, 422, saw the birth of a daughter, Licinia Eudoxia, to the great joy of the Emperor and his consort; on January 2, 423, probably because of this event, Eudocia was honored by the title of Augusta, Empress.

Three happenings in the following years connected the East with the West. As we have marked, from August 423, until October 425, Theodosius, in his twenties, was in nominal right sole ruler of both parts of the Roman Empire. By his aid the usurper John was conquered and Valentinian the Third was declared true Emperor of the West, in October 425. Already, in 424, Valentinian had been betrothed to that infant daughter of Theodosius, Licinia Eudoxia.

In 425 the Emperor of the East, urged no doubt by his wife, established the University of Constantinople on a firmer and far better regulated basis than it had known since its founding early in the fourth century. Edicts, still extant, tell of this renewal: orders, issued by Theodosius and his co-Emperor Valentinian. Professors must be skilled in teaching and in debate, not in scholarship alone; they must well understand how to hold an audience's attention and interest; their lives must be free from reproach. They must give their lectures in halls appointed for this purpose; by no means will they be allowed to teach in private houses or in their own private homes. Never shall two professors lecture in the same hall, and thus confuse students by two voices declaiming the virtues of two branches of knowledge entirely different. Students are to be carefully examined before they may matriculate; once enrolled, they are to be kept under strict scrutiny, in regard to their manner of living, their devotion to study, their avoidance of indecent or wasteful diversion. Unworthy undergraduates are to be flogged in the public square, expelled, and sent home.

We come now to the vexed matter of theology in this fifth century. From 406 until 425 the Church of Constantinople had been ruled by Atticus from Antioch: a bishop, as Socrates describes him, of marked intelligence and charity, both in his service to his own people and in his dealings with heretics. Anthemius had asked for his advice; Pulcheria and her sisters lived and prayed under his direction.

His death caused intense rivalry in the electing of his successor. Finally the enthusiasm of laymen in Constantinople decided the matter, and one Sisinnius, a priest from a suburb of the city, was chosen as its Patriarch. He, too, was noted for his devotion and kindness to the poor; in character he was sincere but simple, lacking interest and ability in stern matters of business. Through this, Socrates tells, his reputation suffered.

On Christmas Eve, 427, he, too, died, and once again the city was filled with discord of voices crying aloud. Right of election remained with the Emperor, as powerful as in previous years in regard to matters ecclesiastical. But Theodosius the Second was altogether undecided in mind; years later he was to complain bitterly when he talked with Dalmatius, a monk of great influence in Constantinople, concerning all the troubles and worries he had suffered during this crisis of the Church. "I begged you, Dalmatius," he protested, "to take upon yourself responsibility for this election of a Patriarch, and you refused; you declared that you did not know enough. Then I asked another monk to act for me, and he, too, pleaded ignorance. You all said to me: 'Constantinople needs a bishop whom everyone will love, for his words and for his doings: one who will guide the priests and speak for all of us.'

"Dalmatius, I implored the clergy to make their own choice; it was for them, I said, to elect their bishop. I wanted this done in peace and quiet; if done in haste I was afraid that the wrong man would be chosen.

"And more! Am I to tell you how those who were eager to be Patriarch offered me gifts, promises, oaths of loyalty? People came to me, praising the man they wanted, bad or good, telling evil tales of those desired by others. You monks fought the clergy; the clergy disagreed with one another, and so did the citizens, the layfolk. It was I who had the power to elect, but I left the choice to you. And at last you monks came to me and told me to decide."

The Emperor's choice, since no priest, monk, or man in Constantinople was held worthy, fell upon one Nestorius, born in a village near Germanicia in Syria. reared in the monastery of Euprepios on the outskirts of Antioch. There he had passed through his novitiate, and there he had been ordained deacon and priest. He was consecrated Patriarch of Constantinople on April 10, 428. We can see him in the pulpit of his Cathedral there; young, good-looking, not very tall, ruddy-haired, his voice appealing with charm to his people, his eyes, large and eager, darting here and there, his words flowing in graceful elegance, fortified by years of study. As a monk he was gladly accepted by monks in Constantinople.

At this time there were four leading Archbishoprics or Patriarchates in the Roman Empire: the sees of Rome, Constantinople, Alexandria in Egypt, and Antioch in Syria. Rome by reason of tradition and power presided over all; the Patriarchs of the other three, being human and prone to error, were at times moved by jealous rivalry. This had been enhanced at the Council of Constantinople in 381, which held bishops only from the East and no legates from Rome. These bishops had been asked, and had consented, to give among these four Patriarchates second place to Constantinople. Rome had protested long and vigorously, but in vain.

Jealousy, then, provoked ill-feeling. Were not Alexandria and Antioch of Apostolic fame and tradition? Were not their cities of more importance than Constantinople, now called the "New Rome"? Thus their Archbishops reasoned, and none more zealously than Cyril, Patriarch of Alexandria.

As nephew of that Theophilus of Alexandria who had won his carefully planned victory over John Chrysostom of Constantinople, he had precedent in his family of battle between the two sees. A few days after the death of Theophilus, in October 412, Cyril had succeeded him as Patriarch. Not only his place in the Church of the East but also his character itself resembled that of his uncle. He was ambitious, determined to win his way, resolute to the point of persecution against those who differed, or seemed to differ, from him in regard to the orthodox Creed, the Faith of the Catholic Church.

For a moment let us look back again at the history of this Creed. The "Edict of Milan," said to have been issued in 313 by the Emperor Constantine, rests on no reliable evidence. But in the time of Constantine Christianity was indeed acknowledged as lawful; its adherents were no longer to suffer persecution.

Some ten years later Arius, a priest of Alexandria, was teaching doctrine which to the Catholic Church was plain heresy: that the Christ as God was not equal with God the Father, nor of the same substance. God the Father, Arius declared, had created the Lord Christ from nothing, and therefore, as One created, there had been in all eternity an age when He was not.

This divergence from the Catholic Faith had been condemned in 325 by the Council assembled through order of Constantine at Nicaea, in Bithynia, Asia Minor, part of the Empire of the East. Arius, excommunicated by his bishop, was sent into exile.

The equality of God the Son, "of the same substance with God the Father, and begotten of Him before all worlds, Very God of Very God, Begotten, not made," the faith declared at Nicaea, was reaffirmed at the Council of Constantinople in 381, over which the Patriarch of Antioch presided. From this date Arianism declined in strength among Romans of the Empire; in great part it was left to barbarian nations.

At this same Council of 381 another and a different form of heresy was condemned: that of Apollinaris, bishop of Laodicea in Phrygia about A.D. 360. His creed held that the Christ was indeed Very God of Very God, but that He was not truly and fully Man. As man he possessed man's body, man's soul; but he lacked man's human spirit. In its stead the Divine Word, the Divine Logos, filled His being, inspired His thought and His action.

We pass on, then, to the year 429. At this time the see of Rome, the leading Patriarchate, was held by Pope Celestine I; that of Alexandria by Cyril; that of Antioch by one Theodotus, who was to die in 429 and be succeeded by John I; that of Constantinople by Nestorius, a monk trained in religion at Antioch.

It is possible for schools of theology which confess the same Catholic faith to seem on the surface to differ somewhat in their view. This may be said of Alexandria and Antioch. The clergy of Alexandria, and Cyril among them, while they firmly confessed a union in the Christ of two natures, Divine and human, yet dwelt much, even preferably, on the Divine, on Christ as God, to be adored, to be supplicated. On the other hand, those of the school of Antioch, also holding fast this union in their faith concerning the Lord Christ, loved to turn their minds toward Him as Incarnate, born of Mary. The result was that either Alexandria or Antioch, if it seemed to see a fitting occasion, was inclined to suspect heresy in words spoken or written by a sister Church.

This was the situation, sharpened by rivalry, when Nestorius became Patriarch of Constantinople. He was firm in his adherence to the tradition of Antioch. He was also in deadly fear of saying anything which might savor of Apollinarian heresy; he detested heresy and heretics. Moreover, he had a quick temper; he was inpatient of reproof or counsel; he was tactless, even arrogant in discussion or in defence of his faith. Anxious to say the right words, he often became so involved in his effort, so eager to prove himself orthodox, that those who read or heard his argument misunderstood its meaning.

Promptly as Patriarch he began assault upon those who had formed sects apart from the Catholic Church. Socrates declares that in the presence of citizens of Constantinople he said to Theodosius: "Give me, Emperor, the earth purged of heretics and I will make return to you, of Heaven. Conquer the heretics for me and I will conquer the Persians for you!" We are told that Arians, in despair of saving the church in which they held secret worship, set fire to it and that the fire spread to private homes. Not only in Constantinople but in Macedonia, and across the water in Asia Minor, according to Socrates, did this Patriarch wage persecution, and the Emperor aided him. On May 30, 428, some six weeks after the election of Nestorius, an Imperial edict went out from the Palace at Constantinople, forbidding eighteen sects of those who dared to differ from their Catholic brethren to meet for prayer in any part of Roman land.

In 429 Nestorius wrote to Pope Celestine, complaining of Apollinarians and Arians, but—strangely enough—asking consideration for certain Pelagians, those who followed the teaching of Pelagius, a monk of Britain. Pelagius believed that men on earth possess natural grace, by means of which they themselves, without the aid of grace supernatural, are able to obey the will of God.

Nestorius, it would seem, was sorry for the miserable distress of the Pelagians for whom he was pleading.

His request, however, did not please Celestine. But the Pope was more worried, more vexed by the words which followed in this letter: "Men have dared to call the Virgin who is Mother of Christ, that is, Christotokos, by the title Theotokos, 'Mother of God.' In all the preaching of the holy Fathers, up to the time of Nicaea, nothing did they say concerning the holy Virgin except that Our Lord Jesus Christ was incarnate by the Holy Spirit, of the Virgin Mary. I make no reference to the Scriptures; everywhere, through the words of both angels and apostles, they have spoken of the Virgin as Mother of Christ, not of God, the Word."

Somewhat later, when no answer to this letter had reached him, Nestorius wrote again; error in faith was still troubling him. "Great and often recurring is my toil here, as I try hard to root out the most foul impiety, and the evil doctrine voiced by Apollinaris and Arius. I simply cannot understand why some of the clergy themselves are tainted with the malady that has seized the minds of these heretics!"

Not only the Pope at Rome, but also people in Constantinople were now disturbed, even offended by action and words of their new Patriarch. He had persecuted the unorthodox; he was now interfering with the round of daily life in their own city. We read that he forbade games, shows in the theater, songs and dances; in fact, all the joys of recreation so dear to men and women of Constantinople at this time.

Worse still, he was interfering with their faith, their religious tradition. Most firmly did they revere as Mother of God the holy Virgin Mary, and now this Nestorius, Archbishop of the Catholic

Church, was allowing the sacred title to be dishonored in his own Cathedral. What sort of Father in God was he?

Two instances of this concern in Constantinople have been given us. The first, described by Socrates, tells that Nestorius, when in 428 he arrived there, brought with him a secretary named Anastasius, also trained at Antioch. He deeply respected the learning of this priest, and often asked his advice. One day, when Anastasius was addressing a congregation in church, he was heard to say: "Let no one call Mary Mother of God. Mary was a human being, and God cannot be born of humanity." Immediately rebellion broke out among both clergy and laity. Nestorius vigorously supported his colleague, and from that time the Church of Constantinople was torn apart by dispute among theologians and simple folk alike. Nearly all were rebelling against this innovation, this insult, as they held it, to Mary, Mother of God.

The other incident appears in a letter written during 430 by Pope Celestine to Cyril; it is found in the Acts of the Council which was to gather at Ephesus in 431. Its story tells that Dorotheus, bishop of Marcianopolis in Lower Moesia, had declared during a liturgy celebrated in the presence of Nestorius: "If anyone says that Mary is Mother of God, let him be anathema." The Patriarch of Constantinople, it was said, raised no objection; but once again the congregation shouted with wrath.

The monks of the East, always alert for trouble, also made common cause against Nestorius, and they were ably supported by the eunuch chamberlains of the Palace, eager to turn the Emperor Theodosius from his friendship with that Patriarch whom he himself had chosen.

To the Pope, now seriously disturbed, to the clergy of East and West, to the people of Constantinople, now simmering with revolt against this Archbishop who interfered with their freedom and their sense of religion, we can add the devout and intensely orthodox Pulcheria: injured, as she held, by insult to her honor and person. From a letter, written in Greek long afterward to one Cosmos of Antioch, translated into Syriac and now given us by François Nau in French, we learn of various acts of Nestorius which she bitterly resented. As one dedicated in a vow of virginity and therefore revered, she had been accustomed after her communion at Mass on Sundays to dine in the Archbishop's Palace. Nestorius would not allow this privilege; the Imperial Court was deeply offended and the clergy of Constantinople told the story wherever they went. Next, a stole belonging to her, constantly seen around her shoulders when she received communion, or laid upon the altar itself, was greatly prized by her as marking the vow she had made. Nestorius removed it from the altar. Third, under Archbishop Sisinnius the Emperor Theodosius had regularly received communion on Easter Day in the Cathedral's most hallowed sanctuary, and Pulcheria with him. Nestorius did not approve of this; one Easter morning when she was about to enter this sacred chapel he caught sight of her and asked his archdeacon what she was doing? The archdeacon explained; the Patriarch in great haste caught her at the door, stopped her, and forbade her entry. Pulcheria, irritated by what she thought unprecedented rudeness, said: "Let me enter, as I always do!" He replied: "This place is open only to priests." Whereupon in her quick anger she retorted: "Is it because I, a virgin, am not Mother of God?" Without thinking, horrified by her words, he snapped back: "You are Mother of Satan!" and forced her to leave.

She went straight to her brother, the Emperor, to tell him all; Theodosius, as was to be expected, gave her what comfort he could, for once blaming the Patriarch.

Other witness, given by Suidas in his *Lexicon* under the title "Pulcheria" even states that Nestorius accused this Empress of breaking her vow of continence by a love intrigue with Paulinus, that friend of the Emperor. In one of his writings, called "A Dialogue with Sophronius," who, as Nau suggests, may have been one of the bishops who were to work against him in 431 at the Council of Ephesus, Nestorius himself wrote: "You had also on your side a creature of battles, a queen, a young so-called virgin, who fought me because I would not allow a woman corrupted by men to be called the bride of Christ!"

So the assault upon Nestorius in a brief time was growing steadily stronger. If Nestorius would not think of Mary as Theotokos, "Mother of God," what in fact did he believe? All faithful members of the Catholic Church believed in the real, the perfect union of Christ, the Incarnate, the Son of Mary, with Christ, the Divine Logos, the Son of God, in His two Natures, bound in One Person.

Chief among those who assailed the Patriarch of Constantinople was Cyril, Patriarch of Alexandria, who was to carry on his campaign in steady, carefully planned movements.

He began by writing to the monks under his authority in Egypt, and by the Paschal letter which he sent to his clergy every year. The one intended for Easter 429 (No. XVII) held definite statement on the reverence due the Virgin Mary as "Mother of God," and on the Word Incarnate. There was, however, no mention of Nestorius.

Three letters now went from Cyril of Alexandria to Nestorius, and replies came from Constantinople. Cyril wrote: "Certain papers—I might call them treatises—are being handed round here, causing us no end of trouble in trying to bring those led astray by them to a better mind. Some people have almost got to the point of no longer admitting that the Christ is God; they think rather of Him as an organ or instrument of divinity, as a God-bearing man. And what do you expect beyond that? . . . I really have to take counsel with your Piety, because Celestine, most devout bishop of Rome, and other most loyal bishops have been declaring this as a fact: Did those papers, those interpretations, which, I don't know how, have reached Rome, did they come from your Piety or not? The bishops write in fierce anger. How, then, are we going to quiet those who come here from the churches of the entire East and keep on murmuring against these pamphlets? Or perhaps your Piety thinks that for the churches the disturbance aroused by treatises of this kind is a mere trifle? We are all full of struggles and labors, trying to bring back those who somehow have got wrong ideas into the straight path of truth once more."

To this Nestorius made rude retort: "That most devout priest Lampo has forced me to write this letter; he talked so much to me about your pious self—yes, and he heard much, too, in reply! He wouldn't give in until he got the letter written by me. . . . So far as I am concerned, although many of your words to me are scarcely those of brotherly love (one has to speak pleasantly), I write to you as a long-suffering man and with kindly salutation. But how much good this vehement driving of Lampo, the most devout priest, is going to bring us, the future will decide!"

The correspondence continued with rising acerbity. Cyril put together in five books a treatise plainly described as *Against the Blasphemies of Nestorius.* He wrote to the Emperor Theodosius II, on heresies; for the ladies of the Imperial Court of the East, first for Eudocia and Pulcheria, then for Arcadia and Marina, he composed two articles of instruction, *On the True Faith;* he wrote also to Pope Celestine.

In August 430, a Council of bishops met at Rome. Nestorius was not there; those who now judged him declared his words heretical. On the eleventh of the same month a letter for Cyril from Pope Celestine left the city. In it Cyril himself was warmly praised. . . . "But, just as you are a good shepherd of your flock, so can Nestorius be accused, not as a base hireling who deserts his sheep but as one who with his own hands tears them to pieces." . . .

"Therefore by our authority you will in all firmness carry out this decision: that within ten days Nestorius either condemn in writing his evil declarations and confess in all surety that he holds the same faith concerning the birth of Christ as the Church of Rome and the Church of Alexandria and all devout people hold—or promptly your Holiness will see that this Patriarch of Constantinople find himself under sentence of banishment from our body, excommunicate, one who has refused to allow healing for himself and has hastened as one foul with disease to the ruin, not only of himself, but of those entrusted to his charge."

Similar letters went from the Pope at this time to John, Patriarch of Antioch, to Juvenal, bishop of Jerusalem, to the clergy and people of Constantinople.

In November 430, Cyril gathered a synod of clergy and laity in Alexandria; to them he submitted in the name of Nestorius twelve articles of doctrine which he named "accursed things"—anathemata. They were at once condemned. Then he wrote to Nestorius, demanding for each his signature in agreement of condemnation with himself, Cyril. He also forwarded the sentence of excommunication destined by Papal decision for Nestorius, should he refuse to sign. Friends of the accused Patriarch were horrified at this action; John, Patriarch of Antioch, sent him much kindly counsel, and Theodoret, bishop of Cyrrhus in Syria, his sympathy, alive with wrath.

Nestorius sent no signature of condemnation. Already the Emperor, while still standing in support of his Patriarch in Constantinople, knew that nothing could prevent trial and judgment. He therefore had sent out a call to bishops of East and West to assemble in Ephesus, that ancient Apostolic city of Asia Minor which now lies ruined within Turkey near the Aegean Sea. The Council was to meet at Pentecost of 431, on the seventh of June.

To Ephesus, then, in good time came both Nestorius, the accused, with his supporters, and Cyril, the accuser, with fifty bishops and many monks, zealously following his lead, all from Egypt; by Celestine himself Cyril had been given charge of the debate. Next arrived Juvenal, bishop of Jerusalem, with prelates from Palestine. To superintend due provision for order and ceremony Theodosius had sent Candidian, Count of the Imperial Bodyguard at Constantinople; the Count, however, as a layman, was to take no part in the discussion of sacred doctrine.

Now all were awaiting the arrival of John, Patriarch of Antioch; his suffragan bishops, he was to declare in excuse, had not been able to leave their churches and he had therefore been delayed. On his way he also wrote to Cyril that unexpected trouble had occurred.

Until June 22 all waited. Then Cyril decided it was time to get to work. The bishop of Ephesus, Memnon, agreed with him; he was heartily supporting Cyril and his Alexandrians. Word was sent around that sessions would begin at once in the Cathedral of Saint Mary, though Nestorius himself was also absent. Three calls were sent him, for he was near at hand. To no purpose; he feared violence and he refused to appear. Without him and without the Patriarch John, still lingering on his way, whether by design or through accident, the synod opened debate. Count Candidian protested, but in vain.

In Saint Mary's the Nicene Creed was solemnly read aloud, then letters which had passed between Nestorius and Cyril, with one from Pope Celestine. Evidence against the accused was given personally by witnesses, and also quoted from various patristic authorities.

From morning until evening the Council sat, stood, spoke, listened, and summed up. At nightfall the citizens of Ephesus heard the final result: the Patriarch of Constantinople had been condemned and deposed from his see by a vote almost unanimous. At once the streets of the city burst into radiance of illumination; a procession of men carrying torches, of women carrying incense, escorted Cyril and his followers to their lodging for the night. Shouts of joy sounded in his ears as he wrote the words which that very hour he sent by messenger: "To Nestorius, new Judas. Know that by reason of your impious declarations and your disobedience to sacred canon law, on this twenty-second day of June, 431, in conformity with ecclesiastical ruling, you have been deprived of your see by the Holy Synod and that no longer have you any rank in the Church."

Later on, Nestorius was bitterly to reproach Cyril for his action: "It is you," he wrote, "who raised against me a troop of monks and of men called bishops, for the hurt and the troubling of the Church. No one, however powerful, stopped or hindered you. You had all the might of the Empire behind you; and I, I had only the name of the Emperor: nothing else to fortify me, to guard me, to help me, and, above all, to obey me. That is why I came to this pass. . . . I had the misery of being driven out by you. You were bishop of Alexandria and you put your hand on the Church of Constantinople, an act which no bishop of any other city would have borne."

And again: "I was summoned by Cyril; Cyril called the Council; Cyril ruled it. Who was judge? Cyril. Who was accuser? Cyril. Cyril was everything at Ephesus."

The Emperor, even at this point, did not abandon loyalty. To the monk Dalmatius as they talked together he said: "I find no iniquity in that man, nor any reason for his deposing." To Cyril he had written in very sharp tone, accusing him of having caused great disturbance in Church and State before the Council met in Ephesus: "You may be sure that you will not regain our friendship unless all tumult and bitterness is stilled before you come to the debate." Cyril, moreover, he angrily charged, by writing those letters to the Imperial ladies had been trying to sow dissension between him, Theodosius, and his sisters.

On the twenty-sixth of June, four days after Cyril's Council of Ephesus had met, John of Antioch and his clergy arrived there. Intense indignation filled them when they heard on every side the fate of Nestorius; promptly they decided to hold a second, a rival synod of Ephesus. They carried out their decision, and the synod is known by the name of the "Conciliabulum." Count Candidian presided, and John led the discussion. His words were born of stern resolution: "Cyril and Memnon stand guilty of iniquity. They have trampled under foot the decrees of the Church, and, with these, the lawful edicts of our most religious Emperor. It is just and right that they themselves suffer penalty of deposition; and that other clergy present at the recently held Council, led into the same sin, be punished by bond of excommunication until, confessing their guilt, they cast anathema upon those heretical chapters of Cyril." The "heretical chapters of Cyril" were his twelve anathemata, in which after diligent scrutiny John believed he had found serious error.

Cyril, Patriarch of Alexandria, and Memnon, bishop of Ephesus, by vote of the "Conciliabulum," were declared condemned and deprived of their sees.

From both synods of Ephesus the Emperor Theodosius received due announcement of their action; a letter from Candidian and John of Antioch, informing the Empress Pulcheria of the deposition of her deeply respected Archbishop Cyril, filled her with horror and wrath. Legates from Pope Celestine who, like John of Antioch, had reached Ephesus too late to attend its first Council on June 22, hurried to discuss with Cyril what they should do; on July 11, 431, they decided that his action in deposing Nestorius was in accordance with canon law.

Soon Constantinople heard that Cyril and Memnon in scorn

were paying no heed to the sentence of deposition; they were carrying on as usual the duties and privileges of bishops. Theodosius thought long and talked with many. Then, in August 431, Ephesus received an Imperial letter announcing that he had confirmed the decisions of both Councils; Nestorius, Cyril, and Memnon were all by Imperial edict stripped of their sees.

Discord was now at its height; yet its duration was brief. Nestorius declared himself ready and willing to return to his monastery of Euprepios at Antioch. This the Emperor allowed, and the Prefects of the East wrote to this deposed Patriarch that they were sending an escort to give him all comfort on the journey, whether he chose to travel by ship or to ride by road. In the autumn of 431 he was there, welcomed with joy by its community. From Cyril's Council of Ephesus came a letter to both Theodosius II and Valentinian III, also to the clergy and people of Constantinople, stating that the deposition of Cyril and Memnon was indeed no act of its bishops. Members of both Council and "Conciliabulum" were ordered by Imperial summons into session, first at Chalcedon, then at Constantinople itself; on October 25, 431, one Maximian was consecrated Patriarch of Constantinople; on Christmas Day of the same year and on March 15, 432, Pope Celestine confirmed both his consecration and the deposing of Nestorius, his predecessor.

By this time Cyril had contrived his escape from Ephesus to Alexandria, where he boldly entered again his Cathedral; Memnon at Ephesus was also assuming episcopal right. All were longing for peace, and Theodosius did not venture to deny it; the return of both to their bishoprics was allowed. On March 15, 432, the Pope could write to those who had deposed Nestorius: "Now at last we must exult in the ending of evil; now at last with one voice we can say: 'Thy right hand, O Lord, is glorified in power; Thy right hand hath utterly broken the enemy'. . . . We rejoiced in the witness of our most benign, most Christian Emperor, when we saw that his decision approved yours."

Theodosius the Second, then, had changed his mind; he was now standing with Cyril of Alexandria and Pope Celestine. On July 27, 432, Celestine died. Four days later Xystus III was consecrated Pope in Rome; he, too, upheld Cyril and his Council of Ephesus.

Yet Cyril was not happy. There remained with him one source of fear, and it ran deep, springing from John of Antioch. John was still unwilling to forsake Nestorius. Shortly before the death of Celestine, Theodosius and Valentinian as Emperors had sent the Patriarch of Antioch a warning: "We have decided," they had written to John, "and the most reverend bishop, Maximian, of our noble city of Constantinople, together with all our devoted bishops and their clergy agree with us in this, to bring together in harmony the members of the true faith, once so well united and by unhappy misfortune torn apart. By this we mean that you and the most religious Cyril, bishop of Alexandria, should meet in friendship, should lay aside the hostility and dispute which divide you.

"For those bishops whom we mentioned before have declared that if by your signature you approve the deposition of Nestorius and cast anathema upon his teaching, then no reason for controversy will remain; then Cyril and the saintly bishop of Rome, Celestine, together with all priests of orthodox faith in all places, will be in union with your Piety. . . .

"Knowing, then, that this is our earnest wish, our will and our purpose, pay heed to nothing but the casting out of all strife and jealousy, that peace abide steadfast in our holy Churches. . . . And show your zeal without delay! Know that we have also sent Imperial word to his Holiness Cyril, in request that he meet you with the same readiness. We have told him not to come into our presence before you and he have met and have made sure your peace."

Cyril knew well that John of Antioch had read with keen suspicion those twelve anathemata, those descriptions of "accursed" doctrine which he had required Nestorius to renounce. Doubtless, he feared, John was now thinking and would soon declare that he, Cyril, was also caught in snare of heresy. This could not be borne, especially as Cyril was only too sure that others shared John's thought. The Patriarch of Alexandria had done all he could to promote his cause, to defend himself. Not only had he poured out words against those who cast doubt upon his faith; he had sent, and he was still sending, gift after gift to those whose support he hoped to gain. We possess a list of these presents, which many with irreverent truth have called bribes, described by him as "eulogies," "benedictions": a list given us by François Nau and taken from a manuscript of Monte Cassino. Among them were valuable tapestries for the covering of tables or beds; furniture wrought in ivory, in silver; money in gold of great value, many pounds in weight. All were accompanied by appropriate greetings; many were welcomed with secret understanding by the officials of the Court in the East, by chamberlains and domestic servants of the Imperial family.

The year 433 found all four—Theodosius as Emperor, Maximian, Patriarch of Constantinople, Cyril, Patriarch of Alexandria, and John, Patriarch of Antioch—bound together by an agreement, put into words as a "Formula of Reunion." It brought a peace neither entire nor lasting; and the price paid by both John and Cyril was heavy. John had been forced to desert Nestorius, so long his friend, who loved with him the Church of Antioch; Cyril had accepted, but with reserve, a creed drawn up by that same Church. The title of "Mother of God" for the Virgin Mary was declared orthodox and true by both Patriarchs, ordered held by all the faithful with proper reverence.

In his joy, however, that the shadow of heresy which had seemed to threaten him had now faded away, Cyril wrote to John those well-known words: "Let the heavens rejoice and let the earth be glad; for the middle wall of partition has been broken down"; and to Maximian, sitting in the seat of Nestorius: "Now are we all crowned with one faith; now we have driven from our sacred folds Nestorius, the inventor of impieties; we have banished the false shepherd from our goodly flock."

Was Nestorius guilty of teaching or allowing false doctrine? The question is still met by answers of "yes" and "no." Many were the accusations cast against him: that he refused to believe in Christ as God; that he believed in two Sons of God; that the two Natures of the Christ were not completely and perfectly united one with the other.

All down the years until his death, probably in 451, he was to protest against these charges; his, he was to claim, was the faith held by Flavian, himself Patriarch of Constantinople from 447 until 449, and by the saintly Pope Leo the First (440–461). Socrates, the historian, refused to believe that Nestorius thought of Christ as merely man. He attributed his failure to declare Mary "Mother of God" to his muddled ignorance, his refusal to study tradition of authority, his proud reliance on his own fluent tongue. Yet it is Socrates who gives us two sayings of Nestorius which might seem to point in a contrary direction. In dispute with Cyril of Alexandria when they met at Ephesus in 431 he is said to have cried out in anger: "I wouldn't call a baby two or three months old by the Name of God!" Bethune-Baker here defends Nestorius: "Nestorius meant that he would not call God a babe, *not* that he could not call a babe God." Some time afterward, when argument had gone on for long and words had turned to bitterness, he impatiently snapped: "Call Mary Mother of God if you like, and let all this quarrel stop!"

Encouraged by words given us by Nestorius himself in the *Book of Heraclides,* we may well hold these stories evidence of utter weariness, hold that Nestorius firmly believed in Christ as One Person in Whom two Natures were united, Godhead and Manhood; that merely fear prompted his refusal to name the Virgin Mary as Theotokos; that he did not understand the mystery of the perfect union of the two Natures in One Person, and that he refused to accept faith in place of understanding with regard to the Mother of God. He did not view tradition in the simple manner given in the English rendering of the well-known *Histoire ancienne de l'Eglise* by Louis Duchesne: "Mary, according to orthodox tradition, is Mother of One Who is God; she is His Mother, not that He owes her His Divinity, but because He has taken from her His humanity."

Courageously Nestorius suffered his fate. Four years he stayed in the monastery at Antioch, and then further trouble came upon him, through his own fault. In defence of himself and of his words in past time, he talked and argued long and strenuously to sympathetic listeners. At last John, Patriarch of Antioch, in fear of resentment and of division among his monks, requested the Emperor to remove this man, a source of constant contention, from the city's gates.

Theodosius was more than willing, and Nestorius was sent into exile at Petra in Arabia. The year was now 435; about this time, in 435 or 436, we find him, together with those who sympathized with him and his words, under penalty ordered in an Imperial edict.

The edict was issued in the month of August and it was stern:

"We command that all, wheresoever they may be, who are known as followers of the accursed suppositions of Nestorius, shall be called 'Simonians.' It is only just that those who turn from God to imitate the impiety of Simon should share his name. . . .

"Likewise we decree that no one shall publish, possess, read, or copy the impious treatises of the nefarious and sacrilegious Nestorius. With all diligence and zeal his writings are to be sought in every quarter and publicly burned by fire."

Soon exile in Petra seemed too lenient a penalty, and Nestorius was removed to Oasis in the Egyptian desert. There he remained, alone and desolate. Maximian wrote from Constantinople to Cyril, his "fellow-minister": "Satisfied now is your keen desire; that cause which you embraced for the sake of religion is fulfilled, the prayer of Your Piety has attained its goal. You have won glory in the sight of angels and men, of all the priests of Christ. For not only did you have faith in Christ; you also shared His afflictions. You alone have been held worthy to bear with Him His sufferings."

And Cyril answered: "No party am I to the notions of Apollinaris. True and rightful doctrine do I maintain, casting anathema upon Apollinaris, upon Arius, upon Eunomius, and with them upon Nestorius. The faith handed down to us from the beginning do I hold as an anchor for my soul, safe and firm."

We now return to matters domestic and political. On October 29, 437, the marriage of Valentinian III, Emperor of the West, with Licinia Eudoxia, daughter of Theodosius II, was celebrated at Constantinople. The next year saw an event which was long remembered. Proclus, who had succeeded Maximian in 434 as Patriarch of Constantinople's Church, joined Pulcheria in a petition that the relics of John Chrysostom be now at last brought back from their tomb at Comana, in Pontus, near the Black Sea, to their proper restingplace within the city he had served. Theodosius gladly gave consent. In his *Ecclesiastical History* Theodoret described the journey in boats across the dark waters of the Sea of Marmora, their waves hidden under the light of many torches; the arrival at Constantinople, where the Emperor, his eyes fixed upon the coffin, prayed the Lord of Heaven to forgive those, his own parents, who in their ignorance had done so grievous wrong to this great Patriarch. The sacred relics were then laid to rest within Constantinople's Church of the Holy Apostles.

It was also in 438 that Theodosius with full consent saw his wife Eudocia depart on pilgrimage to Jerusalem. It would seem that she had vowed to pray in its holy places if her daughter Licinia should be happily married while she herself still lived. Another daughter, Flaccilla, had died in 431.

On her way she visited Antioch and was asked to speak in public before a gathering of its citizens. There she won tremendous applause at the end of her speech by quoting a line from Homer:

"Of your own race I came, from your blood I draw my pride."

In great delight the townspeople set up in her honor a statue of bronze. At Jerusalem she made her own offerings, many and rich. Gladly she met Saint Melania the Younger, that woman of intense zeal and rash enthusiasm.

The invasion of Alaric and his Goths drove Melania and her husband, Pinian, from Italy to Africa, where she spent many years, founding monasteries, to her joy meeting Saint Jerome. Then they went on to Jerusalem. Pinian died there, and his widow lived in a convent for eight years more, until her own death in 439.

She also visited Constantinople, drawn by a fierce desire to convert her uncle Volusian, Prefect of the Empire, who was in the dark depths of paganism. Nothing would stop her. She found him in the Imperial City, laid low by serious illness, led him to Catholic baptism, and saw him die in peace. Then, as her *Life* declares, she went hard to work against Nestorian blasphemy. She also found time to enjoy an audience with Theodosius the Emperor and Eudocia, and to beg Eudocia to come as pilgrim to Jerusalem.

After Melania had returned home to that city, Eudocia came; she met Melania and the nuns of her convent, greeted them happily as her "sisters," and felt toward Melania as "a daughter to her Mother in the faith."

In 439 Eudocia was again in Constantinople; with her in great pride she had brought from Jerusalem sacred relics, said to be those of Saint Stephen. Further pride was hers when on August the sixth of this year her daughter Licinia received the title of Augusta, probably because Licinia's husband, the Emperor Valentinian III, was delighted by the birth of their first child: a daughter, who was named Eudocia after her grandmother.

But the pride of this youthful grandmother, Eudocia, now in her mid-thirties, was soon to crumble away before three disasters; how far two of these were her own fault, it is hard to say.

The first occurred, we may believe, in 440. Paulinus, comrade in boyhood of the Emperor Theodosius, his counselor at the time of his marriage with Eudocia, was now Master of Offices, and therefore constantly in the Palace with Eudocia and her husband. Now he was to fall from favor, and the story of this fall is told in detail by several Byzantine historians. On January the sixth, the Feast of the Epiphany, Theodosius was on his way to church when he was stopped by a man who said that he was desperately poor, that he came from Phrygia, and had ventured to speak to the Emperor because he wanted with his own hand to give to him an apple of extraordinary size and richness. The gift was graciously accepted and the giver, as he had hoped, received liberal recompense. Theodosius then proceeded to church, heard Epiphany Mass, returned to the Palace and decided to send this marvelous product of fertile earth to his wife as an Epiphany present. Eudocia greeted its arrival with equal wonder and admiration. It seemed too good to keep for herself; why not send it, she thought, to Paulinus, who was very unhappy, in bed with a sore foot? Paulinus, directly he saw the ripe, red fruit, said to himself: "It is a King's apple," and at once called a servant to take it to the Emperor.

Theodosius, of course, recognized it as the gift he had sent to Eudocia. She, he at once saw, had sent it on to Paulinus. An apple was the gift of love; were Eudocia and Paulinus carrying on an affair in secret in the Palace itself? Was not Paulinus, known everywhere for his handsome face and figure, attracted to women? The Emperor ordered an attendant to summon the Empress Eudocia to his apartment.

A stormy scene followed. "Where is that apple," he asked her as soon as she appeared, "which I myself gave you?" "I ate it," she replied. "Did you indeed eat it," retorted Theodosius with rising anger, "or did you send it as a gift elsewhere? Answer me, if you dare, upon your soul's salvation!" Solemnly Eudocia answered him: "Upon my hope of salvation I swear the truth: I ate it, I gave it to no one."

But Theodosius did not believe her. In his wrath he ordered death for Paulinus; he was executed at Caesarea in Cappadocia. The date 440 for this tragedy follows that given by the chronicler Count Marcellinus; other sources place it later, in 444. To the end of her life Eudocia denied guilt for both herself and the man she called her friend.

Trouble also came to her from her connection with another man well known in public life. He was Cyrus, from 435 onward Prefect of the city of Constantinople, Praetorian Prefect of the East since 439, and honored, we read, by the title of Patrician. It was not, however, the political standing of Cyrus which had attracted the Empress, but the fact that he was of Greek birth, coming from Panopolis in Egypt, that he loved Greek literature and wrote poetry in Greek. We have in the Greek *Anthology* five epigrams from his pen; two of them describe the house built for him on the coast of Bithynia, Asia Minor, not far removed from Constantinople itself. There he had a glorious view:

> Beauty around me lies, stretching without end.
> Here, there, behind me lies the City; then, in front,
> Open to meet me comes the wonder of Bithynian land.

He also delighted in using the Greek language for his political decrees. John Lydus mentions this in his *Magistracies of the Roman Government:* "Cyrus, still admired by us for his poetry, dared to break an ancient custom and to put forward decrees in Greek; with the Roman tongue his office also lost repute."

Yet Cyrus gained much. Other Byzantine narratives tell that as Prefect of Constantinople he rebuilt the City wall, fallen and crumbling, brought it to such great height and strength that it looked entirely new. The citizens were astonished. One day, when the Emperor came riding into the Hippodrome, all the crowd which gathered there shouted a most unwelcome greeting: "Constantine built this city; Cyrus has renewed it!" Theodosius, sore with jealousy, determined then and there to seek revenge. Pretending to approve this exultation and hiding his resentment, he accused Cyrus of favoring the Greeks. Everyone understood this as meaning that Cyrus was a pagan at heart, no Catholic Christian. By way of removing pagan influence from his government he deposed Cyrus from office in 441—Cyrus was consul that year—confiscated his possessions, and, in mock mercy, ordered his consecration as bishop of Cotyaeum in Phrygia, Asia Minor.

It was no joyful prospect; Cyrus himself had feared Imperial wrath when he had heard applause from the people in the Hippodrome. "Fortune, when she smiles too warmly, is no friend of man," he is said to have wryly remarked. Perhaps it was at this time that he wrote another epigram assigned to him:

"O that my father had taught me to tend the well-fleeced sheep! Sitting beneath the elms or making music with my flute beneath the rocky ledge, in joy would I comfort the sorrows of my heart! Pierian Muses, let us flee the well-built city; another fatherland we must seek. To all will I tell that the murderous drones have done grievous mischief to the bees!"

The citizens of Cotyaeum had no love for their bishops; they had murdered already, one after another, four of them. Now this new one was bringing notoriety with him of heathen, pagan religion; they would soon make an end of him! And, of course, the Emperor, who had driven him out, would be vastly pleased.

Cyrus, however, pagan praetor or Christian bishop, was a diplomat. Christmas of 441 was drawing near when he arrived in Cotyaeum. As he entered his Cathedral to celebrate the Feast, a vast congregation called aloud: "Speak! Speak to us!" hoping to shout him down. Cyrus quietly walked up the steps of his pulpit. When he reached its stand, "Quiet, all of you," he ordered. Then with perfect calm he said: "Brethren, Christmastide is here. It is right and fitting that the day which saw the birth of God and Our Savior Jesus Christ be kept in silence. For by listening alone was the Word of God conceived in the Holy Virgin. To Him be glory for ever and ever, Amen."

The crowd was quick to recognize a subtle mind; hostility turned to shouts of approval and Cyrus held his see for years. After Theodosius died, in 450, he resigned and went to live long as a layman in Constantinople. Near that city, at Anaplus on the shore of the Bosporus, in 462 was the famous Pillar Saint, Daniel, worshipping God and caring for his fellow-men from the top of his column. To him Cyrus brought a daughter, troubled by an evil demon; Daniel prayed and she was released from captivity. In deep gratitude Cyrus begged to be allowed to engrave on the pillar some verses of his own making; Daniel hesitated long, but in the end gave consent:

> Between earth and heaven stands a man, fearless of winds that blow from every side,
>
> .   .   .   .
>
> holding firm stand upon his pillar's height; nourished by hunger divine, by thirst that knows no pain, praising the Ever-Virgin Mary's Son.

The banishment of Cyrus, together with the death of Paulinus, left Eudocia worried and anxious. A third conflict with authority was due to her own foolish ambition. She had always felt jealous of her sister-in-law, Pulcheria, who for many years had held greater influence at Court than she herself had enjoyed, as Empress, as wife.

But recently, as Eudocia knew well, another power had risen, slowly and surely, until it now held the Emperor fast under its control, the control of the Court chamberlain Chrysaphius. True, he worked in secret; Pulcheria was still in formal courtesy head of the Imperial household, even declared as such by Theodosius. Yet Chrysaphius had access at all times to the Emperor in private; Theodosius relied upon his advice; it was he who was now guiding Imperial policy, in matters both of State and Church. So crafty was he in his bland hints and suggestions that finally Eudocia herself yielded to temptation. One day Chrysaphius said to her as they talked: "You are the Empress. Why does the Lady Pulcheria order things in the Palace? Why does she have in her service the one and only Comptroller of the Household? Why don't you tell the Emperor that this is unfair to you?"

Eudocia did complain to him, but she received no comfort. The Emperor's reply was short: "Don't please, get into a temper about that. It is impossible for you to have a Comptroller. Not even I give orders to my sister; she runs the Palace too well."

Then Chrysaphius went to work again; he was not easily defeated. This time he even dared to approach the Emperor in his eagerness to weaken Pulcheria's power. "The Lady Pulcheria is so religious," he said, "so dedicated. Why could you not request the Patriarch of Constantinople to ordain her deaconess?"

This, of course, would safely remove Pulcheria from life in the Palace. She heard of the suggestion and in her anger she despatched her Comptroller immediately to Eudocia, left the Palace, and went to live in the Hebdomon, a seaport seven miles from Constantinople. It, also, possessed a Palace in which by tradition announcement was made of a new Emperor's accession to the throne; churches were there, of Saint John the Apostle and of Saint John the Baptist.

For a while in Pulcheria's absence Eudocia enjoyed some power at Court. Yet her husband had not forgotten the affair of Paulinus. He missed the presence of his sister, while his wife grew more and more discontented and unhappy. Finally she could bear this no longer; she asked Theodosius for leave to return to Jerusalem, this time to stay. Her petition was granted, and in 443 she departed again on her way to the Holy Land. In Jerusalem she remained until her death in 460; a marriage of twenty-two years had been broken. Pulcheria promptly returned to the Palace in Constantinople, once more to struggle with Chrysaphius in problems political.

There were, indeed, gruesome facts to face. Vandals had been worrying both West and East to a point unendurable. In 441, as aid for the Empire, Theodosius had ordered a fleet of eleven thousand vessels, under five commanders, to sail for Sicily, which was being ravaged without cease. To no purpose; the leaders of the fleet—so Prosper tells—by their unending negotiation with the Vandal enemy were more of a burden to Sicily than a protecting force for the West. In 442 the Emperor had issued orders from Constantinople for their return home; both leaders and men of the rank and file were needed for defence of the East against barbarian invaders of its own territories. In 441 and 442 Persians, Saracens, and Isaurians were plundering far and wide the lands of Armenia and Cappadocia; Huns under their co-kings, Attila and Bleda, were harrying Moesia, region of the Lower Danube.

We now come to the long struggle of the Eastern Empire with the Huns. Demand constantly made by Attila upon Theodosius was twofold: annual tribute of money and the return to their own land of Huns who had deserted it for some part of the Roman Empire in the East. The year 441 had seen the Huns of Scythia capturing cities and fortresses on the Danube, including Viminacium of Upper Moesia, many of Moesia, and others of the Roman diocese of Dacia. Moreover, Hun envoys had declared that the bishop of Margus, another city of Roman Moesia, had invaded their country, had robbed their royal fisc and had stolen hidden treasure. Unless the government of Theodosius delivered this bishop as prisoner to them, together with the Scythian deserters who had fled to Roman territory, they, the Huns of Scythia, would make war upon the Empire of the East. In terror lest he should be surrendered, the bishop secretly had made agreement with the Scythians to betray his Roman city of Margus and hand it over to them, if only they would save him from harm. And so Margus had been surrendered by treachery, to become a mass of ruin.

Attila, king of the Huns, continued his work of destruction. In 443 he ravaged Roman lands on his borders; he wrecked fortresses; he made inroads into Ratiaria, capital of Dacia Ripensis; he won victory in Thrace.

During this same year a longing for peace drove the Romans to accept a treaty on the terms offered by him, which were costly. The words of Priscus describe them for us: Deserters from the Huns who had been received by the Romans were to be surrendered to Attila; six thousand pounds of gold were to be paid as arrears of tribute due in the past; for the future, the Romans were to render twenty-one thousand pounds of gold each year; for each Roman taken prisoner by the Huns and subsequently escaping back into his own Roman land without payment of ransom, a fine of twelve gold coins was imposed; if the fine was not paid, those who had received the fugitive were to surrender him to the Huns once again; the Romans were to receive into their country no one of barbarian race seeking refuge there.

Of sheer necessity these conditions were accepted by the Empire of the East, but with bitter suffering. Each citizen was ordered to deny himself to the limit. From a reckless spending in past time of public funds on theatrical shows, on ambitious follies, from lazy indifference concerning defence, the lands of the Roman Empire exposed to attack by Huns turned now to intense effort. Tax collectors worked busily, stripping women of their jewels, forcing the more prosperous of their fellow-citizens to put up their valued furnishings for sale in the public market. Famine was rampant; many died of starvation; others were strangled by their own hands.

But at last the conditions of the treaty were fulfilled; the gold was delivered, the Imperial treasury was empty and bare. All the deserters were sent back to their own Empire of Attila, except some who flatly refused to return to his rule, and these the Romans murdered without mercy. The peace that followed lasted four years.

The months of 443–444 brought further fear and mourning, even horror. First, the winter was without end, it seemed to the citizens of Constantinople. "For six months"—so Count Marcellinus wrote in his *Chronicle*—"snow fell constantly, scarcely did it melt at all; people and animals in their thousands perished through the cold." Among those who died in 444 was Arcadia, sister of the Emperor, in her mid-forties.

News of horror came from overseas. When the Empress Eudocia in 443 had left Constantinople forever, on her way to Jerusalem, she had taken with her two of her close friends among the clergy: Severus, a priest, and John, a deacon. Theodosius heard that she was often to be seen talking with them in Jerusalem. Whether through fear of rebellion or through jealousy, in 444 he sent Saturninus, Count of Domestics, to see what was going on; and Saturninus (possibly, if we may trust the historian Cedrenus here, with consent from the Emperor himself) ordered both put to death. At this, Eudocia broke out into anger so violent that, according to Marcellinus, she "then and there murdered Saturninus": words which, as Ernest Stein literally interprets them, mean that he was "either assassinated by her or at her command." Theodosius at once deprived his exiled wife of the Imperial retinue he had allowed her.

Calamities continued for the Imperial city, of both natural and human origin. In 445 political discord among its people burst into a passion of revolt, bringing death to many; many also, both men and cattle, died from disease. In 446 famine set in, followed by epidemic of plague. A terrific earthquake rocked the city in 447; walls here and there fell crashing down, with more than fifty towers. Hunger again took lives without number.

Then, in 447, Attila once more marched his armies to war against the East. As the *Chronica Gallica* tells: "Again ruin rose afresh for the East; there no fewer than seventy cities were laid waste by the ravaging of the Huns, while no aid came from the West." Count Marcellinus gives the same story: "A vast war, greater than the former one, was inflicted on our people by King Attila; cities and fortresses he attacked and destroyed; almost the whole of Europe he left in ruin." His Huns fought savagely near the river Utus, a tributary of the Danube; they advanced as far as Thermopylae, on the border between Thessaly and Phocis; in another direction they marched to capture Marcianopolis, not far from Constantinople itself. And once again Attila sent envoys to Theodosius, demanding tribute due long ago, left unpaid.

The situation was impossible; the Empire of the East could pay no more. Attila, despite his hunger for gold, had to make some sort of treaty without revenue. He was still hungry for money, still demanding that fugitives from his lands be surrendered by the Romans. The Emperor could do nothing. But his ambitious and powerful chamberlain, Chrysaphius, was more daring. Might it not be for him, Chrysaphius, to save the Empire, to gain his own supreme success? Without Attila the menace of these Huns, these barbarians, would surely wither and vanish; were Attila but once dead and buried, the East might indeed be at rest. Attila must die!

So the Imperial Chief Chamberlain reasoned, and Priscus tells the story of his cunning.

An envoy from Attila, Edeco by name and Scythian in race, delivered to Theodosius at Constantinople during 448 a letter which held a threat of war; the Romans, declared this king of the Huns, were interfering for their own gain with land now his by right of capture in battle. Attila also complained that the Roman Emperor of the East was sending to him as ambassadors mere ordinary citizens; the royal Court of the Huns expected to receive men of aristocratic birth and standing, men of consular rank.

Edeco brought with him one Bigilas as interpreter during his visit; he himself did not know Greek. Bigilas did, for he was Roman by origin and had lived in the Roman Empire of the East; he also knew the Hun language well. Both men, after delivering the letter at the Palace, went to call upon Chrysaphius, who received them most graciously in his magnificent mansion. "You Romans must be blessed with great wealth," said Edeco in envy. "Why," answered Chrysaphius, "you, too, Edeco, could own a house roofed with gold and be lord of wealth if you would leave the land of the Huns and come to live with us, the Romans, here in Constantinople." And he invited both him and Bigilas to dine with him. There, after they had feasted well, and Edeco had sworn to keep all that was said secret, Chrysaphius revealed his thought. "If," he said to Edeco, "when you return to your own land of the Huns, you will remove Attila by death from this earth and then come to live in our Roman Empire of the East, you will live happily, blessed by great wealth." The promise was given, provided that Chrysaphius furnish fifty pounds of gold, as reward for the Hun soldiers who would carry out the deed by Edeco's order. All, then, was arranged; Bigilas, present as interpreter, would offer some explanation of the gold as a "gift" from the Romans; Attila would surely ask whether they had offered money as propitiation for himself.

Promptly Chrysaphius, in secret conference with the Emperor, won his consent; Theodosius was desperate. Then, accompanied by an envoy bearing an answer to Attila's letter, Edeco and Bigilas started their return journey to the land of the Huns. Priscus, the historian, himself also traveled with them, and thus has left us a full account of all that happened.

As the journey drew toward its end, Edeco began to doubt, to fear that trouble was in store for him. Doubt was followed by decision; directly the travelers reached Attila, who was in camp just then, Edeco in private told him all that had been planned against his life.

Edeco, therefore, escaped judgment. But Bigilas was received by the king with a torrent of abuse, though nothing was said of the plot. Abuse could be endured, but an order for the immediate execution of his son was too much; in his terror Bigilas also poured out the whole story of the plot.

He was delivered as captive to guards, there to stay until Attila had decided upon his fate; in the meantime Chrysaphius and the Emperor Theodosius must be dealt with, as vitally implicated in this treachery and crime. Two envoys, Orestes and Esla—so Attila decided—were to be despatched to Constantinople, there to seek immediate audience with the Emperor. Before they left on their errand, Attila gave them instruction. Both were to appear together in the Palace, Orestes with the bag which had contained the gold provided by Chrysaphius as reward for the murder of Attila, hanging from his neck in plain sight. Chrysaphius the chamberlain would of course be present; face to face with Theodosius the Emperor, Orestes was to point to this bag and ask Chrysaphius whether he recognized it? Then Esla, turning to the Emperor, was to say that "Theodosius was son of a noble father, and King Attila had both received and kept alive his own inheritance of upright character from his father. But now Theodosius had fallen away from this high repute and had made himself a slave to tribute. Against right and justice, as a dishonest servant he was secretly plotting against one who was superior to himself, one whose fortune had made him, Attila, master and lord. Never would Attila cease to accuse Theodosius of sins against himself, if Theodosius did not send him Chrysaphius, the eunuch, for due punishment."

Faced by this crisis, Theodosius ordered two of his leading ministers at once to take the road for Attila's dwelling across the Danube: Anatolius, Master of Soldiers, and Nomus, also of magisterial standing, both of them Patrician in title of honor. Nomus was wealthy, ready to spend his money when occasion offered itself, a friend of Chrysaphius and ready to save his life by generosity.

They set out, therefore, eager to bring about peace, and Attila, moved by respect for these men of so great distinction, met them directly they arrived in Scythia. He addressed them first of all, it is true, with haughty, arrogant words; soon, however, even these were conquered by the multitude of gifts brought by these delegates and their courteous approach. As the talk went on, his barbarian ambition, covetousness, and pride yielded to their diplomatic skill. He now swore to keep peace in accordance with a treaty made in 448: to yield the region on their side of the Danube to the

Romans as of their own rightful jurisdiction; to worry Theodosius no longer by demands that Hun deserters be returned, to expect only that in the future the Romans deny them refuge in their land. Finally he set Bigilas free, at a price of fifty pounds of gold, and delivered to Anatolius and Nomus, without demanding the sum of money required for ransom, a multitude of Roman prisoners. It was a great victory for the Roman Empire of the East.

We return from State politics once again to ecclesiastical matters, in which Chrysaphius was as keen to play his part as in civil government. Proclus, Patriarch of Constantinople, had ruled from 434 until 447. Now Flavian, a priest of no bold character but devoted to orthodox doctrine, and entirely opposed to the Monophysite creed, was enthroned in his place. Cyril, Patriarch of Alexandria, had died in June 444, and in the same month one Dioscorus had been consecrated as the head of its Church.

We have now to link in action Flavian of Constantinople, Dioscorus of Alexandria, and Chrysaphius, all-powerful minister of the Court of the Emperor Theodosius. Nicephorus Callistus, writer of Church history, tells that the appointing of Flavian was not welcomed by Chrysaphius, who at once made it his business to see that it should not be welcome to the Emperor. He therefore persuaded Theodosius to suggest to Flavian that he offer to the Imperial Court a gift in gratitude for his reception of honor as Patriarch. It was customary for priests to send, to both the rich and the poor among their people, "eulogies," gifts of blessed bread, at times of feast and friendship. Flavian therefore duly offered to the Emperor his "eulogy" of white bread, blessed by him, and Chrysaphius took it upon himself to write in answer that the "blessing" should have been given in gold. The Patriarch replied that he had no gold to offer, unless he were to strip the altar of its sacred vessels. The chamberlain passed on this answer, carefully spiced with ugly words, to the Emperor, and Theodosius was no longer Flavian's friend. Another version of the same incident, given by François Nau in the *Livre d'Héraclide,* shows the Emperor as himself demanding this gift in the Cathedral of Constantinople at Eastertide.

These versions are but stories which may be true. In grave earnest of truth, the working, the conflict of Flavian and the Emperor, together with Dioscorus and Chrysaphius, now in 448 centered in one Eutyches.

Eutyches, according to his own statement, in 448 was seventy years old. For many of these years he had lived in a monastery on the border of Constantinople; there he had been ordained priest and in course of time had been appointed archimandrite, "abbot" in Western title. His reputation for holiness and austere living was widespread.

Unfortunately, however, he thought it his duty and felt it his joy to take a prominent part in theological debate; for this he was entirely unfitted both by temperament and by mind. He was no theologian, except in his own fancy. When first we come upon him he was engaged in keen warfare against Nestorianism and in firm declaration of the Virgin Mary as Theotokos. A letter written to him by Saint Leo I, Pope from 440 to 461, ran in part: "To our well-beloved son, the priest Eutyches: Your words written to us have told that the Nestorian heresy is once again coming to life; your anxiety concerning this is indeed welcome. . . . With God's help we must see that this detestable evil, recently condemned, be destroyed, root and branch" (Epist. XX).

Eutyches looked back to Cyril of Alexandria as the upholder of his faith; we have observed in regard to the school of Alexandria that while those trained in it did confess a union in the Christ of two natures, human and divine, "they dwelt so much on the Divine that at times their words seemed to point to only one nature in the Lord!" And indeed Eutyches looked back to Cyril in the error of his own mind; trouble was to come upon him in his zeal to combat heresy. His trouble began with one Domnus, who in 442 had succeeded John as Patriarch of Antioch. It was, as we have seen, the privilege and the right of the Emperor to call into action Councils of the Church for the trial of those charged with heresy. So Domnus knew what he was doing when he wrote to Theodosius: "I feel it my duty to inform Your Piety that the priest Eutyches is striving to renew the impiety of Apollinaris the heretic, to upset Apostolic teaching. He is corrupting doctrine in regard to the mystery of the Incarnation, declaring the Divinity and the humanity of the Only-begotten Son to be one Nature, with mixture and confusion in the same."

Another prelate of the Church, however, was also on the trail of Eutyches: Eusebius, bishop of Dorylaeum in Phrygia, Asia Minor. He, like Domnus, was ever ready to ferret out errors in theology; twenty years before, he had boldly accused Nestorius. Now in 448 he was on a visit to Constantinople and he seized his chance to talk with Eutyches. Talk led to argument, and argument to conviction in the mind of the bishop of Dorylaeum: the faith of this archimandrite, whether he knew it or not, was certainly tainted with heresy concerning the Christ. He was preaching rank Apollinarianism, and no words of Eusebius could change his obstinate stand.

Here was a difficult problem. Eutyches was an abbot of wide repute throughout Constantinople, and his determination was as great as the respect given him on all sides. Nestorius, in that same *Livre d'Héraclide,* wrote: "Since Eutyches was not a bishop, he gave himself another part to play, by grace of Imperial support: he was bishop of bishops. It was he who directed the business of the Church in Constantinople, and he used Flavian as a servant to carry out the orders given there. Flavian was so sincerely humble that he did not grasp the meaning of what was going on."

For Eutyches was a very close friend of the all-powerful Chrysaphius, and his godfather in religion. The two made a combination which few would dare to attack; with Chrysaphius to support him, Eutyches was also under the protection of the Emperor himself.

Nevertheless Eusebius, as resolute and determined as Chrysaphius, prepared for battle. On November 8, 448, a "Home" Council of bishops, then in Constantinople, resident and visitor alike, assembled there to settle a dispute between Florentius, bishop of Sardis in Asia Minor, and two of his suffragans. They had finished their business and were about to leave when, to their utter astonishment, Eusebius rose to make formal accusation of heretical teaching against Eutyches, of all men.

For long—so Eusebius told—Eutyches had dared to differ from the apostles themselves, as also from the Fathers gathered at Nicaea, in his theological position. The bishop of Dorylaeum defended his very serious charge by stating that he had evidence from the lips of Eutyches himself. The archimandrite was now maintaining that Christ, Our Lord, after what the Church held as His Incarnation, had, not two Natures, as the Church taught, but only one, a Nature Divine; as man He, Eutyches was saying, was not of our human substance. Not in truth, but only in figure of speech, was the Lord said to have endured hardships of the body in life, to have died on the Cross, to have risen from the dead.

This was the Docetic doctrine which—so Eusebius stated—Eutyches now held and desired to spread abroad.

The bishops of this Council of 448 prepared to sit again for action, and a call was sent to Eutyches. Twice, as the days went on and the Council sat again, he refused to come; he had vowed, he said, never to leave monastic enclosure. Moreover, he pleaded frailty, sickness, old age.

The "Home" Synod of Constantinople had gathered for its

seventh session and it was November 22 when word arrived that Eutyches was on his way with a multitude of soldiers and monks as escort; also the Emperor himself was sending with him for his comfort another Florentius, an official of high rank at Court, Patrician in title. Florentius at once informed the bishops assembled that Theodosius wished him to take part in the trial of Eutyches, since this concerned the faith of the Church, to which he himself was firmly loyal. The request was granted, both by the Council and by Eutyches, the accused.

Now the seventh session opened; minutes of the previous six were read, followed by a statement of orthodox doctrine. Directly after this, Eusebius burst out: "That man here before you does not confess this; he believes precisely the opposite!" So Eusebius continued to argue, and Flavian, who as Patriarch of Constantinople was presiding, had a hard time trying to keep him silent.

Flavian then proceeded to question the aged archimandrite and priest under trial, and Eutyches, now in irritation, now in uncertainty, in the end weary and flustered, endeavored to defend himself, to satisfy his judges, even offering to say what they said and directed him to say. Flavian on this occasion showed himself a hard examiner; he accused Eutyches of declaring in his answer, not his own belief, but what he knew his judges wanted him to say, of trying to accuse them themselves of importing new doctrine into the Church.

At last came the final question, put by Florentius: "Do you confess Our Lord, born of the Virgin Mary, to be of the same substance as ourselves, and of two Natures after His Incarnation?"

And Eutyches, tired out, drew himself together to make the last and final answer: "I confess that Our Lord was of two Natures before the union in the Incarnation; after the union I admit only one Nature, and that is my truth."

It was to the bishops present what they had been expecting, some of them doubtless with hope: a flat denial of the true humanity of the Christ. He had but one Nature, it said in their ears, and that Divine; it declared that the Christ was not of like substance with man on earth. Now Eutyches, after all his wavering at last had said what he really believed. Eutyches himself in his own mind believed that he had authority for this final statement, authority from patristic source. If he had given the answer which the Council required of him, he feared that he would have been casting anathema upon certain Fathers of the Church, even including Cyril of Alexandria. "If, however," he had said during his examination before this Council, "if the Fathers of Rome and of Alexandria were to order me to confess two Natures in the Christ after His Incarnation, I am ready to do so."

The words were those of an old man, baffled and bewildered by Christological argument, trying both to be loyal to Cyril of Alexandria, whose theology he did not understand, and at the same time to escape condemnation for error in a matter so vital to him as abbot and priest.

"Anathema to Eutyches!" cried the Council, and Flavian prepared to pronounce judgment, saying: "He who does not confess 'Of two Natures' does not hold the true Faith"; he was answered by a shout: "Faith forced by necessity is not Faith!"

Eutyches was then deposed from all priestly office, deprived of communion with the Church, and the leadership of his monastery. All who in the future ventured to speak or to meet with him faced penalty of their own excommunication.

The sentence caused furious anger in Chrysaphius and the Emperor. To Eutyches it seemed the end of all things. In his misery he appealed to Pope Leo, declaring "that at the Council he had been full of fear, not daring to bring accusation against bishops of the Church; that also he had not dared to pronounce his own judgment on the Word of God, and that he had wished to receive judgment from Pope Leo himself." . . .

"I who cast anathema upon Apollinaris, upon Valentinus, Manes, Nestorius, and those who say that the human body of Our Lord and Savior Jesus Christ came down from heaven, came not from the Holy Spirit and of the Virgin Mary; I who abhor all heresies, up to Simon Magus, I nevertheless run risk of my life as heretic! . . . Do not allow me to be cast forth from the number of the faithful! Do not allow one who has lived seventy years in continence and all chastity to suffer shipwreck at the end of his life!"

The letter reached Rome and caused Leo to write, on February 18, 449, both to Flavian and to the Emperor Theodosius. Flavian was asked why, for what just reason, Eutyches had been excommunicated? He, the bishop of Rome, had not been informed. Why? And Eutyches had said in his letter that he was ready to receive correction, should he be proved guilty of error. To Theodosius Leo declared that he did not see, from the information so far received by him, that the charge of heresy against Eutyches was proved. Had not Eutyches confessed firmly the faith of Nicaea?

About the same time Flavian was writing to the Pope; Leo received his letter in the month of March. A second explanation arrived in Rome in May, sent by Flavian in answer to the Pope's complaint. In May of this same year Leo acknowledged this, and now granted that Eutyches had indeed fallen into grave error. On June 13, 449, he sent off to Flavian a treatise on Catholic doctrine, known in history as the "Tome of Leo." Its opening words stated that Eutyches, who had once seemed to merit respect as priest, was now shown to be very foolish and ignorant, even one of whom the prophet well might say: "He willed not to understand, to understand for the sake of doing good." "What," the Pope continued, "what learning did Eutyches gain from the sacred pages of the New and the Old Testament when he does not understand even the first words of the Catholic creed? Truly he has not even grasped what the newly baptized know and declare!" Yet Leo did not cease to hope that he might be brought to penitence, to recognition of the truth. "Eutyches," the Pope remarked at the end of his letter, "was not rebuked by your knowledge of the truth. Use your diligence and care, dear brother Flavian, that if by the mercy of God his case be cleared, this foolish and ignorant man may be freed from the plague which haunts his mind!"

But Chrysaphius would own no defeat, and the Emperor followed him as closely in matters of religion as he did in those of politics. A wide gulf of difference now divided brother from sister, Theodosius from the devout and orthodox Pulcheria. On this same thirteenth of June, 449, the Pope addressed a letter to her which told of his deep confidence in her firm following and knowledge of the Catholic Faith. She was, however, as he knew well, subject in all outward action to the Imperial power, now guided by Chrysaphius. Yet, in the hope of putting an end to strife between Church and State, he as bishop of Rome was sending three of his clergy to represent him at another trial of Eutyches.

That trial, by order of the Emperor Theodosius, was to meet early in August 449. Eutyches himself had asked for this and so had Dioscorus, now Patriarch of Alexandria.

Eutyches, thought Chrysaphius, must by all possible means be defended and he quickly went to work upon the Emperor, with success. Theodosius sent word to the Patriarch of Alexandria: "We make you, Dioscorus, President of this Council, and we know right well that the most reverend Juvenal, Archbishop of Jerusalem, is of the same mind as Your Holiness." Theodoret, bishop of Cyrrhus in Syria, a prelate of differing view, he ordered excluded from the gathering.

On August 8 it met at Ephesus in the church of Saint Mary; history knows it as the *Latrocinium,* "Robber Council," a name given it by Pope Leo. Throughout its brief proceedings the influence of the Emperor, of his representatives, and of those who professed Monophysitism, the doctrine of the one Nature of the Christ after His Incarnation, steadily gained strength. The legates sent by Pope Leo asked that his "Tome" be read. It was of no great length; but the request was disregarded. Eutyches made a very long statement concerning his faith and creed; boldly he declared that he was a follower in this of Cyril of Alexandria. A multitude of monks from Egypt and Syria, headed by an archimandrite named Barsumas, caused great confusion by jumping up and down, uttering loud yells of approval or dissent. The Acts of the Council of Constantinople which in 448 had deposed Eutyches were read; at the moment when they told that Seleucus, bishop of Amasia in Pontus, had joyously confessed two Natures of the Lord Incarnate, the monks with one voice howled: "He did *not!* That is Nestorian! *No one* admits two Natures!" At the mention of Eusebius of Dorylaeum all around Barsumas shouted: "Away with Eusebius! Burn him alive! Cut him in two!" When the reader reached the words of Eutyches: "I confess that Our Lord after His Incarnation was of one Nature only," Dioscorus, who was presiding, broke in with a loud "We all agree!" And some among the audience sitting in Council called back: "We agree!"

Finally the vote was taken and by overwhelming consent Dioscorus pronounced its decision: "The judgment of this sacred and ecumenical Council, supported by my own will, is that Eutyches be restored to the order of priesthood and to his rule as archimandrite in his monastery."

Action did not end here; the judges of Eutyches at Constantinople in 448 were yet to be held responsible for error. Amid utter confusion and fierce protest Flavian and Eusebius were deposed from their sees, as guilty of changing the form of the creed of Nicaea; at a later session on August 22 Theodoret of Cyrrhus, Ibas of Edessa, and, still later, Domnus of Antioch, met the same dishonoring. As the words of Dioscorus rang out in the chamber: "Flavian and Eusebius, sources of scandal and confusion to the sacred churches and also in all places to Catholic peoples, we judge unfitted for priestly and episcopal office," Flavian cried "I appeal from your witness"; Hilary, a deacon, and one of the Papal legates, uttered but one word, heard by all: CONTRADICTED!"

Eutyches retired to stay outside his monastery but in or near Constantinople; Flavian was banished from the city. On his way to the place designed for his exile, Hypaepa in Lydia, his troubles on earth ended in his death. It was still August of 449, and he was worn out by the Council of Ephesus, and by the brutal cruelty of those who were hurrying him away.

It was the turn of Pope Leo to burn with wrath. In October he wrote twice to the Emperor; implored him to call another Council for the righting of error, and this time within the bounds of Italy. He wrote to Pulcheria, pleading that she do all in her power to persuade her brother to act "before civil, ruinous war gain force within the Church." To Pulcheria came also a letter from the deacon Hilary, who had fled from Ephesus without bag or baggage, thanking the Lord Christ that he was not guilty of the evil worked against Flavian. Through paths and trails unknown to him and almost impassable he had reached Rome to pour out the story of disorder and hatred seen and heard by him. The Pope was horrified; on Christmas Day he made one more appeal to the Emperor. Nothing was done.

Yet Leo did not cease trying. On February 22, 450, three of the Imperial family of the West were in Rome: its Emperor Valentinian III, now in his thirty-first year; his mother, Galla Placidia; and his wife, Licinia Eudoxia, daughter of Theodosius. It was the Feast of Saint Peter's Chair, and the three came to Mass in the Cathedral. There they met Leo himself, and he asked each of them to write to this silent Emperor in Constantinople.

We have their letters, and the answer to each. That of Valentinian to his father-in-law was dignified and courteous; that of Galla Placidia to her nephew pictured the Pope as bitterly distressed, calling for their own lamentation from his Imperial friends; that of Licinia Eudoxia to her father was full of graceful pleading and compliments. Far more interesting is a letter from Galla Placidia, now past her sixtieth year, to her niece Pulcheria. "The Catholic Faith, held fast by our ancestors since the time of Constantine," she wrote, "has now been assaulted; some wicked action is said to have been stirred up against the bishop of Constantinople. Word has reached us that in the Council at Ephesus no one respected Holy Order or priestly character; with utter presumption, injustice, and no thought of God in His heaven, everything was done to drive certain prelates from their sees. Such doings in our days are simply horrible! So now, my daughter, most sacred and reverend Empress, do please work with us that the acts of that disorderly, most miserable Council be reported for judgment to the Apostolic See of Rome!"

Not until the spring of 450 did answers arrive from the Emperor in Constantinople. To Valentinian he frankly admitted that his order had called together the bishops of the Second Council of Ephesus. So far as he could see, nothing contrary to orthodox faith or rightful justice had been done by it. All dispute had been investigated by reverend authority. Flavian, found guilty of harmful innovation, had received his due; peace, concord, and unalloyed truth now reigned throughout the Churches.

To his daughter, Licinia Eudoxia, Theodosius sent a brief reply. He was always delighted, he said, to hear from her and to grant her petitions. This time, however, he had written to the Pope. Holy judgment had removed Flavian from this life on earth and therefore all doubt and contention were at an end. Nothing remained to be done.

In his letter to his aunt, Galla Placidia, the Emperor defended himself with care and caution. Of course he knew well what the Pope had asked of her. Neither he, his argument declared, nor the bishops gathered by his order at Ephesus, had defined, decreed, or even had had in mind anything except patristic faith and God-inspired doctrine. Flavian, leader of the quarrel, by episcopal judgment had been deposed from office in the Church: "Knowing these facts, Lady and reverend Empress, do not assume or think that we, as is said by some, have purposed anything contrary to the Faith given us of old."

As winter drew near in 449, a new Patriarch was elected for Constantinople: Anatolius, who had been in the service of Dioscorus at Constantinople and was Alexandrian in training. From his association with Dioscorus he shared doctrine with Eutyches. Before his consecration, Anatolius wrote to inform Pope Leo of what had been happening in the Imperial city and its Church. The Emperor Theodosius had requested his clergy to name men whom they considered best fitted for the high office of Patriarch; then, he had said, he would elect one from names given him. At once "immoderate discussion" had broken out; in hope of peace, power of election had been given also to clergy from other places who were on a visit to Constantinople. The vote had fallen upon himself, Anatolius; his consecration was ordered and was to be carried out.

But it was followed by trouble. On July 16, 450, Pope Leo wrote to the Emperor that he did not feel happy concerning doctrine held and declared by this Patriarch of Constantinople; Anatolius had better make clear his theological position before an assembly of clergy and people there.

In this same month the Emperor one day went out riding; he was thrown from his horse, seriously wounded in the spine, and carried back to the Palace on a stretcher. For two days he lay on his bed, knowing that death was near. To his bedside he called Pulcheria and told her that one Marcian, known as both a soldier of skill and a confidential adviser of Aspar, son of Ardaburius, now Master of Soldiers, was to be his successor on the throne. "This," he said, "has been revealed to me by Divine will." The influence of Aspar had been at work and Pulcheria promptly accepted Aspar's counsel, while deciding that she herself would reign with Marcian, as Empress and wife. On July 28, 450, Theodosius died; in August Marcian was proclaimed Emperor and the marriage took place. Never, indeed, Pulcheria resolved, would she break her vow of virginity; within her secret mind she knew well that her wedding with Marcian would maintain for the House of Theodosius Imperial rule and allow her to exercise her power in politics as before.

Marcian, however, was no Theodosius; he cooperated with Pulcheria, he did not follow her. He is variously described as born in Illyricum or in Thrace; John Malalas tells that he was tall, his hair gray, lank and straight, his feet drawn and stiff. Evagrius praises him as one devoted to the Catholic Church, a just man in his dealings with his subjects, one who held rule not by inheritance, but as a reward of manly virtue. Against enemies of the Empire he stood firm. Without hesitation he allowed his Empress to mete out due penalty to Chrysaphius who had so sorely vexed both Empire and Church; Chrysaphius was delivered to execution this same year.

Our knowledge of this Emperor and of his brief reign, from August 25, 450, until January 26, 457, centers largely in the history of the Church, in the details that have come down to us concerning the Fourth Ecumenical Council, assembled in 451 at Chalcedon in Asia Minor, on the Bosporus.

Before that date, however, the Empress Pulcheria had written to Pope Leo, telling him that Anatolius, Patriarch of Constantinople, had declared his loyal allegiance to the Catholic Faith, rejecting all erroneous doctrine held by Eutyches and accepting in full loyalty that put forward in the "Tome," the letter written by the Pope himself to Flavian.

In the letter of Pulcheria, and also in one written by her husband, the Emperor Marcian, petition was made to Leo that a General Council of bishops of the Empire of the East might be called, to put a firm ending to error concerning the Faith of the Church and to give a clear statement of its substance. Leo again and again had insisted upon a Council in Italy; then, finding that this was not favorably viewed by Constantinople, he had suggested postponement in the hope of a more propitious time.

Finally, he had yielded to the Imperial petition; the meeting was to be in the East and he would send Papal legates. Nicaea had first been chosen, and many actually arrived there; then by wish of Marcian Chalcedon was preferred as nearer his Palace.

At Chalcedon, on October 8, 451, in its Church of Saint Euphemia, Martyr, between five and six hundred bishops gathered, including Dioscorus of Alexandria. We do not know where Eutyches was at this moment. In June 451, four months before, Pope Leo had written to Pulcheria: "With regard to Eutyches, author of all the present scandal, would Your Clemency give order that he be transferred to some place remote from Constantinople? Far away, he would not enjoy so often comfort and encouragement from those whom he has drawn into his impious belief. And would you see, also, that his monastery, so near Constantinople, be given over to rule by a Catholic abbot who would free it from that belief?" The Council of Chalcedon, therefore, did not trouble about Eutyches; and, indeed, on July 28, 452, the Emperor Marcian was to issue an edict of banishment for both him and his monks.

It was Dioscorus who now became target for accusation. He had not given assent to the "Tome" of Pope Leo; he had deposed Flavian, Patriarch of Constantinople, to whom it had been sent; against all canon law he had readmitted Eutyches the Monophysite into the communion of the Church; he had repeatedly defied the summons to appear at Chalcedon. Most heinous sin of all, absolutely unthinkable, he had actually dared to issue sentence of excommunication against Leo, the Holy Father himself.

So now he was himself sentenced to deposition from his see, and shortly afterward to exile in Gangra, Paphlagonia. Theodoret of Cyrrhus and Ibas of Edessa were reinstated in their bishoprics; Domnus of Antioch had already been allowed to return to his Cathedral. Prelates who had voted against Flavian at the "Robber" Council of Ephesus were now heard crying: "We all have sinned! We all ask forgiveness!" They were forgiven. Prominent among them was Juvenal, bishop of Jerusalem; he hurried across the aisle to join those who sat as defenders of Flavian. Not so did Dioscorus, now present at last; he uttered no word of appeal, of penitence.

The high point of the meeting was reached in its "Definition of Faith," declared valid in its second version during the fifth meeting, on October the twenty-second. It confirmed again the faith of Nicaea:

"Following in the steps of the holy Fathers we all with one consent declare Our Lord Jesus Christ to be one and the same Son, perfect in Deity, perfect in humanity, truly God and truly man,

of rational soul and body; consubstantial with the Father in regard
to Deity, consubstantial with us in regard to humanity; in all
things like unto us, save in sin; begotten before all ages from the
Father in regard to Deity; born, late in time, for us and for our
salvation, of the Virgin Mary, Mother of God: One and the Same
Jesus Christ, Son, Lord, Only-Begotten; in two Natures, without confusion, change, or division, the difference in the Natures being in
no way destroyed through their union, the character of each Nature
being retained; subsisting in One Person or Hypostasis, not divided
or set apart into two Persons, but One and the Same Son, the Word,
the Lord Jesus Christ; even as of old the prophets, as the Christ
Himself, taught us, when He gave to us the creed of the Fathers."

Marcian and Pulcheria were present at the sixth session, on the
25th of October. After hearing himself and his wife hailed as "A
New Constantine!" "A New Helena!" the Emperor ended the day
with these words: "We render deepest thanksgiving to Christ,
Savior of all, for that the discord of many who erred in faith has
been cut away; that with one will we have all come together into
one and the same creed. And we hope that through your prayers
right speedily will peace in all things be given us by grace of the
Lord God."

The belief voiced at Chalcedon was indeed that of the Catholic
Church; but it was not unopposed. Eutyches has been called "the
Father of Monophysitism"; his belief in the one Nature of Our
Lord Incarnate was to be held by a swelling flood of those who
lived in the East; long and sternly the Church was to fight it.

Another, lesser cause of conflict, but acute and lasting, was the
twenty-eighth canon of this Council, which confirmed by vote the
action of the Synod of Constantinople in 381. Once again it declared that the Archiepiscopal See of Constantinople, "New Rome,"
was second in dignity among the Patriarchates of the Roman Empire, second only to Rome itself. It added, moreover, that the
Metropolitans of Pontus, Asia, and Thrace were henceforth to be
under the jurisdiction of Constantinople's Patriarch. Papal legates
from Rome protested. Pope Leo showed his wrath; on May 22, 452,
he wrote to Marcian, to Pulcheria, and to Anatolius, Patriarch of
Constantinople, accusing Anatolius of sinful pride and ambition, of
disobedience to the sacred canons of Nicaea. But Constantinople
continued to hold its place.

From Constantinople and Chalcedon we pass to Palestine,
where Monophysites were already fiercely at work, stirred into
action by those who had disagreed with the creed proclaimed at
Chalcedon in October 451. Juvenal was one of those who had re-

pented; he, as we saw, had crossed the aisle to sit among those who upheld it. Shock awaited him upon arrival at his see of Jerusalem. Rebel monks of Monophysite mind were now raising tumult in that city; one of them, named Theodosius, had seized authority, had even won illegal consecration as bishop of Jerusalem. In 452 Juvenal was forced to flee for refuge to the Desert.

Among the many who joined this Monophysite rising and supported the rebel Theodosius, was the Empress Eudocia herself, still in exile. As Empress she had loyally followed Catholic practice in Constantinople, and afterward as exile in Jerusalem. But she had been brought up at Athens in pagan ways; she had ever been devoted to the literature of her native Greece. Moreover, she knew little concerning Catholic creed; all the strife and struggle of Councils, of Ephesus and of Chalcedon, had confused her mind.

Pope Leo was distressed and worried by the news from Jerusalem. On June 15, 453, he wrote to Eudocia, praying her to hold fast the Faith. Would she not work with him to turn these Monophysite monks from blasphemous words to the acknowledgment of truth?

Theophanes in his *Chronographia* draws a lurid picture of their leader Theodosius, one "bent on evil." Theodosius, he writes, worked hand in hand with Eudocia, "appointing men in her service as his assistant bishops, bishops of sees rightfully held by prelates still absent in Chalcedon. He did not hesitate to pursue, to rob, even to kill; he persecuted men of high ranking in the Church. For twenty months this Theodosius held Juvenal's see, until the Emperor Marcian learned of his doings and ordered his arrest. Then he in his turn rushed for shelter, at Mount Sinai, and Juvenal in 453 was once more in law and right seated in his Archbishopric of Jerusalem.

But Eudocia, as time went on, met happenings which troubled her conscience. In 455, as we shall see, her daughter, Licinia Eudoxia, and her two granddaughters, Eudocia and Placidia, were seized and carried off by the Vandal king, Gaiseric. Was the Lord of Heaven angry with her for deserting the faith of the Catholic Church? Long she brooded, and at last she decided to seek counsel of that Church. First she went to the Pillar Saint, Simeon Stylites; he told her to ask this from an abbot, Saint Euthymius, who ruled a monastery some miles from Jerusalem. Euthymius not only confirmed her fear but brought her to penitence; for the rest of her life she as a devout Catholic patiently hoped for release from this troubled world.

She had not long to wait; in 460 she died at Jerusalem. Many memories she left, there and elsewhere. She had built and had seen consecrated, its magnificent church of Saint Stephen; she had given rich gifts in plenty to aid things and persons dedicated to religion, men and women suffering from poverty, from disease. Always she had loved to write, and her verses are still in our libraries. Most of them are hexameter lines which tell of scenes from the Bible and the lives of saints. The scholar, A. Ludwich, who described her work in 1882 and edited it in 1897, saw it as dependent on other writing: clumsy, laborious, sinning against good taste and artistic character. In her own time, however, it was held of value. The best known of her compositions, the story of the life and martyrdom of Saints Cyprian and Justina, has been termed, in the 1956 edition of Alban Butler's *Lives of the Saints,* "a moral tale, utterly fabulous."

The year 451 saw also, we may believe, the death of Nestorius in exile. The Emperor Marcian had allowed his return home; but this he had refused, preferring to die where he had lived so long. About 436 we saw him sent to Oasis in Egypt; there barbarians known as Blemmyes had carried him away and for some time held him prisoner. He was taken by them with other captives into the Egyptian Thebaid, as far as Panopolis on the bank of the Nile. In this city he made himself known to the governor of the Thebaid, declaring his ready submission to the Imperial will. He was afraid lest he be accused of attempting escape; or, on the other hand, of actually preferring to remain in barbarian hands rather than accept mercy from the Emperor of the East. From Panopolis he was sent to Elephantine, a city on an island near Assuân; next, worn out by travel, sickness, and the burden of years, he was ordered to return to Panopolis. Even there he was not allowed to rest; other journeys were forced upon him.

Much of his time he had spent in writing, in trying to defend himself against his accusers. Of special interest among his works are two which Evagrius, Byzantine historian, was glad to read: his *Tragedy* and his *Book of Heraclides,* both written in Greek. The latter, found in Syrian text and now ours to read in the French of François Nau and the English of G. O. Driver and Leonard Hodgson, is indispensable; it has given support to an orthodox view of his creed.

Nau has given us in French the last words of this *Book of Heraclides;* I give them here in English to tell of the last hours of Nestorius on this earth:

"For myself, I have seen the sufferings of my life, and all that has been my fate in this world, as the suffering of a day;

and I have not changed in all these years. Now the time of my death draws near, and every day I pray God to deliver me: me, whose eyes have seen His salvation.

"Rejoice with me, O Desert, my friend, my nurse and my home, my fellow in my exile: my mother, thou who even after my death by the will of God wilt guard my body until the Resurrection shall dawn. Amen."

From 450 until 453 Pope Leo I sent letter after letter to the Empress Pulcheria. In April 451, he wrote: "It was your care which brought to light the things contrived by the Devil through Eutyches; you must know that the whole Church of Rome is filled with joy through the workings of your faith, seen everywhere. Catholic priests driven by unjust sentence from their churches you have restored; the relics of Flavian, saved in memory, you have brought back to that Church of Constantinople which he ruled so well." In July 451, he said the same. In May 452, as we saw, he poured out for her sympathy his wrath against Anatolius, holding place of honor after the Papal legates in the Council of Chalcedon: "What greater honor does Anatolius desire than that of Patriarch of Constantinople? To strive beyond the decent limit is a mark of pride without bounds." In March 453, he thanked her for wise action concerning the rebel monks in Palestine.

That same year Pulcheria died. She left all her property to the poor. Three churches were declared built by her, in the words of Theodore Lector, the ecclesiastical historian; all were in Constantinople, and all were dedicated to Mary, Mother of God. She also gave from her wealth the comfort of monasteries for the religious, of hostel to strangers, of hospital to the sick, of rest to the weary and the old.

Hard words have been attributed to those who heartily disliked her devotion to her religion or as heartily resented her proud confidence in her authority, her right to act and to command. But they lack honest support. Those of Eunapius, as has been remarked, were the words of a determined pagan. In spite of the narrative of Seeck (*Geschichte des Untergangs der antiken Welt* VI, page 201) we cannot with any confidence accept the story of her intrigue in love, traced to Nestorius. It would seem better to place mention of this by Nestorius as one of his unwise remarks, based on foolish gossip and uttered in his wrath.

CHAPTER SIX

Valentinian III and Honoria

We now return to the Empire of the West, and to the cities of Rome and Ravenna. There, at the end of our fourth chapter, telling of the usurpation of John, we saw Valentinian, son of Galla Placidia, crowned Emperor on October 23, 425. His mother, as we also said, was appointed Regent for him during his minority, which lasted literally until in July 434, he reached the age of fifteen, and very probably until his marriage in 437.

It would seem that Valentinian the Third was no better than his uncle Honorius, either in character or in rule. So, at least, thought Procopius of Caesarea, who pictured him vividly:

"Placidia, his mother, who brought him up, allowed him to grow into a man weak and womanish. Indeed from a child he was utterly worthless and bad. His special friends dealt with sorcery and poisonous drugs, or guided their lives by the stars. He delighted in love affairs with wives of other men; he was known as lascivious and lewd, though he had himself a wife most charming, of rare beauty. And more than this. He did not recover any one of the possessions lost by the Empire: he lost Libya and other lands, too; he lost his own life. And when he died his wife and his children were captured and carried off by the spear."

But, though she neglected her son, or, rather, indulged him to excess, the Empress Placidia had her own ambition as Regent. She influenced and was influenced in turn by three men, each eager for power and distinction: Felix, Aetius, and Boniface.

It was Felix whom she made her chief minister of government at Ravenna, and from 425 to 429 he rose higher: as Master of Both Services, of cavalry and of infantry, as consul for the year 428, as Patrician, a title of special honor, gained by him in 429. Moreover, in 427 he wrested from the Huns a part of Pannonia which bordered on the Danube, held by them illegally, according to the Roman mind.

Meanwhile Aetius had been winning distinction in Gaul; with fierce assault he drove away Goths who were attacking the region occupied by them along the Rhine. In 429 he, too, in reward had been made Master of Both Services. But his rival, Felix, was Patrician, and Aetius was bitterly jealous. At last, so men said, resentment brought him to treachery, even to murder; in May 430, he stirred up a riot among soldiers at Ravenna and thus deliberately caused the death of Felix and his wife Padusia, a woman of noble line, as they stood on the steps of one of Ravenna's churches. Had he not acted, he declared, Felix would have killed him. His act was readily forgiven. Placidia had no love for Felix and she promptly made his murderer the leading director in affairs of the West. Such is the story told in chronicle.

Boniface, tribune in Roman Africa and from 423 its governor as Count, we have seen through the eyes of Procopius. Another description comes from Olympiodorus, of Thebes in Egypt, who ended his *History* with the year 425, when Boniface was Count of the Palace Guards. In it he pictures Boniface as a man bold in battle, a firm supporter of justice; and, to make his picture more vivid, he tells a story of Boniface in action: "A peasant of the countryside in Africa, to his great distress and shame, discovered that his wife, a girl of radiant beauty, had been yielding her charm to a barbarian soldier in the Roman army. What was he to do? In his trouble he turned to Boniface. The Count gathered from him both the situation and the name of a field where the lovers met, and then told him to return on the morrow. That same night Boniface, alone and in secret, made his way to the field, some nine miles distant, found the soldier with his mistress, seized and killed him, cut off his head and carried it back with him. The husband appeared next day as bidden. Directly he arrived Boniface held out to him the severed head. 'Do you recognize this?' he asked. For a moment the man was too horrified to answer; then he gave fervent thanks for justice done and joyfully returned to his home."

The story may be true; its bold and independent action tallies with the loyalty of Boniface to Placidia in her exile.

More reliable, however, is evidence given by letters of Saint Augustine, bishop of Hippo in Roman Africa from 396 until 430.

About 417 Augustine had written to Boniface, then tribune in Africa, concerning work among the erring Donatists, who demanded a second baptism from converts to their sect. The letter was warm and friendly: "I praise and I congratulate and I admire you, my very dear son Boniface, in that among all the cares of battle and providing of arms you long so keenly to learn the things that pertain to God" (Letter 185).

"Battles and arms" meant the struggles by the Roman army of Boniface against native barbarian piracy and raid.

The next year Augustine was gladly sending counsel to his "deservedly distinguished and honorable son, Boniface": "My son Faustus says that you are eager to hear from me for your soul's health. . . . I have written in haste what I could, while the carrier waited, and I thank God that in some way I have not failed your good desire" (Letter 189).

Boniface had asked whether the life of a soldier, leading his men to battle against the Moors, who were constantly invading and pillaging Roman land, was consistent with that of a loyal Christian? The answer was definite: "Do not think that no one who fights as a soldier with weapons of war can please God. . . . Each man, the Apostle tells us, has his own special and different gift from God. Some men, then, fight for you in prayer against invisible enemies; you in war for them against visible barbarians. . . . So remember, first of all, when you arm yourself for battle, that the very strength of your body is itself given you by God. Your will must be for peace, but necessity brings you war; you fight in order that God may free us from necessity and keep us in peace" (Letter 189).

The years passed, and with them Boniface gained rank and power as governor of Africa. In 427 Augustine was writing markedly different words to him. Boniface had lost his wife by death. Never again, he had said to his counselor, would he marry; he would forsake public life and live as a monk in retreat from the world. Augustine, however, had asked him to carry on his military duties: "Your work as a soldier" he had said, "will be of great service to the churches of Christ if you do it with this thought, this will, alone in mind, that these churches of ours, protected from barbarous raid and ravage, may live in peace and tranquillity."

Boniface had not kept his resolve. He had taken a second wife, Pelagia, very wealthy and of the Arian profession, that creed which denied that the Christ was truly and fully Divine; a child born to them had been baptized in Arian ritual. It was even rumored that Boniface had not been faithful in this Arian marriage, that he had yielded to temptation from other women.

Frankly, Augustine now wrote, if Boniface were not a married man, it would be better for him to withdraw at once from war and politics, to enter a monastery and there to fight against the Devil and his angels. If he did continue to live amid the struggle of

Africa with barbarians, he was not to use the things of this world for evil ends.

"Who would fail to see that men cling close to you to guard your power, your safety, men who are indeed loyal to you, from whom you need fear no treacherous act? And yet who does not see that these are men who want to gain through you things which are not of God but of this world?"

Later on, the words of this letter grew sharper, in rebuke for actual neglect of duty:

"What shall I say about the plundering of Africa, carried on by African barbarians while no man resists, while you are occupied with your own affairs and do nothing to arrest disaster? Who truly could believe, who could even fear, that under Boniface, Count of Domestics, Count of Africa, placed in command of so great an army, of so high power, that same Boniface who once as tribune brought peace to all in this land with only a few native allies to aid him, that Boniface who once conquered and terrified our enemies—that now under him the barbarians could dare so boldly, could advance so far, could work such widely spread ravage, could reduce places teeming with inhabitants to nothing but a desert? Did not everyone say, when you became Count of this land of Africa, that its barbarians would not only be conquered, but would be subject for the years to come, paying tribute to the Roman Empire?

"How false this prophecy was, you yourself can clearly see!" (Letter 220).

Not only was Augustine as bishop in Africa distressed; rumors of growing pride and arrogance in Boniface had reached Ravenna. In 427 Felix had recalled him to Italy; he had refused to come. Then Felix had deposed him from office, had declared war against him, and had sent to Africa a force commanded by three generals: Mavortius, Gallio, and Sanoeces.

Their campaign had entirely failed through dissension among its leaders. By treachery of Sanoeces both Mavortius and Gallio had been killed, and soon afterward the traitor himself had met his death.

In 428, after Augustine's rebuke to Boniface, the command against this rebel was given to one Sigisvult, also ranking as Count, who hurried with an army to Africa. His efforts to overcome Boniface were hampered by Moorish raids, and soon he was in trouble. When report of his difficulties reached Ravenna, Felix sent to Africa an envoy named Darius whom both he and Placidia felt capable to deal with the situation there. He was successful; by spring of 429 Boniface yielded; Darius brought about truce between him and Sigisvult. Nevertheless Boniface remained in Africa; in the same year Placidia as Regent restored him to favor and office.

Of interest in connection with Darius are letters which passed in 429 between him and Augustine of Hippo. The bishop wrote to him after hearing of the truce: "Great indeed in their own glory, and—a source of truer praise—faithful warriors are they by whose labor and peril the unconquered enemy has been subdued; peace has been given to government and provinces once more are tranquil. It is a greater glory to kill wars with words than to kill men with the sword, to gain and hold peace by peace, not by battle." To this praise Darius modestly replied: "You say that I kill war by words. Quite briefly and simply may I say that if I did not extinguish wars I certainly, God helping me, banished them for the time; the evils which had reached their summit of tragedy are now dead and gone" (Letters 229, 230).

The reason behind Placidia's quick decision to restore Boniface as governor of Roman Africa was fresh and unexpected action by the Vandals in Spain. From 406 until 428 they were ruled by their king, Gunderic, who had brought them across the Pyrenees in 409, and terrible is the picture drawn by the chronicler Hydatius of the ravage worked by them at their entrance into Spanish territory. Through it they marched, sacking and plundering, while famine and pestilence followed in their path. Its people, we are told, were driven to feed on human flesh, mothers to kill their own children. Wild animals roamed the land freely, feasting upon the corpses of those who had died by the sword, of hunger, of weariness, of plague.

In Baetica at last these Vandals settled; in 428 Gunderic died. Tradition tells that his death came upon him by judgment of God, after he had laid hands in violence upon one of the churches of Seville, a city captured by his command. His brother Gaiseric succeeded him as king.

Of this Gaiseric we shall hear much. Chronicle has it that he had once been of the Catholic faith. We meet him now as a most zealous Arian, determined that all under his power, Vandal or Roman alike, must embrace the Arian creed and practice or suffer grievous penalty. The Gothic historian Jordanes has described him for us in his *Getica:* "Neither short nor tall, of middle height, lame through a fall from his horse, deep and subtle in mind, a man of few words, caring nothing for luxury; given to violent outbursts of rage, eager to have and to hold, doing all in his power to gain for himself the barbarian peoples of his world, ever ready to sow seeds of strife, to stir up enmity."

In 429 his ambition drove him to a decisive and all-important act. With all his Vandal warriors and their families, he crossed the Straits of Gibraltar, to land in the month of May upon the shore of Mauritania.

We have a vivid description of what followed this invading of Roman Africa, in the narrative of Victor, bishop in this fifth century at Vita, a city in the African province of Byzacena. About 488 Victor wrote his *History of the Persecution of the Province of Africa;* its first book tells of oppression and cruelty due to the will of Gaiseric. As this affliction came upon the Roman dwellers in Africa nearly sixty years before he wrote, Victor was relying here on what he had heard from others. But he took care to find reliable sources for his story, and we may believe that much of it is true. In translation from his Latin his first pages run thus:

"It is now, as you know, the sixtieth year since that cruel and savage Vandal people landed on the shore of unhappy Africa, after an easy crossing of only twelve miles through the Straits between Africa and Spain. Gaiseric was their leader. Craftily he worked to make their name terrible to hear; he declared the number of those whom he brought, old and young, children, slaves and masters—eighty thousand in all.

"They came to a province lying tranquil and in order, a land of charm and delight on every side; wherever they went they brought with them devastation: destruction by fire, by slaughter and the sword. Not even the trees which bore fruit did they spare, lest those who had fled before their march to hide in mountain hollows or underground caverns should steal out and find food. Nothing remained untouched by the blight of their hands.

"But their utter determination and will was set to work ruin upon the churches and basilicas of the saints, upon cemeteries and monasteries; they longed to burn houses of prayer in even fiercer fires than the flames which swept away whole cities and towns."

The record then goes on to tell of bishops and priests tortured to death, forced to yield the treasure of their sanctuaries, driven from their homes; of women brought to shame, of little children torn apart before their mothers' eyes; of proud and noble buildings wrecked, of land lying desolate.

Against Gaiseric Boniface did what he could. He mustered an army, marched out to battle and met defeat. Soon only three cities remained: Carthage, Cirta, and Hippo Regius, see of Augustine. There Boniface took refuge, and there from June 430 until July 431 the Vandals held siege. Within its walls Augustine was lying sick, hearing the roar of battle in his last days; on August 28, 430, he died. Whether the city actually was captured in 431 or not is a question under debate; very probably the barbarians left their target free and retreated to fight elsewhere. Procopius tells, truly or not, that they were suffering from lack of food. We know, however, from the *Life of Saint Augustine* written by Possidius, bishop of Calama in Roman Africa and friend of Augustine, that they returned to the city, in the year 432, it would seem, and destroyed part of it by fire. Now only Carthage and Cirta remained intact.

Boniface had left Hippo to make another effort. Again he had gathered an army, and this time he was supported by troops from Constantinople under the command of Aspar. Once more the Vandals had won victory; then Aspar went home to Constantinople and Boniface to Italy, where Placidia welcomed him as one who had faced bravely the impossible.

But there was another reason for this welcome. Aetius was now in Italy, chief minister under the Regent Placidia. His praise was on the lips of all men; he had repeatedly won success in Gaul, where he had defeated and subdued the rebellious Franks. That was excellent; but on the other hand he had renewed his alliance with the Huns and had even restored to them land secured from them by Felix. Their king, Rugila, was his firm friend. Placidia was finding it very difficult to work with this ambitious and self-willed counselor.

In 432 she decided to dismiss Aetius and to give his place in her government to Boniface, whom she now made Master of Soldiers, on horse and foot. Aetius promptly rebelled. In hot anger he marched against Boniface with a strong force of soldiers and fell in with him near Rimini on the Adriatic, south of Ravenna. The chronicler Marcellinus declares that Placidia had encouraged the struggle which followed; in it the men of Boniface gained victory. The two leaders, however, during the battle had met in single combat, and Aetius—wielding, according to Marcellinus, a particularly deadly spear—had wounded Boniface so severely that after a short while he died. It was still the year 432. Aetius escaped to Dalmatia, and from there to shelter in Pannonia among the Huns.

But his absence from Ravenna was brief; in her need Placidia recalled him. To Sebastian, a son-in-law of Boniface, she had given, as kinsman, his place of honor as Count and Master of Soldiers. Aetius, once back in Ravenna, made short work of Sebastian; he had no desire to live as colleague in the Palace with any one related to Boniface. Sebastian departed into exile. He does not, indeed, seem to have been a man of high distinction, but he had tragic adventures. First he fled to the East and remained for a while in Constantinople under the protection of its Emperor. The hostile influence of Aetius forced him to leave and he next sought aid in Toulouse, occupied by the Visigoths. But their ruler, Theodoric I, had made his peace with Ravenna and therefore could not give shelter to one whom Placidia and Aetius had exiled. Sebastian, after a short stay in Spain, finally fled to Vandal Africa, to beg protection from Gaiseric.

Victor, bishop of Vita, gives at this point a story concerning Sebastian which is no doubt mere legend but perhaps worth repeating (I, 19ff.): "The king hoped for nothing but his death, since Sebastian was a zealous Catholic. So one day, when Arian bishops and secular ministers were present around him in his royal hall, he said, and all heard him: 'Sebastian, I know that you have sworn loyalty to us, and your constant service proves you sincere. But that your friendship with us may remain firm and lasting, our bishops here want you to follow the religion which we and our people honor.'

"The request was entirely unexpected and one that demanded a direct answer. But Sebastian skillfully evaded it. 'Lord King,' he said, 'would you request that a loaf of bread be brought here at once?' Gaiseric had no idea what this meant, but he gave the order. The loaf was brought into the hall, and Sebastian, taking it in his hands, said as he looked at it, freshly baked: 'This bread gained its wonderful, shining grace, its purity, by passing through water and fire. So I, too, ground in the mill of our Catholic Mother Church, cleansed in the sieve of stern searching, have been renewed by the water of baptism and the fire of the Holy Spirit. If you will, let water once more be poured upon this bread, let it again be put into the oven; then, if it comes out as better bread than now, I will do what you ask.' "

Gaiseric could say nothing; he was defeated. But not long afterward he gave order for Sebastian's death.

This last detail is true; but we do not know its motive. Schmidt, following Prosper, dates it as probably taking place in 440; Hydatius places it in 450.

In 434, Aetius, still Master of Soldiers, was honored by the title of Patrician. The same year his friend Rugila, king of the Huns, died and was succeeded by two nephews, Bleda and Attila. Bleda did nothing of great importance; Attila, however, was one of the dominant figures of this century. His earlier years of rule were largely occupied with aggression against the Empire of the East; the chief matter of interest regarding Huns in the West of this time was the destruction wrought by them in 436 upon rebel Burgundians in Gaul and their king, Gundahar. The campaign against their revolt was first waged by Aetius, who defeated them and allowed a treaty of peace. It was an assault by the Huns which shortly afterward brought to these Burgundians fatal ruin; whether Aetius had a hand in this or not is still a question.

Meanwhile the Vandals under Gaiseric, steadily winning their way in Roman Africa, had been also looking outward; they had sailed to invade Sicily and southern Italy. The attempt had been checked; but in 435 Placidia and her son Valentinian, now in his sixteenth year, had held it prudent to send to Africa an officer named Trygetius. On the eleventh of February in this year by treaty at Hippo, now once again in Roman hands, division had been made of Roman Africa between Romans and Vandals. Procopius of Caesarea tells that Gaiseric promised to render to the West an annual tribute of money, and that he also sent his elder son, Huneric, to Italy as hostage for the keeping of peace.

Gaiseric continued his work of persecution in Africa. Against the year 437 Prosper records that he drove out certain bishops from their churches, even from their cities, among them Possidius of Calama. They went, compelled by force, but in complete defiance of this tyranny. Four men of Spain, Prosper continues, who were held by Gaiseric as his true friends, were asked as token of their support to offer themselves for rebaptism as Arian converts. Upon their firm refusal the Vandal king in his rage ordered first their arrest, then exile, then torture, and finally a martyr's death.

In Europe this year 437 saw far happier fortune, a firmer bond between East and West. Valentinian the Third went to Constantinople to take as wife and Empress Licinia Eudoxia, daughter of Theodosius the Second. We saw them betrothed when she was two years old; she was now almost fifteen and her bridegroom was three years older. With high ceremony the marriage was celebrated, in October; they spent the winter in Thessalonica and then returned to Italy. In 438 a daughter, Eudocia, was born to them; on August 6, 439, her mother was honored by the title of Augusta, Empress. Then, about 440, baptism gave a second daughter the name of Placidia, a name proper for the child of Placidus Valentinianus.

By 437, the year of the marriage, the regency of Galla Placidia had ended. Now, still under her influence, but outwardly guided by Aetius, it was the duty of Valentinian the Third at the age of eighteen to reign and rule as Emperor in union with his father-in-law, Theodosius.

The Spanish poet Merobaudes, who was as noted in his time for military service to the West as he still is through his verse, has left in that verse a description of Valentinian and his family as they appeared in mosaic portraits and patterns which adorned a room in the Imperial Palace at Ravenna. Here he describes Licinia Eudoxia, shining as a star in the height of heaven; here is Galla Placidia, arm in arm with her son, the Emperor; by his side is his sister Honoria; and all are standing around the baby, Placidia, shortly after her baptism into the Church: "confessing with a cry the presence of God within her." Above them in the ceiling, the poet tells, are cunningly woven the figures of Valentinian and his Empress, together with scenes telling of his life as child and youth.

Merobaudes, however, was above all the poet who wrote in praise of Aetius, who told of his exploits in Gaul, of his second consulship in 437, his third in 446.

It is of interest to note also that on this occasion of Valentinian's marriage in 437 the quarrel over the ownership of Illyricum was finally settled. As Ernest Stein points out, the town of Sirmium, a bridgehead on the river Save, was now yielded by the West to the Empire of the East, and thus the West finally gave up its claim upon Illyricum, claimed by it so long a time. Cassiodorus (*Varia* xi, 1, 9) writes that Galla Placidia "by the loss of Illyricum gained a daughter-in-law; and the union of royalty, East and West, caused grievous division in the provinces." They resented the cession of Sirmium.

In Gaul during 436 the West had come to rejoice; Count Litorius, an able officer serving under Aetius, distinguished himself by rescuing Narbonne from long siege and famine. Joy nevertheless was soon followed by tragedy. Three years later, in 439, he was captured at Toulouse as he fought the Visigoths, again in revolt. It was his own fault, men said. Among his critics was Salvian, historian of these days, who traced his fall to arrogance and pride: "Litorius believed that the enemy could be caught by him without any aid from God, and therefore he himself was taken." Isidore in his *History of the Goths* declared that since his triumph at Narbonne "Litorius had been led astray by demoniac portents and the oracles of soothsayers." His captors after a few days ended his imprisonment by death.

The Visigoths had conquered, but at a great price. Many of their men had died in battle, and now in 439 they were willing enough to make peace, even on less favorable terms than they had once demanded. Credit for the settlement now drawn up between their king, Theodoric I, and the Empire of the West was due to the skill and shrewd common sense of Avitus, Praetorian Prefect of Gaul. Apollinaris Sidonius, poet in this century, gives him full praise:

> After on all sides there was naught, naught, Rome, of protection left us for thy leaders. Avitus, thou dost renew the treaty; thy words of joy conquer the savage king; it is enough for thee to have ordered that which the world doth ask. Will ever future tribes and peoples hold this true? A Roman's word thy conquest killed, barbarian!
>
> *Panegyric on Avitus,* 306ff.

Aetius was still in Gaul, assuring peace before his return to Italy. In Ravenna all men were confident that the treaty of 435 with the Vandals still held its force, that no trouble would come to Italy from their king.

They did not yet know Gaiseric. He had been awaiting his chance, and now he seized it, while Aetius was still absent from Ravenna. Word arrived there that suddenly and treacherously he had seized Carthage, a capital city of vital importance to Roman Africa, on October 19, 439. Its treasure, the Romans heard, and they heard the truth, was being thoroughly plundered, its inhabitants beset by every kind of pain and distress, its churches looted, their holy vessels carried off in raids, their buildings turned over to Arian clergy or private owners, their priests forbidden to serve. "You could not tell," wrote Prosper, "whether war had been levied more directly on man or on God."

Early in 440 a second shock struck Ravenna; report now came that Gaiseric was again sending a fleet to ravage the shores of Sicily. Valentinian issued decree after decree in his anxiety to protect, to reassure. On March 3, 440, he declared in union with the Emperor Theodosius: "So far are we from neglecting care of our venerable City of Rome that we are indeed working in all ways for its peace and plenty." There followed an order that Greek merchants, at that time banished from Rome, be at once allowed to return and to give of their supplies to its people. No Roman citizen was to be compelled to enter military service; but he was required to guard walls and gates, should need arise, and to obey all orders of the City Prefect. "This," the Emperor continued, "will include the repairing of walls, towers, and gates: a duty expected from every man." On March 20, 440, the two Emperors wrote to Count Sigisvult, Master of Both Services, informing him of a decree recently issued by them: "Any man who shall give refuge, either in town or countryside, to any deserter from the army, whether a new recruit or one experienced in former service, shall not only surrender the fugitive to authority, but shall also suffer due penalty by supplying three other men fit and able to bear arms for the Empire."

Again, on June 24 of the same year, Valentinian ordered that every citizen must willingly work for his own safety by joining in resistance to raids of pirates. Gaiseric was said to be on his way from Carthage with a large fleet. "We ourselves," the Emperor told his people, "in our watchful care have posted guards in various places; the army of the Emperor Theodosius is now approaching; soon Aetius and Sigisvult will be here with reinforcements of soldiers and barbarian allies to protect our cities and coasts. Yet, as we do not know where the enemy may attack us, we bid you, all and each, to keep courage and discipline, as befits men of Roman heart."

Gaiseric's fleet arrived; his men landed in Sicily and proceeded to assault Panormus by siege. Everything was done to harm and vex the Catholic population, to favor the Arian. Hydatius states that the Vandal king was encouraged in this by Maximin, Arian bishop in Sicily, who craved revenge for his own condemnation by Catholic prelates. Panormus, however, did not yield, and in this same year, 440, Gaiseric held it prudent to order a retreat to Africa. Then in 441 Theodosius sent to Sicily a fleet of his own, and much time was lost by negotiations between Gaiseric and Eastern authority.

At last, in 442, these conversations produced another treaty, a second dividing of Northern Africa between the Vandal king and the Roman Empire. The Vandal invaders of Africa, it was decided by Roman ministers, must be kept quiet in peace even at heavy cost to Rome. There were other enemies at work, threatening both Roman East and West; Bleda and Attila, co-kings of the Huns, had long been working havoc in Illyricum and Thrace.

So the better and richer and greater portion of Roman Africa, including Carthage, passed into Vandal possession. Our sources of information here are decrees of Valentinian the Third, and the words of Victor, bishop of Vita. Mauritania, part of Numidia, and Tripolitana remained to the rule of Valentinian; Gaiseric from this time held for his own governing the provinces of Byzacena, Abaritana, Gaetulia, and a portion of Numidia, while he gave to control by his army those of Zeugitana and Proconsularis. Thus he could well afford to seem friendly to the men who fought for him.

Yet more than peace was in the mind of this Vandal king, as we learn from the *Gothic History* of Jordanes. Gaiseric was ambitious

for closer union with the Imperial House of Italy. Witness to this
is given by the poet Merobaudes:

> Now, stripped of the foe, he longed for closer contract, uniting
> of himself with Rome as friend, kinsmen of Latin blood to
> own, to weave an allied clan.
>
> *Panegyricus* II, 27ff.

These lines, we may believe, were written in 446, part of an
offering of praise to Aetius, consul for the third time. About 444,
through encouragement by Aetius, Gaiseric had sent envoys to
Valentinian, suggesting the betrothal of his son Huneric, now well
known in the West, to Valentinian's elder daughter, Eudocia, some
six years old. True, Huneric already had a wife, and she was of
royal blood; her father was Theodoric I, king of the Visigoths.
What did that at the moment matter to Gaiseric? Skillfully he set in
motion a charge of plotting to poison, and punished her justly, as
he maintained, by ordering her nose and her ears cut from her. In
this hideous state he sent her back to her father; Gaiseric was to
dread retaliation from king Theodoric later on.

From Africa and Gaiseric we turn for a moment to record
what had been happening in Britain. We saw that one Constantine
had been declared in 407 "Emperor in Britain and in Gaul"; in
409 he had been invited by Honorius to share his Imperial throne.
But with all vigor Saxons had descended on the shores of Britain
to work destruction against its people, deserted by their "Emperor"
Constantine. Zosimus tells that in this crisis "the Britons, taking
up arms and boldly facing every danger, had themselves freed their
cities from the barbarians pressing down upon them."

As years passed, their efforts had not been able entirely to protect them. Usurper had followed usurper; Honorius had given no
aid. In 410 he had written a letter "to the cities of Britain, bidding
them see to their own defence." In 411 Constantine, and in 413
Jovinus, who had followed him in seizing an Imperial crown in
Gaul, had both been put to death.

So at last Gaul, and with Gaul Britain, had been freed from
illegal rulers, had been restored to the Imperial government of the
West, under Honorius, under Valentinian the Third. In Britain a
"Count of the Britains" had then held guard with his soldiers.
From 428 onward, it is true, the Saxons had constantly landed on
British shores and had stayed there; yet Roman rule had still been
maintained.

Then at last the Roman Empire had abandoned its charge of
Britain. There was reason for this action. Fear once more haunted

Roman lands, fear coming from both East and West. The historian Priscus wrote in 447 that the Romans were dreading war from the Huns; they were facing threat of struggle against the Parthians; in spite of the treaty of 442, Vandals were worrying them along the shores; the Isaurians were rioting and ravaging; the Saracens were laying waste the lands of the East. Gaiseric, as Martroye remarks, might observe peace outwardly, but he judged it prudent to keep stirring up this many-sided menace against his so-called allies.

Of the year 442 the *Chronica Gallica* gave significant evidence: "The inhabitants of Britain, up to this time suffering from various disasters and casualties, are now brought under the power of the Saxons."

Four years later, in 446, had come from Britain a cry of appeal to Aetius. A British monk, Gildas, recorded this in his *De Excidio et Conquestu Britanniae,* written during the sixth century: "To Aetius, thrice consul, the laments of the Britons. . . . The barbarians drive us to the sea, the sea drives us back to the barbarians. There rises for us a twofold death: either our throats are cut or we are drowned." But Aetius at this time was busy in Gaul, and by Valentinian nothing was done; nothing could be done.

From Britain we come to the Huns. In 444 or 445, Bleda, co-king with his brother Attila, was killed deliberately by violence, through the treachery of Attila himself.

Attila from this time was sole king, and as such he is vividly described by Jordanes, borrowing from Priscus: "All his people he gathered around himself. A multitude of other nations he also brought under his rule; above all he longed to subdue the foremost in his world, the Romans and the Visigoths. His army was said to number five hundred thousand men. He was a man born to shake the nations of the earth: the terror of all lands, who—by what fortune I cannot tell—struck fear into all things by his dire repute, spread far and wide. Proudly he walked, his eyes darting hither and thither; his power was seen in the high bearing of his body as he strode forth. Wars indeed he loved, though his own hand he kept under guard; of surpassing force in purpose, he was merciful to those who sought his aid, gracious to those who once for all had pledged to him their loyalty. In appearance he was short, broad of chest, his head unusually large, his eyes small, even tiny. His beard was scant, streaked with white, his nose flat and snub, his skin foul and muddy, as was common in his race.

"Always he was confident of his own great authority; and still stronger grew his confidence through an unexpected incident: the finding of the sword of Mars, ever held sacred by Scythian kings."

Priscus, of Panium in Thrace, in his *History* told much concerning Attila, and we read of this event in the *History of the Goths* by Jordanes, who once again took description from him: "A shepherd, Priscus told, one day noticed that a heifer in his herd was lame. On examining it he found a deep wound, and could not imagine what had caused this. Anxiously searching, he followed its trail, marked by blood, and at length came upon a sword, on which the animal had trodden by accident as it browsed amid the grass. This he pulled out from the field and took at once to Attila, who recognized it with high joy, a wonderful gift. Ambitious as he was, Attila decided that it meant he was destined to be Lord of all his world, that by this delivery to him of the sword of Mars victory in war would be his."

In 447 Attila's armies swept the world, laying in ruins seventy cities according to one report, a hundred according to another, advancing to work destruction even as far as Thermopylae in Greece. It was left to Theodosius, Emperor of the East, to meet this onslaught; the West gave no resistance. It remained for Constantinople also to send envoys, and in 449 to gain brief renewal of peace.

That same year saw a new problem facing the West. Three writers tell its tale: Priscus, John of Antioch, and Jordanes.

It concerned Honoria, sister of the Emperor Valentinian III, a woman now over thirty years of age. She had inherited much of the spirit of her mother, Galla Placidia, who had refused the distinguished Constantine in favor of the barbarian Athaulf. As a child she had been given Imperial rank, created Augusta; now in 449 she had her own apartments in Ravenna, her own retinue of servants. But she was bored to death; there was nothing of importance for her to do, and no prospect of marriage. The Court of the West was apparently determined that no son of hers should inherit Valentinian's throne; he and Licinia Eudoxia had no male heir. Year after year passed in monotony, while Licinia Eudoxia, her sister-in-law, was constantly presiding over brilliant social functions in the Palace.

One man gave her sympathy: Eugenius, Comptroller of her household. This was pleasant, and often she talked with him. Then from sympathy grew desire, and from desire passion; soon he was her lover. Months went by and rumor, true or not, but recorded by Marcellinus (under the wrong date of 434), whispered that she was pregnant: a terrific shock to the Court and especially to her brother, the Emperor. His wrath exploded in stern, even savage decrees. By his order Eugenius was executed; Honoria was banished from the Court into strict seclusion, there to redeem her shame. Very possibly, as we are told, she was sent off to Constantinople, to discipline in the sternly religious house of Theodosius the Second.

Before long, however, she was again in Italy, and betrothed to Flavius Bassus Herculanus, one who had held office as consul in the West, a man of blameless life and no ambition whatsoever: a husband, in fact, entirely safe.

For a while she endured with what courage she could master. Then despair drove her to a wild attempt at escape. She sent off one of her attendants, the eunuch Hyacinthus, to Attila himself, king of the barbarian Huns, with this prayer: Would he take her as wife if a sufficiently attractive dowry came with her? As pledge of her true intention she sent also a ring.

Of course Attila saw at once what he could gain from this proposal. Did he not want to gain Imperial power, with land in the West, especially in Gaul? It would be wise to get Aetius out of the way, if possible. Discord and division were already working there for his purpose. Promptly he put forward to Valentinian his claim to the princess on the ground of her offer. Theodosius wrote in haste to his son-in-law in Italy, advising him to deliver his sister to this barbarian monarch; he had suffered much from Attila.

Valentinian did nothing of the sort. After much questioning under torture Hyacinthus was beheaded by the public executioner; and only the pleading of her mother, the Empress Placidia, induced the Emperor of the West to grant Honoria a pardon without penalty.

In July 450, as we have seen, Theodosius the Second died. He was succeeded at Constantinople by Marcian, who was accepted at once, as a soldier of note, by the army of the East.

Quickly Attila despatched envoys to the Eastern capital, demanding that same tribute which had been yielded him by Theodosius. A firm refusal met him: "I will give you gifts," Marcian replied, according to the historian Priscus; "but if you threaten war, I shall lead forward weapons and men equal in power to yours!"

The king of the Huns then sent to the West, to Valentinian III, a demand for Honoria in marriage, and here again received denial. Honoria could not marry him, he was told, since she had already been promised in marriage. This counted for nothing with Attila, who already had wives in plenty. He was very angry, the more so since there was now no prospect of enrichment by dowry. He had fervently hoped that rule over lands in the West, especially in Gaul, might be granted to him as husband of Valentinian's sister. Might he not himself, he now asked, hold them in her name? "No," replied the Emperor of the West; "the lands of the Roman Empire are held by men, not by feminine authority."

But Attila did not give in; he even increased his demands. One half of the Empire in the West was his due, he declared, as dowry of his future wife, Honoria. This belonged, he added, by right of inheritance to the Emperor's sister: a legacy from their father, torn from her by her brother's evil greed.

It was all in vain, and Attila decided upon war; war, he believed, would bring him Honoria swiftly. From Pannonia he led his army; as it marched it grew even greater and more threatening, until it seemed to descend dark as a thundercloud, coming to destroy all in its path. It crossed the Rhine, making for Gaul; the king of the Visigoths in that country, Theodoric I, hastened to unite his army with that of Aetius, who himself was gathering every soldier from every nation or tribe who would answer his call.

Attila, once in Gaul, marched in 451 for Metz; he entered that city to slay by fire and sword its people in their homes, its priests before their altars. On to Orleans he went, strewing havoc in his way, with every intent to storm its walls.

In fear and dread its citizens watched the Huns as they set up their engines of destruction. Yet not in panic or disorder; the bishop of Orleans, Saint Aignan, was at their head, commanding courage and presence of mind, trust in the Lord of hosts, God in His heaven, even trust in Aetius. "Surely," said Aignan, "he will hear; surely he will come!" So much we may well believe, though the story told in the *Life* of Saint Aignan savors of legend. Later in this same fifth century Apollinaris Sidonius, while writing to Saint Prosper, then himself bishop of Orleans, referred to this descent upon the city in these words: *oppugnatio, inruptio, nec direptio:* "a storming, an invading, but not a destroying." It is clear, then, that the prayer of Bishop Aignan was answered by Heaven, that Aetius arrived with his troops in time to save Orleans from ruin.

The Huns finally encamped near Troyes, on the wide flatlands of Champagne; the battle which followed is described as that "of the Catalaunian or the Mauriac plains." There Aetius also drew up his forces in position. In the center he placed the Alans, for he distrusted the loyalty of their king. The right wing was held by Theodoric with his Visigoths, the left by Aetius with his Romans. All were standing upon the slope of a hill which rose above them; each army fought to gain the crest and the advantage of its height.

According to Jordanes, Attila was nervous; he could not fully trust his huge army, assembled from so many sources. We are even told that before he dared enter upon the struggle he consulted soothsayers. After making sacrifice of cattle and inspecting their fibers, bones, and veins for omens of destiny, they made report of good fortune for the Huns. With one other item of comfort: the enemy would lose by death upon the field one of their chief leaders. This, Attila decided, would certainly be Aetius. Both cheered and troubled by the thought of death, he gave signal for battle. The time was, we may think, an afternoon in June 451. Afternoon was safer; if things went badly for the Huns, night would come and they could escape.

The king took his place in the midst of his men, directing all their effort to capture the ridge above. It failed; Aetius and Prince Thorismund, son of his Visigothic ally, King Theodoric, outdid in speed the Huns and their supporters, who were driven down as they fought to climb.

Again and again Attila called aloud to encourage, to exhort; man rushed against man, troop against troop. Soon the plain ran with blood, and the dead lay thrown on every side. Among them lay King Theodoric himself, bringing in his death grim truth to prophecy. Attila barely escaped assault by the Visigoths as he rushed to shelter within the Hun camp, barricaded by wagons.

Night came down upon the field, bringing peril to all. In the confusion Thorismund suddenly found himself among the chariots of the Huns, mistaking them for those of his own men. One of them hurled him from his horse, and only just in time was he rescued by one of his Visigothic soldiers. Aetius had the same narrow escape. As he ran to encourage his allies, he, too, saw himself surrounded by the enemy, and by desperate effort reached his men, only to throw himself exhausted on the ground and wait for the dawn.

Dawn saw the struggle ended. Neither side had won a decisive victory; but the Romans proudly maintained that success lay on their side, in that Attila ordered his army to retreat, not only from Champagne, but from Gaul. By counsel of Aetius both Frankish and Visigothic armies left for their own lands. He is said to have warned them of danger; the Franks that Attila might occupy their lands, were they left undefended; and Thorismund—now, as eldest son of Theodoric I, heir to the Visigothic kingship—that one of his brothers in his absence might seize the crown.

Authorities also suggest other reasons for this advice. One (*Consularia Italica,* ann. 451) declares that Aetius acted here "with cunning, that he might enrich his own army with the spoils left by the Huns" on the plains of Champagne. Another (Jordanes) holds that "Thorismund, courageous as ever, longed to lead his men once more against the Huns for the avenging of his father's death.

He asked counsel of the Patrician Aetius, as one older and wiser than himself, and Aetius sent him and his Visigoths home, in fear that if the Huns were thoroughly conquered and deprived of power by them, the Roman Empire would be the next victim of Visigothic triumph." We may remember that Aetius had consistently relied upon the Huns as his friends and his resource in need.

Attila retreated from Gaul to make for Italy. Across the Julian Alps he marched early in 452 with his army, now renewed and strengthened, and no one hindered them. It never entered the mind of Aetius that, after the terrific struggle of 451, Attila would make ready for a new campaign in the very next year. The Roman commander never even thought of barricading the high passes through which his enemy came unhindered. Was not Italy in 452 harassed to death by famine and by pestilence? All that Aetius at this moment desired with bitter longing was to flee from Italy altogether with the Emperor and find some place of sure refuge.

Once in northern Italy, Attila took his revenge. In savage fury he laid bare its fields, its villages, its cities; their people, men, women and children, fled in terror from their homes, leaving all to bands that seized and tore apart. It was ironical that in that year of 452 Flavius Bassus Herculanus, husband of Honoria and a man without ambition, was holding office as consul in the West.

Above all, the Hun assault centered upon Aquileia in Venetia, that Imperial city at the head of the Adriatic. It was left a mass of ruins by those who burned, crushed, and carried away its wealth. And not only Aquileia, but Venetia throughout its lands knew this wild tide of wrath.

But, wrote the chronicler Hydatius, God was still in His heaven; plague and hunger were striking not only citizens of Italy but Huns with them. The Emperor Marcian sent troops to aid Aetius; Aetius himself awoke from weariness and desire for escape into a feeling of the shame and dishonor of this mood. At Rome, Emperor and senators debated on the best course to follow in this time of misery. After long hesitation they decided to send envoys to Attila, seeking peace from this scourge of war, and word to the Pope himself, Leo the First, praying him to lead them in their hope.

With Avienus, who had been consul for the West in 450, and Trygetius, who had acted for the Romans during negotiations with the Vandals in 435, the Pope met Attila at the fording-point of the Mincio, that river which flows around Mantua and northward into the Lago di Garda. Attila was deeply impressed; the head of Rome's Church had himself come to plead with him, barbarian, though king of a mighty empire. Before Leo's power and presence his angry passion sank, and submission to peace rose in him even against his will. Promise of undisturbed retreat was given, and he led his men homeward across the Danube. Yet as he turned to go he renewed his threat concerning Honoria: "Worse things than I have done will I do to Italy if she be not delivered to me, with the due portion of her royal wealth!"

He never returned; the following year he died in his own land of Pannonia. To the many women whom he had taken as wives he added, one day in 453, a girl of marked beauty named Ildico. Festive revelry rose high on that day. Marcellinus Comes in his *Chronicon* tells that in the night which followed "a woman" stabbed him with a knife; he was found dead next morning. Suspicion, of course, fell upon Ildico, weeping by his body. But Jordanes, again relying on Priscus, gives another version, also brought forward by Marcellinus, and no doubt true: "Overcome by too much merrymaking, he was lying on his back, heavy with wine and sleep, so heavy that a stream of blood which usually flowed from his nose, could not escape by that passage; in a death-dealing flood it rushed from his throat and killed him."

And so, its great king no longer in command, gradually the empire of the Huns passed from a world that so long had lived under fear.

Yet even now the Furies which beset Italy were not content: the years 454–455 were to bring upon it horror as yet unknown.

Down the length of his reign the Emperor Valentinian had depended constantly upon Aetius, Commander-in-Chief and Patrician. Now another and a foul tide of influence was setting in, from the ambition of one Heraclius, a eunuch who was Chief Chamberlain in the Palace. Again and again we find these servants possessed of high importance at Court; they knew the secrets of their Imperial master or mistress and often used this knowledge for their own gain. Heraclius had long been bitterly jealous of Aetius; now he was determined, first to remove his all-pervading presence, then to win his own place in control of Valentinian's mind and heart. Was not Aetius boldly planning marriage of his younger son, Gaudentius, to Placidia, younger daughter of the Emperor himself? Doubtless this was to lead to the Imperial crown itself. And Valentinian seemed willing to allow this union. It was time to act.

Therefore the Chamberlain, who was himself deep in the Emperor's confidence, used every opportunity to turn Valentinian's friendship with Aetius into enmity, and by using all his skill and cunning he succeeded. It may be that Aetius unconsciously in some measure aided this diabolical work, by constant urging that the proposed marriage take place. Heraclius could easily point to the ambition of Aetius as the cause of evil work.

But Valentinian had another determined enemy in his Court, and one of aristocratic order. He was Petronius Maximus, possibly a descendant of that Maximus who as usurper of Imperial rule had dared to invade Italy in 387. High offices, one after another, Petronius Maximus had held in the West: Count of the Sacred Largesse, twice Prefect of Rome, twice Praetorian Prefect of Italy, twice consul, invested as Patrician. He was now nearly sixty, but his honors had fed his desire for even more honorable estate. For him, also, the removal of Aetius was necessary; with all caution and craft he added his own evil working upon Valentinian to that of Heraclius.

Thus by degrees the Emperor was persuaded to see in Aetius a deadly enemy and rival, and at last to believe that only the latter's death could save him from humiliation and fall.

And so, one day in 454, when Aetius had entered the Palace for consultation and debate with Valentinian concerning politics and finance, the Emperor, overcome by jealousy and fear, suddenly sprang from his seat, crying aloud that it was Aetius who had brought trouble upon both East and West, that he was trying to seize Imperial rule in Rome. In astonishment Aetius tried to calm him. But Valentinian rushed forward, with Heraclius at his side, the Emperor pulling his sword from its sheath, the eunuch holding a knife under his cloak. Down came sword and knife upon the victim, and in a moment all was over. The Patrician was dead.

It is John of Antioch, the historian, who most vividly describes the scene; he ends with a summary of the Patrician's deeds and achievements: his protection of the Regent-Empress Placidia and her son; his final victory over Boniface; his slaying of Felix who, he said, longed to murder him; his subduing of the Goths who invaded, of the Armoricans who rebelled; his command of situations political and military, at home and abroad. With deeper insight Marcellinus declared: "Aetius was the strong salvation of the Empire in the West, and with him it fell dead." Another remark of interest has come down to us from the Salmasian fragment included in excerpts from John of Antioch by Müller in his edition (No. 200): "And when Aetius lay murdered, the Emperor said to one who would understand his words: 'The death of Aetius was no happy thing for me.' And the man to whom he spoke replied: 'Whether it was a happy thing or not I do not know. But I do know that you have cut off your right hand with your left.'"

Together with Aetius on that morning of September 21, 454,

his close friend Boethius, Praetorian Prefect of Italy, also fell victim to the sword of hatred. John of Antioch tells that the Emperor ordered both bodies to be carried, uncovered and dripping with blood, to the Forum of Rome. There he gathered its senators, and there he made long observation against the dead, "taking care not to incite rebellion among friends and supporters of Aetius."

Now Petronius Maximus was nursing his hope; and Heraclius, jealous of one who aimed at a crown which he, the eunuch, could not hold, was doing his best to defeat him. Persistently this Chief Chamberlain warned the Emperor not to sink under the oppression of a second Aetius.

At last Maximus could bear the struggle no longer. Into his confidence he called two men of barbarian birth who had fought well and loyally under Aetius and were longing to avenge his death. "Justice should and must be done," he told them. Their names were Optila and Thraustila.

With these same men among his guards, on March 16, 455, the Emperor rode out from Rome to the Field of Mars, to watch the public games. He had left his horse and was walking toward the archers on the field, when Optila ran forward and struck him twice, on the side of his head and on the face. Revenge had done its work; the Emperor Valentinian III was dead. Thraustila also killed Heraclius. Seizing the Imperial crown and Valentinian's horse, the two murderers hurried away to find Maximus. Neither of them was brought to punishment. All those present were stunned by the shock of the moment, and when they had recovered from this they prudently decided to leave justice alone; Optila and Thraustila were bold and forceful fighters.

Some sources state that the scene of the murder was the Place of the "Two Laurels"; one (*Chron. Min.* 1, p. 303) has it that one of the assassins was a soldier receiving pay from Aetius, and the other his son-in-law.

It may perhaps be worth while here to give a tale, insecure both in source and in authority, told by Procopius of Caesarea in his *History of the Vandal War*. It is included in the Fragment 200 already mentioned, and noted by Evagrius in his *Church History*. Procopius had already declared in his *History*, as we have seen, that the Emperor Valentinian the Third was of little moral worth. Yet we cannot be sure of the truth of this evidence, or of this tale.

Translated from its Greek, the story runs: "Valentinian wanted intrigue of love with the wife of Maximus and she would not hear of it. So he planned a way in which to gain his desire. He invited Maximus to the Imperial Palace for a game of draughts. Maximus came, and the two decided how much the loser was to pay to him who won. Valentinian won, and received from Maximus as pledge of payment a ring which he was wearing. At once Valentinian sent off the ring to the house of Maximus as from Maximus himself, with a message bidding his wife come with all speed to the Palace to greet the Empress Licinia Eudoxia. The wife, concluding from the ring that the message came from her husband, ordered her carriage and hurried her arrival. At the Palace she was received with due courtesy and escorted to a room far from the apartments of the Court ladies. There Valentinian met her, did his will upon her, and she fled home in a flood of tears, crying curses upon Maximus, her husband, as the cause of this crime."

In the fury of his anger Maximus—so the story ends—hastened his designs against the Emperor.

That murder once committed, all Rome was in uproar and confusion, while those in power, especially military power, supported each his own choice for the empty throne. Many called for Maximus; others, and among them the Empress Licinia Eudoxia, spoke for Majorian, a soldier who had served under Aetius. So great had been his devotion to his Commander that the wife of Aetius in a rage of jealousy had forced her husband to send him away to private life at home, to the ploughing of his own fields as a farmer. A third party favored Domninus, an Egyptian man of business, a provision merchant, extremely rich and successful, who had supplied the table and household of Aetius himself with every need.

But Maximus was known everywhere, not only for his great wealth, but for his brilliant career in politics, his luxurious house, his hospitality; on March 17, 455, he was crowned Imperial ruler of the West.

At once he set to work for the sure establishing of his throne. He forced Licinia Eudoxia, suddenly left a widow and still, at least, in outward mourning, to become his wife and Empress; he honored his son Palladius with the title of Caesar and with proposal of marriage to Eudocia, the elder daughter of Eudoxia and Valentinian. The news could not have been welcome to Gaiseric, the Vandal king, for she was already engaged to marry his eldest son, Huneric. To Gaiseric's great content, Palladius died soon afterward. At any rate, so we may suppose, with Ernest Stein; nothing more was heard of him.

Two months and a half Maximus reigned. The enemy in Vandal Africa had inpatiently been waiting for his chance. Gaiseric now decided that, since he was no longer bound by a treaty with

Valentinian, who was dead, and he had next to no respect for Maximus as warrior, he might as well descend upon Italy.

Perhaps fate gave him encouragement. John, the historian of Antioch, tells that Licinia Eudoxia, distressed beyond measure by the murder of her husband and the necessity of marrying his successor, secretly asked Gaiseric to rescue her from misery. If the story is true—doubt has been cast on all these tales of appeals by royal women to barbarian monarchs—she did what her kinswoman Honoria had done. Hydatius records Eudoxia's act in these words: *Gaisericus, sollicitatus a relicta Valentiniani, ut mala fama dispergit, Romam ingreditur:* "Gaiseric, urged by the widow of Valentinian, as wicked report tells far and wide . . . enters Rome."

The last two words refer to a time a little later. The Vandal king, we may suppose, duly received this entreaty; but most certainly in the spring of 455 word came to Rome that Gaiseric was on his way to Italy with an enormous fleet of ships. Its citizens, noble and humble, rich and poor, fled in terror, the Emperor among them. This was too much for his soldiers to see; in their fury at his cowardice they seized him, tore him limb from limb, and threw his mangled relics into the Tiber, his only grave.

Late in this fifth century Sidonius wrote to his friend Serranus: "With greater persistence and courtesy than accuracy or truth do you call Petronius Maximus a most happy man because through his very many honors and offices he rose to the crown of Imperial rule. Never shall I agree with you in this; never shall I think those men blessed who tread steep and slippery heights. . . . For he, whose life had been one long round of feasting, of lavish parades, of magisterial record, of noble clientele and kin, he who counted the hours of his life by the clocks, he, I say, once he was declared Emperor and shut up as such within his Palace, was groaning before the day reached its end, simply because he had gained what he had craved. So heavy was his burden of care that all peace and joy of former days was lost; the task of Imperial honor could not go hand in hand with the leisure of a senator. Nor did the future promise better things, poor man! He who had held in peace other distinctions at Court now ruled amid riots and rebellion of armed men, of citizens, of allies. And then at last release, treacherous, swift and bitter, was given him; an ending red with blood was his reward from that Fortune who so long had pampered him, who now struck him as a scorpion strikes, with her tail!"

Gaiseric was soon within sight of Rome, left undefended by its guards. Outside the gates, as he was about to enter, he came face to face with Pope Leo the First. Again a Pope had come to plead with a barbarian king. Like Attila, Gaiseric could not but listen; he gave his royal word not to set fire to the city, not to murder its men. On the third day following he entered Rome.

Yet for fourteen days Rome was robbed and pillaged; when Gaiseric finally ordered his soldiers to the ships, they bore with them captives without number, treasure without end. Among the captives were the Empress Licinia Eudoxia herself and her two daughters, Eudocia and Placidia, together with Gaudentius, son of Aetius, the murdered Commander-in-Chief. On their way to Carthage also went many vessels of gold and silver taken from Rome's Imperial Palace; spoils from the temple of Jupiter on the Capitoline Hill, with part of its roofing, covered in exquisite art with gilded bronze; spoils, also, brought by Titus to Rome after his capture of Jerusalem in A.D. 70.

It may be of interest to follow the future of these Imperial prisoners. Eudocia, the elder daughter, some seventeen years in age but long ago fiancée of Huneric, Gaiseric's son, was now married to him by will of the Vandal king. Sixteen years, Theophanes and Nicephorus tell us, she spent in Africa as his wife and bore him a son, Ilderic. Then, devout Catholic as she was, in 471 she fled from her Arian husband to the holy shrines of Jerusalem. Soon afterward she died there "in peace, leaving all her property to its Church of the Resurrection"; she was buried in its Church of Saint Stephen.

The younger daughter, Placidia, was already wife of Olybrius, a prominent senator of Rome, when Gaiseric carried her off to Africa. Again and again envoys were sent to Gaiseric, requesting for the three women freedom and return to the Roman Empire. Not only did the Vandal king refuse both East and West this right of restitution; he also was constantly harrying with his ships the coasts of Italy and Sicily.

In the summer of 455 Avitus was proclaimed Emperor of the West, in Gaul; then, early in the autumn, he came to Italy to assume Imperial rule. From Sidonius, his son-in-law, we learn of him. It was he who as Emperor appointed one Ricimer Master of Soldiers. Ricimer, as Sidonius tells, was born of barbarian parents, his father Suevian, his mother Gothic; he was also grandson of Wallia, king of the Visigoths. Barbarian he was; but he was master and maker of Emperors in the West for many years. In 456 he caused the fall of Avitus; his influence stood behind the naming of Majorian as Emperor of the West in 457; he caused Majorian's destruction as Emperor and as man in 461, and the raising of Severus as his successor in that same year.

And still Gaiseric with his Vandal fleets continued to assault Italian and Sicilian shores. Ambition still drove him on; he longed for wider power, higher honor for himself, and he thought to gain this through his family. Was not Placidia, daughter of the Emperor Valentinian III and wife of the senator Olybrius, also the sister of Eudocia, his own daughter-in-law? If, then, Olybrius could be pushed upward to gain a throne, and that the Imperial throne of the West, pride in honor would be his to share.

With this thought in mind, he decided to unite assault with courtesy. In 462 he yielded to a request by Leo I, Emperor of the East from 457 until 474; he restored both Placidia and her mother to Constantinople.

In 465 Severus died; in his *Chronicles* Cassiodorus tells of a rumor that Ricimer killed him by poison. In any case, Ricimer influenced the senate of Rome by proclaiming one Anthemius, Greek by birth, as Emperor of the West in April 467. Leo I, Emperor of the East, in 457 had honored him by nomination as Patrician. In 467, the year of his entry upon Imperial rule, Anthemius had given to Ricimer his daughter, Alypia, in marriage, and by Leo I he had been sent to Rome.

Nevertheless, as Bury observes, Ricimer, a barbarian, would not naturally find sympathetic alliance in Anthemius, a ruler trained by Greek scholarship. In 472, a year of tragedy, both Ricimer, the "king-maker," and Anthemius, the Emperor, were in Italy, divided by a bitter quarrel. Ricimer was in Milan, Anthemius in Rome. In vain Epiphanius, bishop of Ticinum, tried to bring them together in peace.

Strife, already intense, became critical when Olybrius, husband of Placidia, arrived in Rome from Constantinople; in April 472, he was declared Emperor of the West by Ricimer and his soldiers: a proceeding intended, not to gratify the ambition of Gaiseric, but to protect Italy against Vandal attack.

Then, also early in the same year, Ricimer moved to besiege Rome, and civil war set in between him and Anthemius. By summertime Ricimer was occupying the region of the river Tiber, supported by his own barbarians, cutting off supplies of food from Anthemius and his followers; Anthemius was shut up in his Palace on the Palatine Hill, with Rome's people on his side, loyal subjects crowded in narrow and filthy streets.

Nothing could be done; famine and disease were laying low his citizens day by day. Soon he could bear no more the reports which reached him in his prison, once his Palace. Deprived of his throne, fearing for his life, he fled in beggar's rags to hide among those who sought alms from passers-by at the Church of the martyr saint, Chrysogonus. It was an empty hope. Ricimer tracked him down; on July 11, 472, he was murdered there by Ricimer's nephew, Gundobad. He had reigned a little over five years, 467–472.

Ricimer gave him burial "worthy of his Imperial rank"; but he at once established Olybrius in the Imperial Palace. Both men died shortly afterward, in this same year, and both of natural causes; Ricimer through hemorrhage in mid-August, and Olybrius of dropsy on the second of November.

By this time Galla Placidia had long left this troubled life on earth; she had died in Rome on November 27, 450. Her memory is still honored by many; not primarily because they have learned of her political doings and influence, but because they have seen the marvel of the art associated with her name.

It was seen and it still can be seen in Ravenna, since 404 the center and capital in this fifth century of the Imperial Court in the West.

There she commissioned architects and artists to build and adorn a Church of Saint John the Evangelist. Agnellus of the ninth century, born in Ravenna and its historian, tells that it was a votive offering. Perhaps, as Bury suggests, in 424 she started with her children by sea for Aquileia, was caught by a storm and had to return to Dalmatia, reaching Aquileia also by land; perhaps, while the ship rocked beneath her and she expected at any moment to be thrown into the huge waves breaking below, she implored the Lord God to save her and hers. Perhaps at this moment of terror she caught sight of a church dedicated to Saint John; at any rate, should they be saved, she vowed to build a Church of Saint John as token of fervent gratitude to God and His Evangelist. The storm readily died down; all on board landed safely, and during the years which followed the Church was erected in Ravenna.

To the devotion of Galla Placidia is also attributed the building and decoration of Ravenna's Church of Santa Croce, some time after 423.

Connected with this church and near that of San Vitale, built at a later time, is the chapel known as the "Mausoleum of Galla Placidia." Much uncertainty surrounds its origin and its character. Tradition has declared that she herself, her second husband, the Emperor Constantius III, and either her brother, the Emperor Honorius, or her son, the Emperor Valentinian III, were laid to rest there. But the tradition rests on no sure evidence. Perhaps she raised it as a Chapel of Intercession for souls in this life and in the hereafter, including herself; perhaps she dedicated it to the Roman martyr, Saint Laurence, whose tomb lay at Rome.

What we do know is that it held, and still holds, marvels of loveliness and mystic meaning in the mosaics that cover its walls within.

It is small, built in the form of a Latin cross. Its outer appearance is of little interest, showing brick and blind arcades. Within, at some distance from the ground, the walls, varied by vault and arch, marked by lunettes and interrupted here and there by little windows, hold the mosaics that are the wonder of Ravenna.

The background is dark blue, and against this stand out Apostles in white vesture; among them Saints Peter and Paul are clearly recognized. Harts, entwined in a circling design of acanthus, draw near to quench their thirst at a rippling spring; the mind at once recalls Psalm 42:

> As the hart panteth after the water brooks,
> so panteth my soul after thee, O God.

Doves perch on the rim of a bowl; vine-tendrils and fruit, in green, gold, and red, with ordered confusion fill the space between beast and bird. High above is the dome. At its center stands a Cross of gold, surrounded by more than five hundred stars gleaming in regular circles against the deep blue heaven. Guarding the Cross are ranged, two on either side, the symbols of the Four Evangelists; that of Saint Mark, especially, is emphatic in the serene but fiercely determined look of his winged lion, ready, if need be, for furious assault.

The chief interest, however, of this Chapel centers in two of its mosaics. One is placed over the entrance door. Here the sky once more is intensely blue; the scene shows boulders lying on the grass of a meadow amid trees, twining plants and shrubs. On one of these rocks sits the Good Shepherd, likened by critics to a youthful Apollo as He gazes with calm majesty of thought into the far distance. A halo of gold surrounds His head; gold also is His tunic, and over it lies a mantle of royal purple. His left hand holds a long cross of gold, supported on the ground beneath; His right reaches out to welcome one of six lambs which stand around Him, three on either side. The lamb raises its head in joy at the touch, and the other five await their turn.

On the wall opposite the entrance another lunette holds a mosaic of different character. The scene of the Good Shepherd is symbolic in its meaning; this second one may rather be thought historical. It shows a holy man, bearded, as the Good Shepherd is not, also with halo of gold, clad in a white mantle which flies out vigorously on either side through the rapid pace of his movement. On his right shoulder he carries a gold cross, on his left hand lies an open book. With intense energy, shown in his face and figure, he is hastening toward a grille, alive with leaping flames. Just beyond this grille there is a bookcase with open doors; within on two shelves one can see the Four Gospels.

Who is this determined Saint? One theory has held that his name is unknown; he is some zealous Catholic now hurrying to cast into the fire that book lying open on his hand; it is full of heretical lies.

Another, and more generally accepted suggestion, names the saint as Laurence himself, marching in joyful haste to martyrdom.

This archdeacon of Rome's third century was one of the holy martyrs constantly called upon, in prayers of the faithful, for aid to those suffering misery during the fifth; his name, as Giuseppe Bovini has observed, would be entirely proper for a chapel dedicated to intercession. Three passages from Latin literature of early medieval days mark his fame.

The first comes from Sermon 296 of Saint Augustine; given, we may think, shortly after the capture of Rome by Alaric the Goth in August 410:

"The body of Peter, men say, lies at Rome; the body of Paul lies at Rome; the body of Laurence lies at Rome; the bodies of other holy martyrs lie at Rome. And Rome is wretched; Rome is plundered, is laid waste, is burned. So many tragic deaths, through hunger, through pestilence, through the sword! Where are our minds? Are they upon the saints?"

Here, then Saint Laurence is one of Rome's greatest Apostles, one from whom support might well be sought.

The second passage tells of Saint Melania the Younger, who was living at Rome toward the end of the fourth century. She longed for the virgin life in solitude of prayer; in obedience to her father's will she was married at fourteen to one Pinian, almost equally young. Her first child she lost soon after birth; now, on August the ninth, 399, she was expecting a second. It was the eve of the Feast of Saint Laurence, and she wanted intensely to keep the Vigil, which lasted all night until dawn. Her father decided that in her case this was not possible; whereupon she decided to stay up all night, praying in her room at home. There she was found on her knees by messengers sent by her father, who wanted to hear how well she had rested; with bribes she begged them to report that they had seen her fast asleep in her bed. This settled, she went off to the Church of Saint Laurence for Office and Mass. On her return she was seized by travail; her newborn child died the next day and her own life was almost lost in agony.

The third passage is more cheerful. It comes from a poem by Prudentius, poet of the fourth century, honoring Laurence himself as hero and martyr:

> That death of the holy martyr
> was true death of pagan temples;
> there Vesta knew Palladian gods
> deserted without penalty.
>
> *Peristephanon* ii, 509ff.

> O doubly, fourfold, sevenfold,
> blessed in truth Rome's citizen,
> who face to face with thee and thine
> honors the place where lie thy bones.
>
> *Ibid.* 529ff.

All her life Galla Placidia, ambitious, fickle in regard to those who worked for her, heedless—so unlike Pulcheria—in the training of a boy destined to be Emperor, was devoted to the Catholic Church. Her son, Valentinian III, has been sternly criticized by writers both medieval and modern. It is refreshing, however, to find Ernest Stein defending him against the charge of corruption and utter unworthiness. As Stein points out, an effort to redeem the low estate of Rome's Empire in his time may be found in his Imperial edicts and decrees; these may not be altogether the work of his ministers.

CHAPTER SEVEN

Dhuoda and Bernard of Septimania

From Greek record of earlier days we pass to Latin of the ninth century. In the third chapter of this book we looked at a man, Synesius of Cyrene, who spent his last years in sorrow, sickness and solitude. We turn now to consider a woman, burdened for many years with the same afflictions, yet ever loyal in generous courage and devotion to Bernard, a husband who left her to suffer alone.

Her name, unknown to most readers, is given us in various versions: Dhuoda, Duodana, Dodana; we will keep here the oldest, Dhuoda. She lived in the ninth century at Uzès, southwest France, in the department of Gard, north of Nîmes and Avignon, west of the Rhône. Muirhead calls it now "a pleasant old town," but gives no mention of Dhuoda; nor does the *Guide Littéraire de la France,* "Bibliothèque des Guides Bleus," published in 1964. In Dhuoda's time we may well think of Uzès as grim and forbidding, fenced in by ramparts; she must often have felt herself a prisoner without hope of rescue.

And yet she wrote a book inside those high walls: the "Manual" of Dhuoda, most of which has come down to us. That in itself is remarkable, as a legacy from this ninth century. In it we find details of interest concerning herself and her kindred, her ancestors and her sons. She was evidently a woman of marked intelligence who had knowledge of Latin writers of former days; and she was born of aristocratic lineage. Not that she boasted of this; wholly devoted to the faith and practice of the Catholic Church, she describes herself in her book as a humble, unworthy sinner, trusting to the mercy of Heaven to save her from misery in the Day of Judgment, to lead her from earthly pain and loneliness to the joy of those who are ever with the Lord.

Moreover, the events of the ninth century could bring her only troubled thoughts; between 817 and 843 the Empire of

Charlemagne was breaking up into various partitions. Let us look for a moment at the story of these years: a story which she knew from the words of others or from her own experience.

Louis, son of Charlemagne, assumed the Imperial crown of the Frankish Empire as co-ruler with his father in 813; upon his father's death early in 814 he held it as sole Emperor. For over three years he longed to hold definite unity of rule in the lands he was governing; in July 817, this, he hoped, was brought into reality at his Palace of Aachen by an Act approved in a General Assembly of bishops, abbots, nobles, with others of lesser rank, clerical and secular. Its provisions declared: that the eldest son of the Emperor, Lothar, now in his early twenties, was to be co-Emperor from this time onward with his father, and as his heir was to succeed him in Imperial rule upon his death; that the two younger sons, Pippin and Louis, were to rule as kings: Pippin as king of Aquitania, an honor which he had already received in 814, Louis as king of Bavaria. Over these younger brothers Lothar as Emperor was to hold authority; in 817 Pippin was only twelve years of age, and Louis eleven. In Italy Bernard, a nephew of the Emperor—Louis the Pious, as he is known in history—was king, a youth of eighteen and foolishly ambitious. In his folly he yielded to persuasion by unworthy courtiers, rose in rebellion against the Empire, and was punished in the following year, 818, by the cutting out of his eyes. He died in agony.

This Act of 817 was again approved by an Assembly called at Nymwegen (Nijmegen) in the Netherlands, on May the first, 821.

In October 818, the Emperor lost his wife Irmingard. Soon many young women of noble rank were invited to court for inspection by His Majesty; among them was one Judith, daughter of Count Welf of Bavaria, who at once conquered Louis the Pious by her beauty, her charm, and her quick, intelligent mind. In 819 they were married, and she became Empress of the realm; from her was to rise the cause, both natural and deliberate, of the first inroad upon the unity devised in 817.

Dhuoda had heard of all these happenings. But the following year, 820, was to rest more clearly in her thought, which now turned from the Imperial Court of Aachen outward to those borderlands of Spain known as the Spanish March. This region, adjoining the kingdom of Aquitania, had been conquered and settled as part of the Frankish Empire by Charlemagne at the end of the eighth century and in the first years of the ninth. Since 801 it had been governed by one Bera, a Goth, holding the title of Count of Barcelona; its power was enhanced by its freedom from dominance by Aquitania's king, Pippin; its own individual name was Duchy of Septimania.

In January 820, however, Bera was publicly accused of high treason in another Assembly at Aachen; he had been plotting against the Empire, it was declared, with Saracens eager to invade its lands. The Emperor Louis, always anxious to allow justice and mercy, gave to the accused benefit of the legal custom among the Franks. This custom decided his innocence or his guilt by victory or defeat in a duel on horseback with his accuser, a Count Sanilo. They fought; Bera was overthrown, and therefore sentenced to death, the penalty for treason. Yet once again the Emperor intervened, and Bera was sent into exile at Rouen, Normandy. Ermoldus Nigellus, Ermold the Black, who wrote during the reign of Louis the Pious a poem in his honor, described in it this battle, fought by the two near the Palace, amid the wide fields on which the Emperor enjoyed his sport of hunting.

Even more readily did Dhuoda remember the year 822, in which that same Emperor Louis the Pious knelt to do penance for grievous sins before a vast congregation of his bishops, clergy, and secular nobles, at Attigny in the Ardennes. He confessed himself guilty of the torture inflicted upon Bernard of Italy; of action against Church and State in sending to exile the monks Adalard and Wala, men high in political esteem who had dared to show their sympathy with that young rebel. In 822 the Emperor also sent his sons Lothar and Pippin away from his Court, ordering them to govern their kingdoms of Italy and Aquitania.

The year 823 saw a disquieting omen of rupture in Imperial unity. On June 13 the Empress Judith gave birth to a son whom his parents named Charles in memory of his grandfather, Charles the Great. From that moment his mother turned all her power, all her influence, upon Louis the Pious for the assuring of her son's future within the Empire. She made Lothar, then at home on a brief visit, receive him from the font as godfather; she exacted from Lothar a promise that, whatever portion of Imperial land the Emperor might decide to bestow upon Charles, never would he, the eldest son, raise or encourage resistance. Lothar went back to Italy with bitter regret, all the more bitter since, some two months before, Pope Paschal I had crowned him in Rome as co-Emperor with his father. He knew very well how forceful the persuasion of Judith could and would be for the husband who adored her.

The following year brought Dhuoda herself into the record

of history; in June 824, she was married to Bernard in the Imperial Palace at Aachen. Bernard was godson of the Emperor Louis the Pious and a man of noble origin.

His father in this world was William, Count of Toulouse: a soldier well respected, even renowned at the Court of Charlemagne for his upright character and his courage in war against the Saracens, invaders of Spanish land under Imperial rule. Above all, he had received high praise for his bold assault during the siege of Barcelona in 801. Yet even more evident was his devotion to the Church; encouraged by Benedict, abbot of Aniane in Aquitania, he finally entered the monastery which he himself had founded at Gellone, in the barren territory near Aniane. There, a simple monk, he had spent his last years; history knows him as "Saint William of the Desert."

His son Bernard was also a soldier, keen in battle, like his father; unlike him, however, he was ever ambitious, proud, coveting influence, power, and rank, using all the means within his reach to gain these ends.

To him, on November 29, 826, Dhuoda bore a son, William. By this time she had learned how to live alone; Bernard was far away, seeking fame. In 826 there was a revolt of Gothic settlers in the Spanish March. One of them, Aizo, formerly, it would seem, a resident or a prisoner in the Palace at Aachen, was leader of the rebels, supported by the Emir of Muslim Spain, Abd-ar-Rahmân II (822–852), who held his Court at Cordova. By the next year, 827, the trouble had greatly increased, and Louis the Pious decided to send a strong army of Frankish soldiers to the rescue. These men were nominally under the command of Pippin of Aquitania, but in fact were led by two nobles of the Empire: Matfrid, Count of Orléans, and Hugh, Count of Tours.

It was a mistaken choice. Both Matfrid and Hugh detested Bernard as arrogant, as one grasping all for himself; after the fall of Bera he had been appointed by the Emperor Louis as Count of Barcelona and governor of the Spanish March. They set out; but dallied so long on their way to Spain that Bernard, left without aid, was scarcely able to remain unconquered, helpless to prevent harm. The land around Barcelona and Gerona was sorely ravaged; the people, farmers, owners of estates, rich and poor alike, saw their fields burned and plundered; they were terrified by strange lights blazing and flashing across the sky: omens of dread death, they said. When the assault finally died down and the enemy retreated with vast gain, Bernard, like his father, at least won much

praise for his unyielding spirit. In 828 Matfrid and Hugh were
deprived of their rank and property.

But trouble was not confined to the Spanish land. Rumors
were soon reaching Dhuoda, at home with her little son, that much
was wrong in the length and breadth of the Empire. On all sides
discontent was stirring men's hearts; the harvests were falling,
farms were poorly stocked; people were hungry; laws were constantly broken; disease was rampant; nobles were dissipating their
resources, heedless of the poverty around them; clergy, of rank
both eminent and humble, were neglecting their charge. Even the
elements of Nature itself were rising in riot, as though in fellowship
with the passions of men. A writer of this time, known to us only
as "The Astronomer," declared: "As Easter of 829 drew near, un-
timely darkness set in; an earthquake shook the land so vehemently
that buildings all around almost collapsed. There followed a storm
of wind, so violent that the Palace of Aachen quivered under its
force and most of the lead tiles were blown from the roof of the
Church of Saint Mary, Mother of God."

What was to be done? To this question the Emperor could
find no immediate answer; but Judith, his wife and Empress, could.
She had heard of the determined resolution of Bernard in the
Spanish March; she had met him, had talked with him, and she had
greatly enjoyed his manner and conversation. Did he not know
much concerning things in which she herself took deep interest—
astrology, divination, prophecy, things supernatural, strange and
curious?

So she brought his name before her husband, declaring him
exactly the man to bring peace and order into both Palace and
Empire. Louis the Pious yielded to her will. Either during an
Assembly held at Worms in August 829, or shortly after this meeting, announcement informed all that Bernard had been appointed
Chamberlain of the Imperial Court. His influence as Chamberlain,
all men knew, would reach far further than the Court.

Two other Imperial decisions were also declared about the same
time. First: an order was given that Lothar, who had been at home,
signing decrees as co-Emperor, was now to return to Italy. Next,
it was made known, in an edict which struck many with fear and
anger, that Louis the Pious had dared to interfere with that Act
of Unity solemnly approved and confirmed in 817 and 821. He
had given to Charles, the little son of Judith, now six years old,
wide lands for his future rule within the Empire: Rhaetia, Alsace,
Alamannia and part of Burgundy; he had also placed young
Charles under the guardianship of Bernard, the Chamberlain.

Wrath, accusation, hostility, and lament now arose from nobles and peasants alike. Yet worse was to come. Great things, a return to peace and prosperity, regulation of life in its varied aspects, had been expected from a firm control by the newly appointed Chamberlain. Altogether different from this expectation was the experience of months, of years to come. In the words of "The Astronomer": "Bernard as Chamberlain did not destroy the seed-grounds of discord; rather, he promoted their increase."

In 830 Dhuoda heard report after report of her husband's perverse and unholy doings. Men of aristocratic rank, folk of simple station, were forever telling of his arrogance, his tyranny. He dismissed, they told, from Court and tenure those whom he did not like, and appointed those he favored in their place. He was constantly with the Empress Judith; it was openly said—though "The Astronomer" stoutly denied it—that in his ambition and lust he had made himself her lover. Paschasius Radbert, who wrote a *Life* of Wala, statesman and abbot of Corbie, a monastery near Amiens, in this work poured out his fury against the Chamberlain: "No day," he declared, "was more unhappy than that when the accursed Bernard" (mentioned here under the fictitious name of 'Naso') "was called from Spain. . . . Like a fool he plunged into all swine-pools of filth; like a wild boar he wrecked the Palace, he destroyed good counsel, he scattered abroad all laws of reason; he banished those who held office, sacred or civil; he took for himself the Emperor's wife. . . . He turned day into night, and night into day. . . . The Palace became a brothel where adultery held rule and a paramour reigned. . . . And when there remained no doubt of adultery, of the tricks of fortune-tellers, of false prophecies, then things were heard of through him, so many in number, of such sort as nowhere men believed to be still existing. From every part of the world they came, just as if Antichrist himself had appeared with his wicked sorceries."

In the spring of 830 men of Brittany revolted—a not uncommon occurrence—and the Frankish army was ordered to assemble at Rennes to suppress them. The day of arrival, however, was in Holy Week, a time of strict fast; the weather was cold, wet, and depressing; the roads were flooded through continued torrents of rain. In their mass the Frankish soldiers defied authority and refused to march.

There was further stimulant for the rebellion. Two sons of the Emperor, Lothar of Italy and Pippin of Aquitania, had themselves risen in revolt against him, induced by misrule in the Empire, by reports concerning the Chamberlain, by the weakness of the Emperor, Louis the Pious.

In March Louis himself set out for Rennes. Most of his army turned aside and made for Paris; excitement and anger by this time were raging among them. They were demanding that Louis, the Emperor, be cast from his throne, that the Empress be stripped of her power, that Bernard the Chamberlain be killed outright.

The Emperor quickly sensed what was happening. He gave Bernard leave to flee for his life, and at once Bernard hurried for refuge to his Spanish March. Judith sought safety within the convent of Saint Mary at Laon, near Soissons. Only Louis the Pious showed courage; he marched boldly to meet his rebel sons: Lothar, who in May came from Italy, and Pippin, arriving from Aquitania. They were stationed at Compiègne on the Oise, a city now the center of revolt. There every effort was made to compel the Emperor to abdicate; his wife was brought to him and ordered to use all her power in persuading him to enter a monastery.

To no end; Louis only asked for time to think, and she was soon carried off to become a nun in the abbey of Holy Cross, founded by Radegund at Poitiers. Two of her brothers, Counts Conrad and Rudolf, were tonsured and sent to monasteries in Aquitania, to be closely watched there under command of Pippin, its king. Nor was Bernard's family spared; his brother Heribert was blinded and taken as prisoner to Italy.

All that summer of 830 Imperial authority lay silent and helpless; in his *History of the Sons of Louis the Pious* Nithard, a contemporary source, told that "Lothar, having grasped power, held his father and his stepbrother, the boy Charles, in theory free, in reality captive."

Then at last, little by little, reaction set in and gained strength. It was felt, especially by men of religious calling, that to keep the Emperor under restraint was akin to treason, that this virtual imprisonment was an intolerable insult to the Frankish throne. The Emperor himself saw the change, and at once turned to make use of it. He despatched a messenger to open the way of reconciliation with his sons, Pippin and Louis; Louis, indeed, had not been active in the rising against his father. According to Nithard, the Emperor used as his envoy a monk, one Guntbald. This may be true; but no other historian tells it. Guntbald, or whoever delivered the Imperial offer, was successful; Louis and his two sons talked themselves into alliance, especially when in return for renewed loyalty he promised each of them a tempting addition to the land they ruled.

Now with even quicker energy the Emperor went to work. An Assembly must be called to punish the rebels of 830 and to reward the faithful. Nymwegen in the Netherlands would be, he knew well, the best place for this meeting of a multitude of his subjects; its men of East Frankish and Saxon descent were always ready to support him. At the same time, fear, still lurking in his mind, drove him to order that no one should attend clad in armor.

In October 830, when proceedings opened in the Imperial palace at Nymwegen, one of the first to enter was Hilduin, abbot of Saint-Denis, a famous monastery on the outskirts of Paris, and he came fully armed. Louis at once commanded his departure, and, before all who were present, sentenced him to exile in Paderborn, Germany. Next, Wala, the monk and statesman who had openly sided with Lothar against the Emperor, and was forever dwelling in public on the miseries of the Empire under Louis the Pious, again was banished from Aachen and its Court, ordered to return to his abbey of Corbie, and to remain there.

Further penalties were dealt out in another Assembly, held on February 2, 831, at Aachen itself. Once again Lothar, heir to the Imperial crown, was dismissed to Italy, forbidden to leave that kingdom without special permission; the rebels of 830 were at first condemned to die, then by mercy of the Emperor were allowed to live: those of the laity in exile, the clergy in monastic cells. Judith, who had been restored to the Imperial Court, now appeared before nobles of Church and State to assert by oath her innocence of the sin of adultery with Bernard. Her declaration was accepted, though doubt was widely felt, even in the mind of her husband. Yet his joy in seeing her safely restored to him drove away that horrid thought.

But the most important acts made known by the Emperor in this meeting at Aachen were additions to the lands ruled by Pippin and Louis, according to his promise, and a substantial further bestowal upon Charles of territory in Alamannia, and in Burgundy, together with the region of Reims.

Some of the exiles received a pardon early in May 831, during a Council held at Ingelheim, on the Rhine south of Mainz. In the autumn a third Council met at Thionville on the Moselle. Here, as Dhuoda must have heard, her husband, who up to this time had remained a fugitive in Septimania, ventured to appear and to declare that he was ready to face in a duel of arms anyone who accused him of lascivious and lewd crime. No one came forward; Bernard gave oath that he was innocent, and, like the Empress, he was accepted as such.

Shortly before Christmas of 831 Pippin arrived at Aachen and was received with no goodwill by his father, who had summoned him before, and in vain. This unexpected reception so annoyed the king of Aquitaine that he stole away in the darkness of night and returned to his own land. The matter seems a small one, but it foretold further evil.

And in 832 it came. First of all, word reached Louis the Pious, with all his Empire, that Louis, king of Bavaria, and his own son, had gathered an army and was about to invade Alamannia, recently given to Charles; that he intended to march from Alamannia against the Emperor himself. At his right hand for his support stood Matfrid, once Count of Orleans, passionately longing for revenge. Had not Louis the Pious robbed him of land, of rank, and of repute?

Nevertheless, his people, Franks and Saxons, rallied around the Emperor in a crowded Assembly held at Mainz. His army crossed the Rhine and Louis soon thought it well to retire into his own Bavarian kingdom. The Imperial soldiers, led onward by the Emperor himself, loyally pursued the rebel; and at Augsburg, Louis the Pious who ever longed for peace offered and gained reconciliation with his son.

Pippin, however, did not submit to reconciliation. In the autumn of 832 he and Count Bernard of the Spanish March were summoned to the Emperor's presence at Jonac, his Palace near Limoges, on charges of disloyalty to the crown. Before long Dhuoda in her distant home heard that her husband had been stripped of his feudal privileges and was no longer Governor of Septimania. Its rule had been given to Berengar "the Wise," Count of Toulouse, who was deeply respected by Louis the Pious and also related to him by birth. In his new office Berengar did well, gaining popularity and honor among his people.

Pippin was accused of disobedience to the throne, of daring to forsake his Emperor's presence in Aachen. He was sent into captivity at Trier and deprived of his kingdom of Aquitania, at once awarded to the boy Charles, now nine years old.

These measures did not make for peace; early in 833 the Frankish Empire was shaken by a rebellion far more serious than that of 830. The Emperor's three sons had all suffered penalty at his hands: Lothar had been held a veritable prisoner in his realm of Italy; Pippin had lost Aquitania; Louis had failed to win success in his rebellion; all three were jealous of young Charles.

And they found support. Agobard, Archbishop of Lyons, wrote Louis the Pious a letter, a "mournful letter," of open rebuke:

"You," he declared, "did everything" (in 817 at the Assembly of Aachen) "which should be done, with such faith and hope that no one doubted this had been the work of God in you. Your other sons you appointed rulers of parts of your kingdom; but that there might be one realm, not three, you preferred before them the son with whom you shared your Imperial power. You gave him authority to write deeds, to sign and confirm edicts, and then, as co-Emperor with you, you sent him to Rome that the Pope might confirm your action. You ordered all men to swear that all would follow and abide by this choice, this division of power. To no one did this oath seem worthy of scorn or needless; but lawful and convenient, in that it made for peace and harmony. As time went on all letters bore the names of both Emperors.

"And then you changed your mind; the orders were shattered; your son's name was no longer seen in edicts. . . . Without any reason or good counsel, him whom once you chose with God, you now have repudiated without God; and you are wise enough to know that it is for men to follow God, not to precede Him. . . .

"Of very love for you we grieve that this deed of yours has brought us this year so great evils, so grave crimes. . . . You must be aware that many people are resenting contrary and different laws: not only do they feel resentment, but in sullen mood they speak evil words concerning you."

It was time, the three brothers decided, to seek revenge. In April 833, Louis marched from Bavaria; Pippin escaped from Trier. They met in Alsace. The Pope himself, Gregory IV, had traveled with Lothar, declaring that he came to restore peace. Others thought differently; even the bishops of the Frankish Empire were whispering that he had really come to "ensnare" in the ban of excommunication not only the Emperor, but also those bishops who would not support his rebel sons. Naturally, the Pope denied these rumors with all the force within him. In high indignation he wrote to Frankish prelates: "This merits all shame, that you say I came to cast excommunication presumptuous and devoid of all reason; we warn you that we do not burst out, either of our own will or at the advice of another, into muddled and confused sayings or sentiments. For the very same reason which you put forward: that it would bring insult and dishonor to the Imperial authority, loss and rebuke to our own."

Far stronger in tone than his previous letter was the defence now written by Agobard for the rebel sons of the Emperor:

"Hear ye, all peoples; let earth and her fullness hear, from the rising of the sun to its setting, from the north and from the sea; Let all men know and recognize that the sons of the Emperor Louis justly were, and are, filled with wrath; that with a good will they are striving to cleanse their father's Palace from the filth of crime and evil factions, and the Empire from most bitter and stormy crises. Their great desire is that brotherly faith and sincerity, working in the sight of God and welcomed by all loyal people, may live among us and endure, unbroken and undefiled."

There follows a fearful picture of the Emperor's marriage; of the love and reverence which he and Judith had once held for one another, of its gradual cooling; of final wantonness on the part of his wife, indulged without shame.

Yet the accusations against Louis the Pious and Judith have not been fully accepted, in both contemporary and modern times. "The Astronomer" called it "a crime" to declare Bernard "the lover of Judith"; Thegan, who also wrote a *Life* of the Emperor Louis, told in it that "the Lord Emperor came from Aachen to Compiègne and there his son Pippin met him, with the leading nobles of his father: the archchaplain Hilduin, Jesse, bishop of Amiens, Hugh and Matfrid, Abbot Helisachar, Godfrid, and many other treacherous men, wishing to drive the Emperor from his rule: action which his beloved son Louis forbade. Those impious men mentioned above brought many charges against him, which it would be impious to speak of or to believe. They said that Judith the Queen had been seduced by a certain Duke Bernard, a man of royal descent and godson of the Emperor; it was nothing but lies, all of it." The historian Bernhard Simson, one of our leading modern writers on Louis the Pious, has written that "although the Emperor was probably not entirely certain of his wife's innocence, yet he still loved her passionately and claimed that, instead of the illegal measures forced upon her, an official inquiry should be made regarding the misdoings of which she was accused."

In 833 Louis himself once again went boldly to meet his sons; he placed his camp opposite theirs, near Colmar in Alsace, on the plain then called the Rothfeld, but described by "The Astronomer" as "The Field of Lies." Promptly the Pope crossed this field to talk with him, and stayed in his camp from June 24, the day when action at Rothfeld began, until June 29, saying again and again that he had come simply on an errand of peace. Meanwhile the sons of Louis were making promises which steadily brought support to their side.

By the 29th of June nearly all those present, and many far away, were eager to dethrone Louis and to give the Imperial crown to Lothar. Now, at the Emperor's asking, all three of his sons rode to his camp, dismounted, and gave him pleasant greeting. It was false; discussion, courteous or rude, was at an end. In the dark of night all, enemies and former supporters of Louis, stole away to join the rebels. At dawn he found himself deserted; only his Empress, their son Charles, and a few faithful friends, were with him. As the sun rose and the scene became clear, a man standing near the Emperor was so overcome by its silent emptiness that he cried out: "The right hand of the Lord has surely done this deed!" Those who had remained with the Emperor now came to ask what they could or should do? Looking around him, he answered: "Go to my sons! I do not want anyone for my sake to lose life or limb!" With tears in their eyes they slowly went away.

So now Lothar assumed Imperial power and rule; Pippin returned to Aquitania, Louis to his German kingdom. By Imperial order from Lothar his stepmother, Judith, was sent off under guard to Tortona in northern Italy, and Charles at the age of ten to the monastery of Prüm, near Trier in Germany: partings which gave the husband and father far more pain than the loss of his throne. For some time Lothar kept his father a prisoner in the abbey of Saint-Médard at Soissons, and then carried him off to Compiègne on the Oise.

It was now autumn of 833; at Compiègne, on October the first, an Assembly of bishops, abbots and other clergy, secular dignities and many of lesser rank, gathered in its Palace. The business of the day, so Lothar as President announced, was to lay bare the charges brought against the Emperor and to decide upon appropriate action.

Accusations, bold and vehement, now came from Ebbo, Archbishop of Reims, who was of humble birth and had been prepared for his high office through the generosity of Charlemagne himself. The assembly was moved by his words; nearly all who were present agreed to a motion that the Emperor, Louis the Pious, should make public confession of his many sins. Lothar had now gained his goal; his father would dethrone himself by his own act, acknowledging himself unworthy of Imperial rule. Had he not already in 822 done penance at Attigny?

In the monastic church of Saint-Médard at Soissons Louis, adorned for the occasion with crown and royal mantle, stood before its high altar, while every one in the vast congregation looked upon this rare sight. They saw him lay his crown upon that altar, put aside his Imperial pride of dress and the sword he always carried, and clothe himself with his own hands in penitential sackcloth.

Then he declared against himself a long catalogue of offences, written, not by himself, but by those who condemned him to humiliation.

The result was as Lothar had foreseen. The Emperor prayed for forgiveness and received excommunication; he read the tale of his sins and was deposed from his throne; finally he was taken back to his cell in Saint-Médard's monastery to begin a long silence, a prisoner in solitude. The silence was only broken from time to time by those who urged him to enter monastic life and discipline; always he declined.

At the approach of winter Lothar carried his captive to Aachen. And there once again, as in 830, wrath and rebellion began to die down. The causes for this were varied. One was quarrel among the rebels; Hugh, now again Count of Tours, Matfrid, Count of Orleans, and Lambert, Count of Nantes, all severally yearned for power and rank in the Empire only second to that of the Emperor; they thought of nothing else. Another was remorse, spreading among the humbler folk, shame that this man, so long their ruler, should be condemned, humiliated, held in prison by his own son. A third cause for this change of feeling was the affection always held by Louis the German for his parent. Now he sent remonstrance to Lothar, and messengers to the prisoner himself. Lothar's answer was brief and rude. Had not the bishops themselves declared the Emperor unworthy of his crown? Had not Louis himself risen against their father? Lothar did indeed allow the envoys to speak with his captive, but only in the presence of guards. Yet the message of hope was in some fashion conveyed by signs, unseen by witnesses. Envoys also went their way from Louis to his brother, Pippin, and here they received much encouragement; Pippin had no desire to serve under Lothar as his lord.

So Louis and Pippin both gathered a formidable army and prepared to march upon Aachen. This news so alarmed Lothar that in January 834 he fled for refuge to Paris, where he gave Louis the Pious, whom he always carried with him, into the custody of the monks of Saint-Denis. Meanwhile Pippin had reached the Seine, but had been forced to halt on account of the wide flooding of its banks. Others were on the same errand of rescue; among them was actually Bernard, husband of Dhuoda and once governor of Septimania. He was marching with Count Warin of Burgundy toward the river Marne; but when they came within sight of it, they, like Pippin, found it an impossible barrier, swollen high by the rains.

Yet for Lothar the near presence of these armed forces brought vivid fear; on February 28 he left Paris, this time without his father, who remained at Saint-Denis.

Now, at last, there was strong hope of reconciliation and peace. On March the first, 834, a multitude of clergy and layfolk descended upon the abbey, claimed the Imperial captive, led him triumphantly into its church, and there celebrated a ritual which healed the wound of 833. Bishops gave Louis the Pious absolution from sin, united him again in fellowship with Christian men, placed the crown of Empire on his head once more, clothed him in Imperial array, while the rafters of the roof resounded with shouts of joy. And again Nature joined them; but now in happy sympathy. Winds that had raged for days calmed to gentle breezes, rains ceased to pour down, skies cleared, the peace was won.

In mid-Lent there was renewed ritual of rejoicing; on "Laetare" Sunday a choir at Quierzy, near Laon, sang a hymn of victory: "Rejoice, O Jerusalem; and keep festive day, all ye who love her!" But the Emperor's gratitude rose to its highest point when Ratold, bishop of Verona in Italy, brought back to him his wife Judith.

Lothar, on leaving Paris, had gone to Vienne, and from there to Chalon-sur-Saône, south of Beaune. At Chalon he did all he could to injure those who had aided his father. In vengeance against Count Warin he besieged the city, killed men, destroyed buildings; and in like fury against Bernard, he seized his sister Gerberga, a nun in one of the convents of Chalon, thrust her into a wine-cask, and hurled her into the river to drown. Openly he declared her a witch.

The Emperor, now at last restored to authority, was eager to live in accord with all his sons. With Louis and Pippin, he encamped near Blois; Lothar, however, stationed at no great distance, was still stubbornly defiant, but could do nothing for himself. His father sent for him, offering a full pardon. In the end he gave way, owned himself guilty of grave wrongdoing, swore never to rise again in rebellion, and was sent back once more to rule Italy.

In February 855 two more congregations celebrated the return of Louis the Pious to power: at Thionville (Diedenhofen) by the river Moselle on the second, the Feast of the Purification, and at Metz, about twenty miles distant, on the twenty-eighth. Here, in the Cathedral of St. Stephen, Ebbo, the leader of those who had censured the Emperor, stood high in a pulpit to acknowledge his action as iniquitous and contrary to all justice. Shortly afterwards he was deprived of his Archbishopric of Reims; Agobard for the same reason lost his Archsee of Lyons.

In the summer Louis held an Assembly in the vicinity of Lyons. Lothar pleaded sickness, but Pippin and Louis of Bavaria were there to support their father. Discord among the Goths in Septimania was the subject of debate; they were divided in allegiance. Some loyally upheld Berengar, their governor; others openly spoke and acted in favor of Bernard, dismissed from rule in 832. The meeting had barely ended when Berengar died, most unexpectedly, on his way home. Many, including nobles of the Imperial Court, lamented his death. Nevertheless Bernard gained immense power in Septimania; before the year 835 ended he sat proudly once again as its governor: a reward given him by the Emperor in gratitude for his vigorous support the year before.

Even so, however, complaint arose. Noble land owners from Septimania flocked to the presence of Louis the Pious, petitioning that he send magistrates to protect their estates from ruffians and robbers who came constantly to plunder, with no respect for things sacred or secular. Bernard, it would seem, had taken little thought for private properties; his people badly needed aid to sustain law and order within their land.

Neither had hostility ceased for the Imperial family. In 837 Louis as Emperor gave a wide portion of Belgian territory within the Empire to young Charles; in 838, when at the age of fifteen Charles received the sword of knighthood, another gift of land was his, granted in honor of the day. These donations, of course, widened the rift of jealousy between him and his elder brothers. Trouble was not greatly lessened when in December 838 Pippin, king of Aquitania, died, leaving two sons. The elder, Pippin the Second, held his own share in the conflicting ambitions of his Imperial family.

The year 839 saw a most serious step on the road to conflict; a dividing of the Frankish Empire into two principal parts, of land in the East and of land in the West. Division was made between Lothar and Charles. Lothar, as the elder, had privilege of choice and decided to rule the East; the West then went to Charles. Only his kingdom of Bavaria was left to Louis the German; and the nephew, Pippin II, received nothing at all.

As was natural, Louis of Bavaria gathered his soldiers for a march in revolt. The Emperor was failing in health; but at once he started out in opposition, crossed the Rhine and forced Louis to retreat into Bavaria. For the father the effort was too great; his sickness became critical, and on June 20, 840, he died on an island in the Rhine. Lothar, now legally his successor on the Imperial throne, prepared for war against both Louis the German and

Charles of the West; he was in no way content to rule half an Empire.

In 841 Bernard, Duke of Septimania, comes again into the story, told here by Nithard. Charles had asked Bernard to meet him at Nevers, where the river Loire receives its tributary, the Nievre; he wanted the Duke's support. But Bernard refused to come; he said that he had sworn an oath of loyalty to Pippin the Second. If, however, Pippin did not keep faith with him he would forsake his oath within fifteen days and make his submission to Charles as his lord.

Yet after all they met in Bourges, near the river Cher, and Charles during their talk discovered that Bernard had no thought of loyalty to any one, to Pippin, to Lothar as Emperor, or to Charles himself. In his anger and in his dire need of support Charles decided upon force; he would suddenly attack and seize Bernard, then hold him prisoner until he swore allegiance. But Bernard was wary. He saw what might happen and escaped just in time, leaving Charles to pour out his fury upon the fugitive's friends.

Then a second time Bernard changed his mind; he decided that the better course would be to yield. Again he sought a meeting with Charles; humbly now he made his submission, and promised to serve him loyally. In return young Charles promised support and true friendship; finally he sent Bernard off to try to bring Pippin the Second into the same bond of alliance.

All this happened very early in 841. On March 22 Dhuoda bore to Bernard their second son. Soon after his birth, before he had even received the name Bernard in baptism, he was taken from her by his father. As a lad, William, the elder boy, had also been carried off. Concerning the infant Bernard Dhuoda was to know nothing; William would, of course, be on feudal service, as page for some noble, very possibly his own father, at Court or in the field.

Meanwhile, quarrel born of ambition and jealousy continued between the brothers: Louis and Charles on one side, and Lothar on the other. Repeatedly Louis and Charles sent envoys to Lothar seeking peace. To no purpose; then Pippin the Second joined Lothar. So the struggle firmly advanced in grim determination until, early in the morning of June 25, 841, a furious battle for dominance broke out at Fontenoy-en-Puisaye, near Auxerre. It is one of the famous battles of the Middle Ages; for long its outcome was in doubt. Finally Count Warin of Burgundy, friend of Charles, came with a strong force to his aid, and Lothar gave up hope, fleeing for refuge toward Aachen.

Yet the *Annales Bertiniani* picture this success of Louis and Charles as no complete triumph; their soldiers were, by the time Lothar turned to escape, so utterly exhausted that they broke down in the race.

Bernard, Duke of Septimania, had done nothing for Charles upon the field of battle; he remained within hearing, but at a safe distance from harm. When, however, he heard that Louis and Charles held the advantage, that they had driven Lothar away in flight, he sent his son William, now serving under him, to swear allegiance to Charles. It was, he thought, a tactful move. So William became liege man and vassal of Charles. As reward Charles handed over to the lad an estate in Burgundy, already bequeathed to William by Theoderic, his uncle, but kept during his childhood by Louis the Pious and, after the death of Louis, by Charles himself.

In his desire for peace between himself and Charles, Bernard proudly declared that he could, and would, persuade Pippin II, ally of Lothar, to swear homage to Charles. The offer was eagerly accepted; but Bernard failed utterly in his attempt.

Little by little, these happenings became more or less known to Dhuoda, waiting in Uzès.

There followed, at Strasbourg on February 14, 842, an exchange of sworn loyalty between Louis and Charles in the presence of their subjects. They vowed to support each other, especially against Lothar, should he attack either of them. Louis gave his oath in the vulgar tongue used at this time in Gaul, very different from its parent Latin; and Charles in Old German, widely spoken by the Franks.

This, and further ominous action by his brothers, brought Lothar to a decision that he had better try to negotiate a peace. A trusted envoy was despatched with orders to tell them that Lothar, the Emperor, was willing to send nobles of the highest rank in his land for this discussion, if he only knew where his brothers might be found. Answer came that he was to send whom he would; anyone could easily find them; at the moment they were on their way to Chalon-sur-Saône. Near that city they met Lothar's ambassadors, who at once delivered his message:

"Against God and against you I have sinned, as now I see well; I desire now no longer to quarrel with you, with any Christian men. If you are ready to deliver into my hands somewhat more than a third part of the Empire, in consideration of my title of Emperor, granted to me by your father, and of the Imperial dignity given to the Frankish kingdom by our grandfather, Charlemagne, then do you deliver it. If you are not willing, then do you grant to me only the third part of the whole, not including in that whole the realms of Lombardy, Bavaria, and Aquitaine.

"So, by grace of God, let each of us rule his own part of the Empire as best he can; let each enjoy the aid, the goodwill, of his brothers; let each of us in his turn give peace and law to his people, and by the will of Heaven may that peace be lasting among us all."

On Thursday, June 15, 842, the three brothers met upon an island in the Saône; each took his oath to keep the peace, to divide the Empire into three portions. Then Louis and Charles gave to Lothar privilege of first choice.

But not until August 843 did this divison gain reality, when the brothers at Verdun on the Meuse confirmed the Treaty which made Verdun's name famous. There, for Lothar, Louis, and Charles, the Empire created by Charlemagne was cut into three parts. And so the Act declared in 817 and confirmed in 821, now some twenty-two years later, fell dead.

Dhuoda must have mourned this tearing apart. Yet a far greater shock, were she still living, would have reached her the following year, 844. Then her husband, Bernard of Septimania, once Count of its borderland, and Chamberlain of the Imperial Court, came to the end of his grasping and covetous ambition. He had longed to make the Spanish March wider, richer, far more powerful, even almost a royal realm; and in the increase of this longing he had found an enemy. Charles, king and ruler, held this land of Spain, bordering upon France, as by law his own, and he would suffer no rival. Captured, we read, under the walls of Toulouse by this enemy, accused of high treason, condemned by Frankish judges in trial, Bernard met death in 844 by public execution.

As time went on, a legend spread concerning that death. Men said that Bernard had made his peace with Charles, had shared holy communion with him at the altar, had knelt before him to offer homage in the monastery of Saint Saturninus near Toulouse. Then came the story of his end. Rumor declared that, after Bernard on his knees had sworn his faith, Charles held out his right hand, seemingly with all courtesy to assist his liege man in rising from the ground. With his left hand, however, it was told, he drove a dagger into Bernard's side, wounding him so grievously that then and there he died. For Charles believed, according to the story, and many with him, that Bernard had violated faith and religion in adulterous union with the Empress Judith. Many even believed, to the intense anger of Charles, that he was himself son of Bernard; their belief was supported by an extraordinary likeness between the two.

In revenge for this popular belief, Charles—so rumor spread the tale—stained with the blood of his victim, gave the corpse a lusty kick, shouting: "A curse upon you, you who defiled the marriage of my father, your lord!"

For two days—so the tale ends—the body lay neglected where it fell, until Samuel, bishop of Toulouse, in mercy gave it burial.

There is, of course, no foundation of truth in this fable, except possibly in its mention of Bernard as lover of the Empress. It is given us by Odo Ariberti in his *Narratio de morte Bernardi,* and may be found in Bouquet VII, 286.

We now come to Dhuoda and her "Manual." We have seen her character: sincerely humble, yet maintaining her right, bearing the marks of courage and determination which she owed to her well-born forefathers. With maternal passion she loved her two sons, William and Bernard, little as she saw of them; she never failed in loyalty to the husband who deserted her, who shamed her by his life and by his death. As she had been trained, so she held fast to the creed and practice of feudal faith. The "Manual" was written for both her sons, but especially for William, then about sixteen years old. In it she exhorts him to be true to his feudal lord, Charles, and to the oath he had sworn:

"To the utmost of my knowledge and ability, by aid of the Lord of Heaven, without craft or beguiling, in my service and in my person, I will be your true and loyal man; for this purpose: that the power which God has given you, for the fulfilling of His will and for the salvation of yourself and your faithful people, you may be able to hold and to control."

In return Charles, once acknowledged as his lord, had promised him protection, justice and mercy, within the bounds of reason and of human power.

Dhuoda began to write her book, she tells William, at the end of November 841, some five months after the battle of Fontenoy; she finished it early in February 843.

Her first words told of her desire in compiling it: "Many children, I know, are happy with their parents in this world. But I, son William, am far away from you, anxious and longing to aid you in need. So I am sending you this little work, written by myself in a way which will serve your young mind. It gives me joy to think that although I cannot talk with you face to face, when you read these pages, you will know what you ought to do."

Verse of acrostic form follows, praying the Lord God to guard, to inspire her son. Then again she turns to counsel:

"Even though many books are yours to read and study, please read this little one, and may God help you to understand it. You will like my words, for they are briefly given; you will find in them a mirror reflecting what is good and healthful for your soul. If you follow this teaching which I give, not only will you be accepted by the world, but by Him Who formed you from clay. And both are absolutely necessary: that you be of use to this world and that you be strong to please God in all things."

Now she begins to lay before him his duty to God and man, with all humility on her part; she hopes that no one will condemn or even criticize her for attempting so difficult a task.

There follows, first, instruction on the love of God; on God in Heaven; on God, Creator and Ruler throughout all ages; on the path Heavenward; on the needful study of books; on the listening to masters of theology; on prayer: "Pray, my son, not only in church, but anywhere and at all times: early in the morning, the last moment before going to sleep; at the Seven Canonical Hours of the day; at the moment of entering upon duty in the field."

Especially must William revere his father, both in fear and in love, pray for him constantly, obey him readily, never make him sad, never scorn him as physically weaker than his son.

So must he be faithful to his lord, Charles. With the older and the younger men at Court or in the field he must work and serve eagerly, remembering that the seed of youth ripens into the fruit of age. He must work with and for the humble and those of high estate: "Love all, that you may be loved by all. Does not Nature teach us here? Animals, insects, plants, all seek aid from one another."

Above all he is to honor the priests of God, chosen by God to serve their fellow-men. It is for them to intercede for us sinners, Dhuoda writes; their privilege to baptize in the Name of the Holy Trinity; their right, as given by their ordaining, to hallow bread and wine for our Communion with the Lord. "So do not rashly judge those priests who seem to you unworthy of their calling; for very reverence say nothing in scorn."

Then comes a reference to the troubles of this ninth century: "We live in evil times, my son; I fear lest disaster come to you and to your soldiers as they fight. You will meet often men ambitious for their own ends, greedy, arrogant, disobedient, pleasing the world rather than the Lord of all."

The latter part of this "Manual" deals with the seven gifts of the Holy Spirit; the eight Beatitudes; tribulations and tragedies, temptations and persecutions, need and necessity; sickness, intercession for those departed this life on earth, especially those of William's house and family; and, strangely enough, unless we remember Dhuoda's training, the allegorical interpretation of numbers.

Toward the end she writes of herself: "You know how I have suffered through many infirmities of my frail body. By grace of God and the merit of your father I have sustained them all, but my spirit has felt their force. Of late I have been slothful in prayer; my duty of the Seven Hours I have neglected to seven times seven. May God of His mercy raise my sick and burdened self to the heaven above! You, and others, also, must pray very often for me; both now, and, yet more urgently, after my death, which I believe will soon come. I am racked by fear of my fate in the future; yet never will I despair of the mercy of God."

At the end she places an epitaph for her tomb; she has written it herself in acrostic lines, and it bears her name.

We may think that she died in 843, and that she was spared the misery of her husband's death in 844.

And, further, she did not live to hear of the fate of her two sons.

After his father's death William, her firstborn, then eighteen years of age, probably lived in Burgundy. Some years later he marched upon Barcelona with a force of soldiers and seized it by craft of strategy; in 850 he captured Aledran, Count of Barcelona, within the Spanish March. The same year he himself was taken prisoner by even deeper cunning and put to death in Barcelona itself.

Dhuoda's second son, Bernard, was only nine years old at this time; he grew up with a fierce longing to work vengeance upon Charles "the Bald," who, as he held it, had murdered his father. In 864, at the age of twenty-three, he was present at the Assembly of Pîtres, near Rouen, and there Charles gave consent that the lands of Burgundy, once owned by William, should now pass to his brother, Bernard himself. Yet this favor did not in the slightest allay the hatred felt by Bernard for Charles; he was secretly hoping for revenge, and at this moment thinking that his chance was near at hand.

The Assembly was still in debate when, by permission, he left its members and hurried, so it was told, to conceal himself and other armed men in ambush within the forest hard by. He had heard that King Charles, with two of his nobles and chief counselors, Robert the Strong, Count of Anjou, and Ranulf I, Count of Poitiers, were to pass that way. He would be there—so he planned—to seize the king, and probably to kill both the Counts outright. Both, he grimly remembered, were enemies of his family and as such deserved to die.

But other eyes had marked his action; there were spies in the service of Charles, and Bernard was arrested in the depths of the forest. By sheer courage and muscular strength he managed to escape, to take refuge in an armed citadel of Burgundy.

He lived a lawless life until 872, when he was thirty-one; at this early age he was killed in a sudden riot. Neither he nor his brother William left any children, and their line died with them.

Even though she never heard of it, this was a tragic ending to the hopes of a wife who loved and honored a husband who, men said, loved, not her, but Judith, wife of another man; of a woman who so dearly loved the sons who both died in their sins; who so deeply revered the feudal loyalty which they all three despised; who so fervently loved the God whom they ignored.

CHAPTER EIGHT

Abelard and Heloise

From the ninth we pass to the twelfth century, to tell once again the most famous love story of the Middle Ages. Men and women have given their varying views of this: in narrative, in discussion and in argument; in drama, in poem, in novel; in skilled translation from its Latin. Yet there may be readers, students of history, who do not know clearly its course, especially as illustrated by those letters which here, following Étienne Gilson, we will hold it wise to regard as genuine.

In 1079 Peter Abelard was born at Le Pallet, a town near Nantes in Brittany. It is fortunate for us that in his fifties he wrote the "Letter to a Friend" from which we gain understanding of his life, his character, and his sorrows. To his Breton birth he traced his ardent enthusiasm for learning; Berengar, his father, had been a student before he entered military service, and he took care that his sons followed in his steps. Peter, as the eldest, was Berengar's special charge; from his earliest years he was encouraged to delight in books. This was exactly what the boy wanted; he was glad, he tells us, to forsake the court of Mars for the embrace of Minerva. The armor in which he chose to defend himself was that of philosophy, and among all branches of philosophy he vastly preferred dialectic, the science of argument based on logical reason.

At last he found that home could teach him no more. Promptly he went out to travel, to enjoy eager discussion with men who held his own views of metaphysics and with those who differed. Throughout his turbulent life he was to love argument, here, there, and everywhere; he was known as "The Peripatetic Philosopher." Finally, at the age of twenty-one, he settled at Paris, in the twelfth century the heart of Europe's intellectual vigor. The head of the Cathedral School of Notre-Dame was William of Champeaux, Archdeacon, famous for his knowledge of philosophic mysteries. For a while Abelard listened, and William was delighted by his longing for progress. Then suddenly he was moved to raise his voice in dispute, when William was lecturing on the theory of Universals. Such daring annoyed his professor exceedingly, as did Abelard's surprising knowledge of the question.

It was, he tells us, the beginning of the storms which were to harass him nearly all his days. Not only was William angry, but many of Abelard's fellow-students resented both his presumption and his brilliance. Was he not a newcomer? He was hardly known by sight!

But he persisted; he was full of bold ambition, as he himself admitted in his story of his troubles. He went further: "At length, trusting my ability beyond the number of my years, as a mere youth I wanted to direct a school of students on my own account."

Before long he did; in 1103 at Melun, a town near Paris, though William tried hard to prevent him. In Paris, while Abelard's repute at Melun rose high, William of Champeaux steadily lost pupils; and even more so when his rival, growing in confidence, moved his school from Melun to a center even closer to Paris, the town of Corbeil.

All this burst of energy, as might be expected, took its toll; Abelard fell sick and was forced to return home to Brittany for a long rest. He remained there two or three years, while students again and again tried to get him to resume his lectures.

By 1108 he had recovered, and soon he hurried back to Paris, where he found that William had gathered a community of young men dedicated to religion. Himself professed in monastic vow, he was now directing these disciples of his in a foundation which was eventually to win high renown as the Abbey and School of Saint-Victor.

William had yielded his chair of philosophy in Paris to another scholar, but he was still lecturing to those who cared to hear him. Abelard listened among the diminishing attendance; once more he broke out into disagreement and once more he conquered his teacher, in a victory for which undoubtedly he had hoped.

But now unexpected success suddenly fell to him. The scholar who had gained William's professorship, in his eagerness to hear Abelard discuss philosophical questions, offered Abelard himself that honor and found ready acceptance.

The thought that Abelard, once his pupil, was now holding a chair of philosophy in the Cathedral School of Paris, drove the jealous mind of William to desperation; he not only tried to turn him out of his office, but he hurled evil accusations against the scholar who had passed it on to him. So evil were the charges that neither the man accused nor Abelard could hold the chair, and soon it was given to one of Abelard's keen competitors for fame.

Quickly therefore he left Paris for Melun and again settled his school there; William's envy followed him, but Abelard's reputation steadily increased. Before long he heard further report concerning William; finding that the dedicated youths in his house of religion were sceptical about his conversion to monastic discipline, since he was still in the secular world of Paris, William had removed his community to a village some distance away.

At once Abelard brought his pupils back to Paris; now that William had departed there was hope for peace. He did not settle them within the city itself, since his competitor was there, in possession of the professor's chair of philosophy; he placed his school upon its outskirts, on the Mont Sainte-Geneviève. He would fight that competitor.

And so Abelard's fame mounted steadily and the competitor suffered. William, when he heard with joy that Abelard was not inside the walls of Paris, returned there with his religious community, longing to win success for himself, while he professed that he was returning to aid Abelard's competitor. He professed in vain, since he himself was now as nothing compared with Abelard, and the competitor, finding no aid, but rather harm in William's endeavor, and no support for his own efforts, resigned his chair and entered a monastery. Students of Abelard disputed and argued with those of William constantly, at times even with William himself; Abelard could quote happily the words of Ovid:

> "If you want to know
> The issue of this battle, I was NOT conquered by him!"

Then he gave judgment in his own words: "If I were to keep silence, facts would cry aloud!"

The joy of conquest, however, was interrupted by a call from his home in Brittany. His father by this time had left that home for a life vowed to cloistered religion, and his mother was planning to do the same. She wanted to bid her son farewell.

His brief visit ended, he returned to Paris. It was about 1113 and he now learned that William had left the city, had received consecration as bishop of Châlons-sur-Marne, and no doubt was at last content.

The road of Abelard's ambition now lay open and comparatively free from hazard. It was characteristic, nevertheless, of this young man of some thirty-four years to long for wider, deeper knowledge; he must add the science of theology to his philosophical research. And for this he decided that he must go to Laon, north of Soissons and of Reims, to study under its master, known far and wide for learning: Anselm of Laon.

With fervent hope Abelard set out, entered Anselm's lecture room, and met with complete disappointment. His words on Anselm are full of scorn: "So I went to this old man, for whom long practice rather than his mind or his memory had won renown. Indeed, if anyone called on him in doubt concerning some matter, that inquirer came away more doubtful than before. Anselm, it is true, was a marvel to the people who listened as he spoke; but just a nobody to the minds of those who asked him questions. Wonderful was his flow of words, but contemptible in their meaning, empty of reason. The fire he kindled filled his lecture room with smoke, no light at all. He was just like a tree which seems to those who see it from a distance marvelous in its foliage; but when they come nearer, they find that it bears no fruit. To me he was the ancient oak tree of Lucan, the Roman poet:

'Standing as a shadow of a great name.' I did not stay long in his shadow!"

Both lecturer and students soon saw and resented this contempt: a contempt, however, which was to draw Abelard into a new path of work. Here he tells his story of the adventure:

"One day, after lecture and discussion we, pupils of Anselm, were relaxing in fun, joking and jesting with one another, when somebody asked me what I, a student of philosophical science, thought about reading theology? I answered that theological study to my mind was excellent for the salvation of one's soul; but to my great surprise I had discovered that scholars do not find the writings of saints of old, or even ancient comment on these writings, clear to their minds! So they have to seek understanding elsewhere.

"This remark of mine raised much laughter, and some of the students present asked me whether I myself could, or in my pride thought I could, understand those holy writings of ancient days without some direction to help me? I answered that if they liked I was quite ready to try my skill! This brought more laughter, and a general shout: 'Of course we all agree to that! Let's search, and find for you some out-of-the-way text! Then we'll see what you make of it!'

"Soon they all agreed upon a most obscure prophecy in Ezekiel. I took it and at once invited them to come and hear me the very next day. Whereupon they gave me advice which I didn't want, telling me not to hurry in such an important matter; I had had no experience and I had better take my time, watching out for mistakes! This made me really angry and I replied that it wasn't my custom to do things through long, long practice but through sheer plain intelligence; either they would come on the day I said, or I would stop the whole business altogether!

"Only a few came to my first talk on that passage in Ezekiel. It seemed to all of them so silly that I, who knew nothing about Biblical prophecy, should attempt to explain it. All the same, every student who did come was simply delighted by my talk, praised me up to the skies, and forced me to go on as I had begun. When others who had stayed away heard this, they rushed to my second and my third lecture; they all, too, tried hard to get copies of what I had said on the first day.

"Old Anselm," Abelard continues, "was terribly upset, envious as could be. Then and there he began to accuse me of ignorance of theology, just as William had done in regard to philosophy. But two of his students—Alberic of Reims and Lotulf of Lombardy— were even more angry at this insult to their pride. It was they, I found, who had suggested to Anselm that he forbid me to interpret sacred texts again, lest I should make bad mistakes, and these be held due to his teaching!

"But," Abelard added, "real scholars were very angry with him, and so his jealousy only added to my triumph!"

A few days later he left Laon for Paris. Now came the years —c. 1114–1118—which saw him at the height of glory in the Cathedral school. There, as he continued his study of Ezekiel, he became no less famous for his knowledge of theology than he long had been in philosophical argument.

Peace was now his, and he enjoyed it to the full. He also gathered a large harvest of wealth; his lecture rooms were crowded, and students paid for their training. His ambition was satisfied; his pride had reached its goal; his fame was spreading throughout Europe, among learned and unlearned alike.

Yet there were tares among the wheat. As he gained wealth, so he became more sure of himself in his own mind. He gradually gave less time, less effort, to the preparing of his lectures, to the care of his pupils. As the years went on, he turned to self-indulgence, to luxuries which he could now afford, to social entertainment. It is true that at no time, even now, did he allow himself immoral or, indeed, doubtful action; he avoided women of all classes, even those of noble rank who would gladly have welcomed this, the most famous man in Paris.

Fortune, he writes, as she smiled upon him, held in store a more convenient way for hurling him from his pinnacle of fame.

To put it better, Divine justice intended to punish a proud, conceited, and ungrateful man!

So now we come to Héloise, with whom Abelard's memory will always be connected. She was a girl of some seventeen years, living with an uncle, her guardian, near the Cathedral of Notre-Dame in which that uncle held office as canon. Where Abelard first met Héloise we do not know; but he must have heard much about her. As a child of extraordinary intelligence she had been taught by the nuns of Argenteuil, near Paris; she had pursued knowledge until she was held one of the most intellectual of her set in France; indeed, in Western Europe. She delighted in books; her uncle, Fulbert by name, was as proud of her as he was devoted in affection; nothing was too good for Héloise; and for her he cheerfully spent his money, very dear as it was to his heart.

Since Abelard constantly heard talk among those who marveled at her brilliance, he grew more and more curious; she was, they said, as charming and pleasant of face as she was intelligent. For the first time he felt the temptation to talk with a young woman. We may think that perhaps he did exchange some words with her in the Cathedral school; there is also some ground for a theory that he wrote to her, and that she answered his notes.

At any rate, he soon decided that he must really get into closer relation, and with great care he contrived a plan. He went to her uncle, Canon Fulbert, and said that he was in need of a lodging near the Cathedral School, that Fulbert's house would exactly suit him, that he would pay for this hospitality whatever was asked of him. More than this; he added that he had heard of Fulbert's niece and her repute as student; he would be delighted to carry on her education. With full confidence Abelard spoke; who, either Fulbert or Héloise herself, could or would resist him? Was he not the most brilliant scholar of his time, a young man in his thirties, handsome and attractive? Did he not know how to win over either man or woman, if he willed it?

At once Fulbert gave consent; Abelard might train, might discipline, that girl of his; he might teach her day and night alike, her mind and its work were entrusted wholly to his care.

About 1117 the lessons began, and so did the course of fate for both master and pupil. Desire within him turned to passion, and Héloise answered his love. Soon Abelard was neglecting his students and his lectures in the school; his teaching of Héloise was being interrupted by words and acts far from the intellectual. He was writing love-songs for her and she was listening to them, enchanted by his voice, his melody.

Months passed, and those in the school were miserably disappointed by Abelard's growing carelessness. Yet still Uncle Fulbert had no fear, no suspicion of what was going on in his house. Then at last the two were caught, forgetful of all but themselves, and Fulbert's deep content turned into fury of anger, misery of shame that this had happened to his niece under his own guardianship. At once they were separated; they could now only reach one another by letter.

One of these letters told that Héloise was soon to bear a child. She wrote in high joy; but her lover was faced by the necessity for action. After long thought he decided what must be done and he did it; in the dark of night she journeyed from her home, disguised as a nun, while Fulbert was absent. She found refuge with Abelard's sister in Brittany, and there a son was born, whom she named Astrolabe.

Meanwhile Abelard himself, filled with worry, perplexity and fear, had reached his own decision; he would pacify the wrath of Fulbert by making Héloise his lawful wife. But the marriage must be kept a secret, for the saving of his own reputation and for his hope of promotion in the Church; he was at this time no priest, but he was a canon and a cleric. Were it known that he was married, he would be forced to resign his canonry. It would also, he feared, lessen his fame as philosopher, as director of the School of Paris, were it known that he was a married man, hampered by family problems.

Fulbert, whose anger had increased tenfold after he found that Abelard had carried off his niece, now saw himself compelled to give consent to the marriage and its secret. Abelard at once went to Brittany to bring her to Paris. Héloise, however, fought a grim battle. Either in talk with Abelard in Brittany, or in letters— our source of information is again his *Historia Calamitatum,* his outpouring of his troubles—she declared her determined opposition to this wedding, fortified by the warnings of Cicero and Saint Jerome.

"To say nothing of the hindrance to your study of philosophy," she argued, "think of your dignity as professor. What have scholars to do with maidservants, writers with cradles? How can books, papers, and pens, fit in with spinning? Who on this earth, absorbed in meditation, things sacred, things philosophic, could live with the wailings of little children, the lullabies of nurses trying to quiet them, the noisy rushing crowd of domestics, men and women, in his house? Who could put up with the nasty, everlasting messes made by babies? Rich men, you will say, could, those whose castles or spacious houses have rooms to spare, who have ample means for spending, who are not tormented by daily worries. Well, we are not rich!

"Philosophers, I tell you, don't live like wealthy men; those who long for money and are bound up with worldly business have no leisure for dwelling on things divine, things philosophic. In ancient days philosophers, those who really were great, scorned this world; they did not merely shut their eyes, they *fled* from the things of their times; they denied themselves all pleasures, that they might rest in the embrace of philosophy alone, their one and only concern. Seneca, who stands among them as greatest of all, tells his pupil Lucilius: 'Philosophy is not a holiday occupation; its study means neglect of everything else; no time is long enough for it. It makes no difference whether you leave philosophy alone altogether or whether you work at it now and then; if you interrupt your thought upon it, philosophy then is no longer yours.'

"For, like those who are true monks, dedicated to their love of God, so in the same passion the truly great philosophers of this world have spent their lives."

Later on, Héloise turned to speak of herself: "It would be a far happier thing for me," she declared, "and more becoming to you, Abelard, if I were called your mistress rather than your wife!"

She ended finally her fierce protest with words of deep foreboding: "One thing remains for us: in the ruin of both, our sorrow will be as deep as the love which went before it!"

Yet her words fell dead before Abelard's desire. Leaving their son with the sister in Brittany, he brought Héloise back to Paris. There, in one of its churches, after a night given to vigil of prayer, at daybreak they were made man and wife by nuptial rite and benediction in the presence of Fulbert and some of their friends.

From the church they went their separate ways, Abelard to the Cathedral School and his new lodging, Héloise to her uncle's house; rarely after this day did they meet. And soon the truth was known; Fulbert, his heart and mind longing for vengeance upon Abelard, upon Héloise also, broke his word and told of the marriage. In vain Héloise declared with solemn oath that the rumors which now ran through Paris were utterly false; her stubborn denials only threw her uncle into spasms of wrath. So cruelly did he insult this once-beloved ward of his that Abelard felt obliged to remove her from his presence. He settled her among the nuns of Argenteuil, in the convent where as a child she had learned her first lessons. Now she worked and prayed with them, clothed in all vesture of religion save the veil which marked those dedicated by profession and vow.

At once her relatives and friends began to whisper, then to cry aloud that her husband was already eager to get rid of Héloise: a stream of gossip which drove Fulbert and others to their final revenge. One night, as Abelard lay alone in a room set apart for him within his guesthouse, a servant, won over by bribery, unlocked its door and conspirators bent on evil silently crept to his bed. Suddenly Abelard awoke, only to suffer torture by mutilation of body, mind, and soul, as his manhood was torn beyond repair.

The dawn of the coming day found him still in agony, not only from assault within himself, but also from the world outside. Clergy and students alike were pouring out their pity and sympathy, to the utter shaming of this man who had in a moment fallen from his height of repute and dignity to a depth of humiliation lower than thought could conceive. What was he to do? Whither could he flee? Commiseration from the public crowd was more than he could bear; he realized that his disgrace was known far and wide, for his unending pain.

At last he felt that only one refuge was his: he must hide behind the walls of a monastery, must, indeed, become a monk. He had no longing for monastic life; but it would at least shelter, it might even heal, his wounded pride.

And what was his wife, Héloise, to do now? He could not endure the thought, let alone the reality, of her united in marriage with another man, even were that possible; or, as a widow, uncared-for, supporting herself and their son; in poverty, perhaps, but certainly in shame. No! as husband, so wife; Héloise, too, must enter religion, leave this world for the cloister, make her profession by vow of lifelong obedience. And she must do this first, before himself, that he might be entirely sure.

It was done; we can read his own words in their clear Latin; translated they tell:

"And so we both took the holy habit of religion; I in the abbey of Saint-Denis" (on the outskirts of Paris), "and she in the convent of Argenteuil. Very many of her friends, moved by sympathy, tried to dissuade her from taking upon herself the really unbearable burden of the monastic yoke. I can think of her now, hurrying, almost running, in her haste to reach the altar, to receive the holy veil from the bishop, to bind herself by profession to the Rule. As she went, she was saying, interrupted by tears and sobs, the words which the Latin poet Lucan placed on the lips of Cornelia,

wailing for the fate she was to bring upon her husband, Pompey
'the Great':

"O noblest husband!
Never shouldst thou be mine! Did fortune hold
Such right over so high a head? Why did I,
Why impiously wed thee, if to misery
I was to doom thee? Now accept thy penalty,
But one which gladly will I pay!"

The year was 1118 or 1119; Héloise was eighteen or nineteen,
and Abelard in his later thirties. Slowly he recovered from his
shame and misery. Clerics were asking him again and again to turn
his mind to the teaching of those who could not afford the customary fees for lectures. For this reason, they declared, the hand of
the Lord had struck him, that, removed from carnal lusts and the
stormy life of this world, he might devote himself to study, a true
philosopher of God.

Gradually he yielded to this encouragement, as day by day he
looked upon the manner of life in Saint-Denis. This was marked by
licentious indulgence, irregularity, and dissipation; its abbot,
superior in office, to the same extent was more worldly, more de-
graded, than all his monks. Abelard could not resist rebuking and
reproaching both individuals and the community as a whole; before
long they hated the very sight of him.

Yet others outside the abbey, students who knew him as teacher, pressed him to return to his teaching; at last he asked and won
from Adam, abbot of Saint-Denis, permission to retire to a small
priory some distance away.

Once more he gained joy; so great a crowd of students gathered
around him that there was no room for their lodging, not even
space in which to grow vegetables and grain.

Theology now absorbed most of his work for them; but "as a
kind of fish-hook"—so he tells—he offered also lectures on secular
philosophy, which was what his pupils wanted, and then quietly
drew them on to theological doctrine. This gave his jealous rivals
further pretext for complaint. They had never ceased to watch
him, and now they protested that as a monk Abelard had no right
to concern himself with lectures on secular theories; nor, indeed,
with instruction in theology, of which, they maintained, he was no
master.

Nevertheless he persevered, and now he set to work in private
on a theological treatise, *Concerning the Divine Unity and Trinity,*

in the hope of aiding many who were perplexed and confused in mind. Many teachers of theology, Abelard felt sure, did not themselves understand what they were presuming to give their disciples, and the blind could not lead the blind.

His effort was rewarded; puzzled students thanked him heartily. This aroused fresh envy in those who held themselves to be now the authorities in philosophy and theology, since both William of Champeaux and Anselm of Laon by this time had died. Especially vehement in accusation were Alberic and Lotulf, now professors in the School of Reims; for their support against Abelard they called to Conan, a Papal legate sent to work in France by Pope Paschal II.

It was soon decided that Abelard's teaching was dangerously erratic; it must be brought for examination before a Council. This drastic decision met with approval and the Council was called to meet at Soissons in 1121. Before it assembled Abelard's two chief opponents took care to spread rumors concerning his views on theology. So sinister were these rumors that, when he arrived at Soissons with his work on the Holy Trinity, stones were thrown at him by a mob, shouting "He believes in Three Gods!"

Day after day the Council met, and nothing heretical was discovered; Alberic and Lotulf were angry and disappointed. It was ready to break up when Geoffroy, a greatly revered bishop of Chartres, rose to defend the accused, proposing that Abelard and his statements should be thoroughly examined in argument between him, their author, and competent critics.

This move was immediately crushed; all had heard of, and some had even experienced, Abelard's skill in debate. By this time many of those present had grown weary, many had left the hall. Geoffroy now suggested that Abelard should be taken back to his monastery of Saint-Denis, and that his writing should again be reviewed there. To this the Papal legate gave consent; but jealous enemies of Abelard would not hear of it. Soissons was in the diocese of Reims, and therefore in Soissons Alberic and Lotulf held influence which they would not have in Paris.

In the end they gained what they wanted; the Papal legate was no theologian and left judgment to the Archbishop of Reims. Geoffroy of Chartres, friend through he was, advised Abelard to submit; worse would be in store for him if he did not. He need not fear; soon, Geoffroy was sure, he would be allowed to return to his own abbey.

Abelard, then, was found guilty of grave and recurring error; with his own hand he was forced to throw his treatise *On the Divine*

Unity and Trinity into a blazing flame and see its charred fragments disappear.

But not even this penalty brought the accusations to an end; a voice was heard crying aloud: "I read in that book of his that God the Father alone is Almighty!" In horror the Archbishop demanded that Abelard declare his faith. At once there rose a shout from the audience: "All he has to do is to recite the Athanasian Creed!" Tired to death, with tears in his eyes and choking in his throat, Abelard struggled through it as best he could.

Immediately, handed over to the abbot of Saint Médard's monastery in Soissons, he was carried off, he himself said, as if to prison. Yet kindly welcome met him when he entered; the community of Saint-Médard was proud to receive so learned and famous a guest. Nothing, however, could comfort him or mitigate his feeling of disgrace and his worry concerning the future. Even his mutilation, the shaming which had made him less than a man, seemed a little thing compared with public condemnation and the destruction of his writing and his words.

His stay in Saint-Médard was brief, as Geoffroy had told him. Then he was sent back to Saint-Denis, only to find further trouble there. Smoldering hostility now rose into open quarrel, for a reason which seems slight but proved serious. Abelard, when reading the Venerable Bede on the *Acts of the Apostles* happened to remark that Bede believed Dionysius the Areopagite had been bishop of Corinth, not of Athens. Immediately from all sides a storm of protest broke out; for this Dionysius was held by all, Abbot Adam and his monks alike, to be founder and patron of their house. Had not Hilduin, writing in the time of Louis the Pious, declared this truth? Abelard defended the authority of Bede; from his brethren arose a cry: "You have always been against us!"

Each side was mistaken in its description of Dionysius; but that was known neither to Abelard nor to those who trusted Hilduin. The abbot felt that the honor of his house was under dangerous assault. He called all his sons promptly together to judge in a General Chapter this brother of theirs who had so rashly sinned in upholding what was not genuine tradition. It amounted to high treason, he declared, so to misname the saint, the great patron of their abbey, favored as it was by royal support. Abelard must be sent for punishment to the king of France himself, Louis VI; until Louis could receive him, he would be kept in the abbey under close guard.

At these words Abelard's power of endurance collapsed altogether; in despair, aided by a few monks who felt pity for him in this crisis, he fled one night from Paris to the lands owned by Theobald, Count of Champagne, a friend of his. Hospitality was given him in the priory of Saint-Ayoul, at Provins near Melun. Its prior was also a friend, and therefore Abelard ventured to ask his support when, during this visit of refuge, Abbot Adam of Saint-Denis came to see the Count on important business and met Abelard himself unexpectedly. Would Abbot Adam forgive him, Abelard pleaded, and would he allow him to live under monastic rule wherever he could find a monastery that would admit him?

The abbot drew a wry face. Did Abelard, he asked, want to live in some other monastery? That indeed would be a great affront to Saint-Denis; Adam was still secretly proud that Abelard, the great scholar, had chosen for his life as monk the abbey which he himself was ruling. No, indeed; excommunication would be cast upon both Abelard and Count Theobald unless the fugitive Brother Abelard quickly returned home.

This threat threw Abelard and his friend, the prior, into deep anxiety regarding the future. Then, a few days after Adam had returned to Saint-Denis, he suddenly died, in February 1122; in March of the same year one Suger was enthroned in his place. Suger was of a different mind; by means of powerful intercession Abelard gained, not punishment, but support from the king of France. All moved smoothly; the king held strong influence over the abbey of Saint-Denis. Now Abelard was permitted to settle in monastic solitude where he would, provided that he did not enter any other community of monks in any manner similar to that from which he had fled.

Before long a solitary home was found by him in a desert and barren region near Troyes, on the bank of the little river Ardusson and in the parish of Quincey, not far from Nogent-sur-Seine.

There Abelard built from reeds and thatched straw a little chapel, dedicated to the Holy Trinity, and close to it he lived under rough shelter, with one cleric as companion. There day by day he held in mind the words from the fifty-fourth Psalm: "Lo, I have got me away far off, and have remained in the wilderness."

Students heard of this retreat where he lay hidden and followed him in their multitude, leaving, as Abelard put it, their cities, their strongholds, to dwell in lonely silence. "They came," he said, "from their comfortable homes to build for themselves little huts, to live on wild herbs and coarse dark bread instead of delicious fare, to sleep on reeds and straw instead of soft beds, to make with their own hands tables from turf. You might well call them hermits, not scholars."

But Abelard's rivals ground their teeth in envy; the greater the flock of pupils, the greater was Abelard's triumph, the more bitter their own humiliation. So the envious professors grumbled among themselves. "See," they said, "all the world has gone after him, and we have won nothing by persecuting him; indeed, we have made him glorious! We tried hard to blot out his name; and instead of that, we have kindled for him a blaze of light." Such, at any rate, was Abelard's thought in his *History of My Calamities.*

Yet the greater the crowd of those who followed him, the more austere, the more difficult, became life and its necessities for Abelard and his clerk. At last he was driven to require recompense from his pupils. He was delighted to teach them, but in their turn by their own labor they must provide necessary food, clothing, housing, with a chapel worthy of its purpose; they must plant, reap, gather in the harvest. He himself had no time for domestic work; he, their teacher, must study, must give his hours to meditation.

Willingly they worked to give him leisure. The oratory of the Holy Trinity disappeared, giving place to another raised in stone and wood, hallowed in the Name of the Paraclete, the Holy Spirit Who had comforted this exile in his loneliness.

Even this dedication raised an outcry among Abelard's enemies. Why build an oratory of God the Holy Spirit? Why not of God the Father? Or of God the Son? Or, indeed, as before, of the Holy Trinity, in whose Name so many churches or chapels had been consecrated?

Who, thought Abelard, was raising this criticism against him? Did it rise from the words of "two new apostles, one of regular canonical life, the other a monk," called upon to bring ruin upon his head? These were once thought to be Norbert and Bernard, both saints of the twelfth century; but neither of them had as yet publicly condemned his writings.

It was dread of attack which was now haunting Abelard's mind. Blow after blow, in Paris, at Soissons, at Saint-Denis, had made him fear that further trouble would come.

He was on the edge of a nervous breakdown, in terror of another charge of unlawful teaching, when suddenly there came a call to rule as abbot the monastery of Saint-Gildas de Rhuys, near Vannes in Brittany, left without guidance by the death of its Father Superior.

Relief and the thought of welcome change drove Abelard quickly to accept this invitation. In years to come he was to write: "Never, God knows, would I have consented but for the hope of escaping my torment of misery. This abbey of Saint-Gildas was in a barbarous region, so barbarous that I didn't even know its language. Its monks were wholly undisciplined, living a life foul with sin; its secular inhabitants were uncivilized and disorderly. . . . I was full of fear and anxiety when I saw what was before me, when I first began to hold authority among those brothers who racked my heart, my mind, both night and day. Did I try with all my power and force to make them obey the Rule, I quickly faced death for my body; if I left them alone and did not do my best in discipline, I faced damnation for my soul.

"Worse still, this abbey had long been under the hand of a tyrant who in its state of chaos had seized his chance to make himself lord of all the land around, even to wring from its monks heavier taxes than the Jews are made to pay. Its brethren kept on trying to get from me their daily needs and supplies, each individual for himself. They had no common purse; each of them supported his mistress, his son or his daughter, one or more, from his own pocket. They loved to see me worried about this; within the monastery they stole, they carried off everything they could, while I had to choose between attempting to keep decent order or retiring altogether. Outside in the open, that tyrant and his men were continually making my life hideous; inside the monastery its monks never ceased planning and plotting mischief to worry me. Those words of Saint Paul might have been written especially to describe my days: 'Without were fightings, within were fears' " (II Corinthians vii, 5).

All this everlasting struggle left Abelard no time to visit Argenteuil or even to write letters for Héloise. His arrival at Saint-Gildas may be placed about 1125, and for two years he bore his burden with such courage and patience as he could summon up. Then, about 1127, a happy chance came his way. Suger, now abbot of Saint-Denis, by grace of a charter issued in the ninth century and confirmed by King Louis the Pious and his son Lothar, discovered that the monastic house of Argenteuil had been willed to Saint-Denis, his own abbey. Promptly he brought the charter into action. He ordered the nuns of Argenteuil, where Héloise had risen to authority as Prioress, to depart, to yield their homes to its proper owners, himself and his monks.

The order was legally allowed, and in 1128 the nuns departed to scattered homes, here and there in France; only the Prioress, Héloise, and a few of her sisters lingered on for a while. A bright thought struck Abelard, and with it in his mind, he decided to visit Argenteuil. There, as he again talked with the nun who some ten years before had been united with him as wife, he offered her the house, oratory, huts and lands of the Paraclete, the Holy Spirit: all, since his departure, lying desolate and empty. With delight this gift was welcomed, and preparations for removal began. In 1129 Héloise and a community of nuns under her rule were established in their convent of the Paraclete; finally, on November 28, 1131, Pope Innocent II issued a Bull confirming their possession. Once again Héloise was Prioress and head; five years later, in 1136, she was the first abbess of the community.

From 1129 onward the convent of the Paraclete saw progress to prosperity. Neighbors were kind to a house of women; Héloise as director won praise from every quarter. Soon Abelard could write: "Its nuns, I believe (God be my witness), in one year gained more of earthly provision than I would have done in a hundred, had I remained there. In that the feminine sex is the weaker, poverty among women is the more to be pitied, and thus it moves human hearts to action. . . . But the Lord granted so much grace to our sister" (as Abelard now addressed Héloise), "our sister, the Prioress, that bishops loved her as a daughter, abbots as a sister, layfolk as a mother; all alike marveled at her piety, her prudence, and the kindness of her patience, unequaled in all times. . . . The more rarely she allowed herself to be seen, the more she devoted herself, behind the closed door of her cell, to holy meditation and prayer, the more urgently did those who were outside ask to see her, to seek from her counsel for their souls."

Abelard, for the comfort of its nuns and for his own support in trouble, continued at first to visit the Paraclete. In this, how-ever, he again provoked complaint. People said that he wanted feminine charm for his delectation, that he yearned for the woman he had loved as mistress and as wife. It was for him a relief to remember what had once been said of Saint Jerome's friendship with Paula. And did not the Lord Christ Himself and His apostles on earth love their friends among women? Did they not talk with them?

Nevertheless he discontinued his visits and his letters to Héloise and her nuns, while things went from bad to worse in and around Saint-Gildas. If he ventured into the lands outside its en-closure, he met dangerous attack; inside the abbey, murder walked secretly. Before he had become its abbot he had received Holy Order as priest, and he regularly celebrated Mass at its altars; one day some one slipped poison into the chalice and he had a narrow escape from death. In vain he tried the dreaded penalty of excom-munication; at Saint-Gildas it had no effect. Then he compelled the most defiant among rebels in the community to promise before their brethren in Chapter that they would leave the monastery and cease in any way to worry him. They gave their oath, but they either broke it and remained, or, if they did leave, they speedily returned. Finally, those who constantly refused to obey their Rule were ordered to take this oath in the presence of bishops, even of a Papal legate, to say nothing of lay nobility. They departed; but when Abelard, happy at this relief, turned, as he trusted, to rule his abbey in quiet and peace, he found that the brothers who up to this day had been obedient, now became harder to deal with than those he had driven out. Every day when the community gathered in chapel or refectory he felt in his secret mind that a dagger was poised to strike.

And so the *History of My Calamities* came to its end while he was still at Saint-Gildas. It was written as a letter to "a very dear brother in Christ," though whether that friend was fictitious or really existed we do not know. In its last words Abelard remembered that he was not alone in his misery; Christ Himself and His followers all suffered persecution.

Yet the day had come when he could bear no more; about 1132 he left the abbey forever. We do not know where he stayed during the next three or four years; perhaps he was with his sister in Brittany. His visits to the Paraclete, his letters, had long lain in the mind of Héloise as joys of the past, perhaps never to be renewed for her comfort.

Then, about 1135, we may think, this *History of My Calamities* reached her. We do not know who sent it to the convent of the Paraclete. At once she wrote to Abelard, pouring out the sorrow of her heart:

"Héloise to Abelard: His handmaid—No! daughter; His wife—No! sister; To her lord—No! Father; To her husband—No! brother."

"By chance, most beloved, your 'Letter to a Friend' has come to me. It came, and I began to read it as eagerly as I embrace in love its writer. That writer's substance I have lost; but at least I did hope to get comfort by some picture of you from its words.

"Now I have read that letter and I think upon words filled with bitter poison: the pitiful story of our conversion and, dear and only love of mine, your constant torture. You wanted that friend of yours to think his troubles a mere nothing when compared with yours. You told of persecution from your teachers; of treacherous evil done to your body; of the accursed jealousy of your fellow-students; it was they, you said, who caused the ruin of your wonderful treatise on theology, who as it were carried you to prison.

Then you came to the contrivances of your abbot and those false brethren, to the slanders of those two so-called "apostles," to the shameful talk against the naming of your oratory, the Paraclete; and then you ended with the doings of those most horrible monks whom you called your sons."

"It all brought back to me my own grief, and the more so since you say that the danger to you is increasing. Now, then, we are all, every one of us here, forced to despair of your life; every day our hearts beat in terror of hearing that you are dead.

"I implore the Christ, Who still protects you as His own, that you write to tell me of those storms in which you are tossing; write again and again, that at least I, who live for you and only you, may share your tragedy or your joy. If for a while the raging of your enemies calms, then speed letters to give us relief; at least this will prove that you have me still in mind.

"You wrote to your friend to comfort him; you wanted to heal his small wounds. But new wounds you have given me, and opened up again the old ones. You paid your debt to your friend and comrade, when you had bound yourself by greater debt to me—to me, not only friend, but the nearest of your friends; not a comrade, but a daughter, or whatever happier or holier name you can think up for me. For it was you alone who founded this house of the Paraclete, who built this oratory, who settled here this present community of ours. Everything here is yours, of your creation.

"This, then, this new garden which you alone planted, is tender and frail, frail in itself, even if it were not new. It needs water for its growth. You at Saint-Gildas are teaching and warning rebels, to no effect. You who give so much to the obstinate, think what you owe to the obedient, your daughters here. And not so much do you owe to these devoted nuns as you owe to me, your one and only belonging among them. The holy Fathers of the Church wrote much for women; neither through reverence for God nor love for us have you tried to comfort me, neither by words spoken face to face nor by letter written far away; and I am so weary in my grief, which never ends. Your debt is the greater because I became one with you in the sacrament of marriage; because, as is clear to all, I loved you with untold love.

"It was you who caused my sorrow, you alone; so I ask you, and only you, to comfort me. All that you ordered me to do I have done, and done so gladly that when I simply could not offend you in anything, I had the courage to lose my own self at your command. At your order I changed not only my clothing but my spirit, that I might prove you to be the one and only possessor of my body and of my mind. Nothing, God knows, did I ever seek in you except you yourself; it was you that I longed for, not what you had. I never looked for marriage lines or marriage dowry, never for my own pleasure or my own will. All I wanted was to satisfy you, as you yourself know. And if the title of wife seems to you too sacred or too binding, the word "mistress" has always been sweeter to me; or, if it does not shame you, let us call me your "concubine" or "courtesan." The greater my humiliation for your sake, the richer will be your gratitude to me, the lesser will be the hurting of your glory."

Later on in this same letter Héloise comes to her professing as nun:

"It was not devotion to religion which brought me as a girl to the stern life of a convent, only your will; and now, if I win nothing from you, in words spoken or written, think how I toil here in vain. No reward for my life here as a nun is to be expected from God; I certainly did not surrender myself through love of Him. It was you whom I followed when I hurried to God in religious life. But no! I did *not* follow you; before you dedicated yourself to religion, you sold me in holy habit through monastic vow to God. God knows that I would not hesitate to go, before you or after you, into the fires of Hell! My heart at that moment was not with me, it was with you; and now, if it is not with you, it is nowhere at all.

"But I *cannot* be without you. O beloved, if only your love for me trusted me less, if it were only more anxious! The more confident I have made you of my love, the more you neglect me. All my pleasures I have sacrificed that I might obey your will. I beseech you, by that God to Whom you have offered yourself, that, in whatever way you can, you come to me or write to me; that through this comforting I may more readily render obedience to Him. When in time past you sought earthly delights, you wrote me often; you made many a song to place Héloise on the lips of all. All the streets, every house, rang with my name. Far more rightly you could now push me toward God: me, whom then you called to wanton pleasure! Think, I beseech you, think of what you owe to me! And keep in your mind what I ask of you, as I end this long letter with a brief word: Farewell, my one and only love!"

Abelard answered, but in a very different tone. He was writing to his "sister," "once dear to him in the world, now most dear in Christ." The letter gave his reason for the long silence:

"The fact that after our conversion from the world to God I have written nothing that could comfort you or encourage you in your present life, is not due to negligence, but to my strong confidence in your intelligence and practical sense. I did not think that that one, to whom Divine grace has given the necessary abilities and power, required such aid from me. You have skill, you have strength, to teach the erring in word and in example, to comfort the weak, to urge forward the languid, just as you used to do when you were Prioress." [Héloise had lately been installed as abbess of the Paraclete.]

So the words of Abelard run, giving counsel calmly, and asking that its nuns offer intercession for him, even giving the words of a prayer to be used in their oratory. If he meets death at the hands of enemies, will Héloise see that his body be carried for burial to the Paraclete? "This finally I ask above all things, that you who now worry too anxiously over the danger to my body, show the same care for my soul."

Even more sad, in its reproach, its love and its yearning, than her first letter was the reply of Héloise to Abelard's tranquil explanation. At the same time, in both letters Heloise made use of her wide and learned reading; her mind, it would seem, was fighting bravely for his heart.

She begins now with a question: Why did Abelard place her before himself in the title and address of his letter: a woman before a man, a wife before her husband, a handmaid before her master, a nun before one who was both a monk and a priest, a mere servant of the Church before an abbot?

Again she begs him not to speak of death; "the very mention of your death is in a way death to me; do not write to me these words! They pierce my soul as by a sword of death, worse than death. The soul that is worn out by worry is not at rest; the mind distracted by fear has no real thought for God. What can I hope for if you are lost to me? What reason have I for remaining in this pilgrimage on earth, where I have nothing to help me but you, and no pleasure whatsoever except the fact that you are alive, the hope that some day your presence, now denied me, may be given me once more? O—if I may say it—O God, ever cruel to me! O merciless mercy! O unblest blessing! that has hurled so many weapons in constant assault upon me, so many that it has now no more for its rage against other victims! If in truth there were some weapon left, it would find in me no spot unwounded. Chosen out by you, I rose higher than all women, and now I lie ruined, suffering a heavier fate because of that very happiness of mine!

"And, while we yielded to the turbulent joys of love, or, to put it in foul but clearer words, yielded ourselves to lawless embrace, Divine discipline spared us; and when we corrected lawlessness by the law and buried the foulness of forbidden love in the honor of marriage, then the wrath of the Lord laid its heavy hand grimly upon us! Then you, as a lawful husband, paid the penalty meet for the most evil crime against marriage. Two of us sinned and you bore all the punishment."

The letter goes on with quotation after quotation from the Bible and the Fathers, directed against women, against sin. Then again Héloise declares: "In every moment of my life, and God knows it, I am still more afraid of offending you than of offending Him! It was your command, not Divine love, that drew me to my clothing as nun. So think how unhappy a life I endure, more in need of pity than all others, if I suffer so bitterly here all in vain, with no hope of reward in the future! My pretence has deceived you, deceived you for a long time, as it had many people. You might well call me a hypocrite living in a convent! And you demand prayers from me, while I look for yours. Please do not think so highly of me; I am afraid you may cease to help me by your prayer. Don't, I beseech you, think of me as whole and healthy, and so take away from me your aid as physician. False praise has injured many souls. The more you praise me, the more real my peril, because I love praise from you; and the greater my delight, the more eager I am to praise you in everything. Be afraid for me, don't trust me; then in your fear for me I shall always find help."

From Abelard in answer to this passionate outpouring there now came a lengthy letter of pastoral counsel: "To the bride of Christ, from His servant."

She had made four complaints, and now he answered them with energy.

He began by repeating her accusations. First: He had placed her before himself; Second: Instead of comfort he had given her even further anxiety and grief; Third: Once again she had lamented the cruel mutilation worked upon him and, after this, the fact that they both had turned to life in religion; Fourth: she had implored him not to give her praise.

These four accusations Abelard treated in full detail which need not be given here. In brief, to the first he replied that the bride of Christ was of higher estate than His servant; to the second, that he had told her of the danger, possibly death, which faced him, simply because she had begged for news concerning him, good or bad; against the fourth reproach, her rebuke of his praise, he declared that those who give this rebuke often do it in hope of further and greater flattery. He was quite aware of her genuine humility. At the same time he advised her not to protest against praise; to those who did not know her she might seem to crave it.

Lastly, he dealt with her third charge, her "old and ever lasting complaint," as he called it, against their profession as nun and monk. Here his counsel grew more commanding, even sharper:

"Since, as you say, you want to please me in all things, do not torment me in one; but rather, that you may greatly please me, stop this lament! By it you cannot give me any pleasure, nor win with me the happiness of the blessed in the realm beyond. Will you let me go there without you, when you say that you are willing to follow me even to Hell's fire? Seek religion for one thing, at least, that you be not separated from me; since, according to your belief, I am hastening toward God. And do not *torment* yourself by the thought that you were the cause of our blessed gaining of life in religion. Do not doubt that God created you for that very reason!

"So let us mellow the bitterness of your grief, and prove how just, how helpful to us, even more right for us as wedded than for us as guilty of illicit passion, was the vengeance of God. You know quite well that, after our union in marriage, when you were living with the nuns of Argenteuil, one day I came secretly to see you, and there, in so sacred a place, dedicated to the Holy Virgin herself, most shamefully I did my will with you in a corner of the refectory, the only retreat we could find. What of the way in which I deceived your uncle and carried you off to Brittany disguised as a nun, pregnant with child, in very mockery of our present life? You did not fear to laugh at the habit you were wearing! Think, then, how wonderfully Divine justice—No! grace—has brought you, against your will, to atone in that same habit for your sin, to make up for pretence by reality! Think, most dear one, think how the Lord has caught us like fish in His net of mercy, how against our will He has rescued us, shipwrecked in the whirling waters of a vast Charybdis. Each of us well may say: 'The Lord took care of me!'

"Yes, I was caught in so deep a desire for you that those miserable and most foul delights, which now we do not like even to name, I held more precious than God or my own decent self. The Divine mercy had no other means of redemption for me than utterly to take them from me forever. God punished me in exactly the right and fitting way, purifying me rather than depriving, removing from me what was for me a source of sordid sin."

At the end of this argument Abelard placed a prayer of intercession, composed by himself, and asked Héloise to offer it every day for his own progress in monastic life.

From this time he had no longer to wrestle with Héloise against rebellion and complaint, shown in her words to him, written in her letters. Yet his victory was but partly won, as we can tell from the reply she quickly despatched:

"Lest you be able by any chance, in any way, to talk henceforth to me of disobedience, the bridle of your command has been fastened down upon my words of extravagant grief. Now at least I shall keep myself from such words in my letters to you, although in talking this is not only difficult for me, it is entirely beyond my power. Nothing, indeed, is so far from our control as our minds; here we are forced to obey rather than command.

"And so I will hold back my hand in writing, while I cannot keep my tongue from words. You can, however, give me some remedy for my grief, if you cannot take it away altogether. As a second nail, driven into the same hole, pushes out another, thrust inward, so new thought drives out that which held the mind before; and really good thought, a stimulant for the mind, seems truly now needful for me, and indeed for all of us here at the Paraclete."

One has to admire the courage with which Héloise set herself to accept the inevitable. She loved Abelard; she could not lose his love for her, even as his "most dear sister." From this time her letters to him were those of an obedient and devout soul. She fought to hold back her tongue from words which he would not welcome, which others should not hear from an abbess speaking to the Father Director of her community.

But this was nothing compared with the struggle in her secret mind and heart. How could she keep herself from passionate longing for his presence, for his love? Night and day, in the oratory, in her cell, in refectory, in her thought and in her dreams, his shadow appeared; and, most of all, as she struggled to concentrate her spirit on prayer and communion with the Lord of Heaven. It was a battle in which she was constantly defeated, which she as constantly carried on. Outwardly she won a splendid victory. Yet we shall never know how far the passion of the woman and the wife was conquered by the discipline and inner devotion of the nun.

Outwardly, then, she turned with determination to the rule

of her convent. Her letter now continued with petition for Abelard's aid, his offering of "new thought":

"All of us, your daughters in Christ, ask earnestly from you, Father, two things. One is that you instruct us in regard to the origin of religious Orders for women, that you tell us what authority gave us profession as religious. The other is that you draw up for us a written Rule, suited for women, describing for us the proper condition and manner of our life. This, as we have discovered, has not been done since the time of the holy Fathers of the Church, days long ago."

Eager questions follow. Here Héloise writes that only one Rule is now followed for both monks and nuns, for the weaker set as for the stronger. "What should be prescribed for women? What about clothing—hoods, breeches, and scapulars? What about tunics and woolen clothing? What about the abbot's reading of the Gospel, or his precenting in the hymn which follows? What about his special table for pilgrims and guests? Is it proper for us—a thing we have never done—to provide hospitality for men? Is the abbess to eat with men? How easy it is to ruin souls when men and women live in one and the same house! Especially when they dine at the same table, where drinking and drunkenness run wild, and wine, that luxury, fills them with delight!"

Two answers quickly arrived for "the most dear sister," giving in great detail just what she had asked: two treatises rather than letters, dealing with both questions, asked by her obediently. Father Abelard wrote and sent to the Paraclete yet a third treatise, on study of the Old and the New Testament. He encouraged Héloise to send him full descriptions of the problems she encountered in her guidance of conventual life; he regularly answered, also in writing, giving their "solutions." We still have forty-two of these questions and replies; they dealt generally with words of Holy Scripture which Héloise wished to interpret for her nuns, especially those of the Lord Christ. Yet the Old Testament also found explanation. Often the "solution" needed but few words; now and again it reached considerable length. Sequences and hymns, propers for the various offices of the day and of the night, for seasons of feast and fast, came to the convent sisters from Abelard's pen, together with sermons, composed by special request of their abbess.

With these sermons came a letter:

"Héloise, reverend in Christ and beloved sister, at your request I have made haste to write some homilies, for you and your nuns to hear in the oratory, although this kind of work is contrary to my custom. I am given to reading rather than to preaching, and I insist on plain writing in sermons, not on elegance of style; on making clear my meaning, not on ornament of rhetoric. Perhaps through this, the lack of ornament, my words will be better understood by simple minds. You will find that they deal with the feasts of the Church in due course, from the beginning of our redemption onwards; that is, from the Feast of the Annunciation to the day which remembers the Holy Innocents."

Lastly, to Héloise, Abelard dedicated his *Expositio in Hexameron,* his work on the six days of creation as described in Genesis. His preface tells that she had entreated, even with force, that he write an interpretation of these most difficult chapters; in her petition she declared that such interpretation was rarely to be found, that even Saint Augustine faced the reading of the Book of Genesis as a formidable task.

In 1136 Abelard was again in Paris, lecturing once more at Mont Sainte-Geneviève, with new and bold confidence, since students in multitude came to rejoice in his presence. Confidence now led to daring ventures, of downright assurance or tentative suggestion, not only in his view of philosophy but also in matters theological. He had no conscious, deliberate desire to reject the doctrine of the Church; but he yearned to be free to think, and to put his thoughts before these earnest, deeply interested hearers.

For a short while, it would seem, he left Paris; but he was there again from 1139 until 1140. It was now that his revolutionary interpretations of theological doctrine, as they seemed to men of traditional faith, were arousing criticism, suspicion, even alarm.

Early in 1140 William, once abbot of the Benedictine monastery of Saint-Thierry near Reims, and now monk of the cloister at Signy in the diocese of Reims, was writing his treatise on the *Song of Songs.* During his study, as he himself tells, he happened to come upon a book by Abelard, or, more probably, two of his treatises: the *Theologia,* his chief work, and his *Theologia Christiana.* The title, or titles, made William curious, and he turned page after page. As he read on, he grew more and more horrified "at the strange novelties of words regarding the Faith, the new inventions, unheard-of meanings."

At once he sat down and wrote to the two men he trusted most: Bernard, abbot of Clairvaux, the Cistercian monastery founded by him in the valley of the river Aube, some forty miles from Troyes,

and Geoffroy, bishop of Chartres. William gave a second reason
for his letter to Bernard: "That man Abelard fears and dreads you,"
he wrote.

Bernard, whom now we know as Saint, was not actively hostile
to Abelard at this time, but he had some knowledge of him and his
mind. In January 1131, they had both gone to Morigny in France
for talk with Pope Innocent II, who was there on a brief visit; no
doubt they had met each other. Somewhat later, probably between
1131 and 1135, Bernard had visited the Paraclete. There, as he listened to its nuns reciting the Office of prayer in their oratory, he
noticed that in the petition of the Lord's Prayer, "Give us this day
our daily bread," said of course in Latin, for *quotidianum,* "daily,"
the word used in the custom of the Church, they substituted *supersubstantialem.* When he inquired the reason for this change,
Abbess Héloise told him that it had been made through counsel
from Abelard. Abelard here was following the Latin given in the
Vulgate rendering of St. Matthew's Gospel, made by Jerome; St.
Jerome had written there *supersubstantialem,* as the equivalent
of the Greek word ἐπιούσιος. The earnest desire of modern scholars
to find the exact meaning of this Greek word has given rise to
considerable study, with suggestion of various English renderings:
"for the morrow," "for today," "day by day." But the correct equivalent lies still uncertain.

At any rate, Bernard objected to the introduction of this
novelty into the Lord's Prayer, and Abelard felt it necessary to
write him a letter:

"Recently I was at the Paraclete on a matter of business, and
the abbess told me with the greatest joy that you had made a long-
awaited pastoral visit, that you had been welcomed, not as a man
but as an angel, that you had encouraged both her and her sisters by
your stirring counsel on religion. She also told me in confidence
that you were somewhat disturbed because the Lord's Prayer was
not said, word for word, in the daily Hours at the Paraclete as it is
elsewhere, and that when you heard this was due to me, you
charged me with introducing what was unknown elsewhere. So I
have decided to write you some kind of explanation. Indeed, as is
meet and right, I should be more sorry to offend you than all the
nuns at the Paraclete."

There follows a long reasoning, of the sort briefly given above.

Of course Bernard knew of Abelard's notoriety, not only for
learning, but for new and different interpretations of doctrine. At
first he did little but write to William of Saint-Thierry:

"I consider your action in writing to us both just and necessary. I have not yet read Abelard's work carefully, as you bid me; but, so far as I can tell from running through it, your attack upon it seems well justified. I think that you have dealt a strong assault against evil teaching. As you know well, I do not trust my own judgment, especially in matters so important; but I do believe it well worth while that, when opportunity allows, you and I should meet and discuss all this business. I am afraid, however, that this could not be managed before Easter; it would not be right to interrupt our course of prayer during Lent."

But before many weeks had passed Bernard had read with due diligence writings of Abelard, had heard the rising outcry against them, and had decided upon further action. First, however, he thought it wise to see Abelard himself, before condemning his work. He would warn him in private that he was deep in error. And in so kindly a way did he plead, that Abelard, touched by his friendliness, promised correction.

But his yielding mood soon vanished. Encouraged by his students and relying on his own skill in dialectical dispute, Abelard said openly that he would face Bernard of Clairvaux himself, and any others who cared to meet him for theological argument.

Bernard had no desire to stand in Council as opponent of this scholar, so famous for debate; "It is not the business of a servant of God to carry on dispute," he protested, "and I am but a child in these matters." Later on, warned by men whom he knew well that his absence from such a Council would shock the faithful and strengthen the accused, he yielded his consent and proceeded to act accordingly. Letter after letter came from him, urging the clergy of high rank—Pope, Cardinal, Abbot—to rise in defence of the Faith. A Council was called, to meet at Sens on the Yonne river, some seventy miles southeast of Paris, in the octave of Pentecost, 1140 (or, as some hold, 1141).

To Pope Innocent II Bernard's words broke out in anger against both Abelard and his friend, Arnold of Brescia. Arnold had been condemned for heretical teaching in Italy; he had been expelled from his native land, had fled to France, and there had found support in Abelard's way of thinking.

"Master Peter," Bernard now wrote, "and Arnold, from whose pestilence you purged Italy, have taken their stand together against the Lord God and against His Son, the Christ. They have become corrupt and abominable in their endeavors; with the ferment of their pollution they poison the faith of the simple, overthrow moral order, defile the purity of the Church.

"O beloved Father, do not deny her your aid; see to her defence; gird on the sword! For now through fullness of iniquity the love of many is growing cold."

To Stephen, Cardinal, and Bishop of Praeneste, Bernard sent a more personal condemnation:

"His life, his words, his books, which came from darkness into the light of day, show forth Peter Abelard as persecutor of the Catholic Faith, as enemy of the Cross of Christ. A monk on the outer side, he proves himself a heretic within; he holds nothing of the monk except the name and the clothing."

To another Cardinal:

"We have in France a monk professed, without rule, without care, without discipline: Abbot Peter Abelard, who discusses theology with children and keeps company with women. In his books he serves to those of his house stolen waters and secret bread; to his lectures he brings profane novelties of word and thought."

To yet another:

"Peter Abelard writes, teaches, argues and divides, just as he likes concerning morals, sacraments, and the Blessed Trinity: Father, Son, and Holy Spirit."

To an abbot Bernard wrote that Peter Abelard held in himself the mingled heresies working among men:

"With Arius he places grades and scales in the Holy Trinity; with Pelagius he prefers freewill to the grace of God; with Nestorius he divides the Christ."

Bishops of the diocese of Sens were called by this abbot of Clairvaux to war against the heretic:

"We are summoned to Sens in the octave of Pentecost; we are urged to fight! Let me think of you as friends, not of myself, but of Christ, Whose spouse, the Church, is crying to you in the forest of heresies, in the harvest of errors! Under you, her guardians, these are budding, these are growing, and she is all but suffocated!"

The Council ran its course, and after it broke up Bernard wrote for Pope Innocent II his description of what had occurred:

"The Archbishop of Sens sent me a word of entreaty, naming the date of the days during which Peter Abelard, in his presence and that of his fellow-prelates, was to confirm, if he could, his perverse doctrines. I refused to come to Sens, for two reasons: First, because in argument I am like a small boy, and Abelard has been a warrior from his youth; second, because I held it unseemly that the basis of the Faith should be laid under discussion by human reasoning; surely it rests upon firm and settled truth. I said that Abelard's writings were enough to prove him guilty; that the duty of judgment in his case was reserved for bishops.

"But Abelard raised his voice louder and louder; he gathered his accomplices. What he wrote concerning me to his followers, I do not care to tell. He spread word everywhere that he was going to answer me on the appointed day at Sens. At first I hid the fact that I knew this; I thought little of common rumor.

"Yet at last I did yield to the advice of my friends; but it cost me tears of pain. They saw that all men were getting ready for a spectacle, and, if I were absent, they feared that people would talk. After all, there had to be some one there to answer and contradict!

"So in the end I hurried to Sens, all unprepared, with no arguments, nothing in my mind, except these words: 'Take no thought how or what you shall speak, for it shall be given you in that same hour' (Matth. x, 19), and, 'The Lord is on my side; I will not fear what man may do to me' (Psalm CXVIII, 6).

"Not only bishops and abbots, but a multitude of monks were there, with masters of schools from the cities and many learned clergy; the king himself had come to hear the trial.

"First of all, with his prosecutor standing face to face with him, passages from Abelard's books were read as evidence of his errors. Then, in the very middle of this reading, suddenly Peter refused to listen any longer; he hurried out of the hall of audience, crying that he would appeal against this trial—a thing I do not believe allowed by law. The trial continued; in the end his passages were condemned, as contrary to the true Faith.

"I have told this for my own defence, lest I be judged heedless and inconsiderate in so important a matter."

Abelard said afterwards to his friends that during this reading of the passages under accusation he had become so troubled and confused that he could remember nothing; dense fog came down upon his mind and all power of reasoning fled.

Another description of procedure at this Council of Sens was written by Bernard to Innocent II, in the names and, as it were, in the persons, of six prelates of France, headed by the Archbishop of Sens.

In this we learn that Bernard at the beginning of the trial informed Abelard that he might choose one of three proceedings, as a man under accusation: confess himself guilty, prove himself innocent, or promise to erase and correct errors, as needed. Then, in the midst of the reading of passages from his work, he had cried out that he would appeal to the Pope himself, and with these words he had rushed away. This he had done, Bernard carefully added, in spite of the fact that he had no reason to fear; his judges were honest men.

The Pope read and deliberated; in mid-July his answers reached France, sent to the Archbishops of Sens and of Reims, to their suffragans, and to Bernard of Clairvaux. After referring to the condemnation of other heretics—Arius, Manichaeus, Nestorius, Eutyches, and Dioscorus—Innocent II continued:

"We grieve to find, from your letters and from the details of errors sent to us by you, Brother Bernard" (and here the Pope was mentioning a lengthy tractate sent him by this abbot of Clairvaux), "that during these latter days, when times of peril press upon us, heresies and perverse doctrine have again begun to grow and spread, through the writings of Peter Abelard."

At the end of his letter the Pope declared sentence: "By authority of the sacred canons we have condemned all the evil theories of this Peter, with their author, and as heretic we have laid upon him the penalty of perpetual silence."

Meanwhile Peter had started for Rome. On his way he had fallen sick and had been forced to seek hospitality in the Benedictine abbey of Cluny, founded in 910 near Mâcon in Burgundy. Its abbot was now Peter the Venerable, a priest of gracious and generous nature; he told the story of Peter Abelard's stay in his own letter to Pope Innocent:

"We asked Abelard where he was going? He told us that he was worried and depressed because men were calling him a heretic, a word from which all within him shrank in utter loathing. So he had appealed to the sovereign power of the Pope in an effort to find refuge."

The abbot of Cluny continued:

"We heartily approved this appeal, and we urged him indeed to seek that refuge in Rome, open to all; Apostolic justice, we said, was denied to none, even foreign or pilgrim strangers.

"Just at this time the abbot of Cîteaux [a Cistercian monastery near Beaune in France] came to visit us at Cluny. He joined us in encouraging Abelard to seek peace of reconciliation with Bernard of Clairvaux; he even said that he would himself take Abelard there.

"And so it came about. Abelard went, and returned to tell us that, with this abbot of Cîteaux as mediator, he had indeed made his peace with Bernard. Then, persuaded by us, or, rather by God Himself, he put away from his mind all the exciting turmoil of the Schools, their students and lectures. Might he, he now prayed us, be allowed for the future to make his home in Cluny's tranquil house?

"He is over sixty years old, Holy Father, frail in health, professed as monk; we think that his presence would benefit the many brethren of our community. So we gave our consent, under condition that you give yours. Therefore now I ask, and the abbey of Cluny in all devotion to you is also asking, that you allow us this joy, that Peter Abelard spend the remaining days of his life, which perhaps will not be many, in this, your monastery. The insistence of enemies will not be able to drive him out from a home; from, as it were, a nest, which, as a wandering sparrow or turtle-dove, he has found here."

The request was granted and Peter Abelard became one of Cluny's brethren. It was probably soon after this decision that he wrote his *Apologia*, his "Confession of Faith." It begins:

"A well-known proverb declares: 'Nothing is so well written that it cannot be disfigured'; as blessed Jerome says: 'He who writes many books finds many critics.' I myself, though I have merely written brief treatises, nothing in comparison with other men, yet have not escaped the scar of rebuke. God be my witness, in those gross accusations cast against me I recognize no guilt; though, if indeed I am guilty, I will not stubbornly defend myself. Perhaps I did make some errors which I should not have made; but I call God to support me as Judge of my will, that I was prompted by no malice, no arrogance. I gladly gave to all men my words, that they might be my judges, not my followers."

Another "Confession of Faith" was sent by him to Héloise for her assurance:

"My sister Héloise, logic has made me hateful to the world! Those who err say in their error, for their wisdom lies in destruction, that I am most excellent in logic but that I stumble badly in Paul; and while they praise aloud the knowledge of my mind, they rob me of purity in Christian faith. They are led, I think, to judge by opinion rather than by mastery of experience. I do not want to be a philosopher in order that I may kick against Paul, nor an Aristotle of the sort which will separate me from Christ. . . .

"Also, that all uncertainties may be driven out of your heart, Héloise, be sure of this: that I have firmly founded my conscience on that rock on which Christ built His Church."

The story of Abelard's last years is told us in a letter written to Héloise after his death by Peter the Venerable. First of all, this abbot of Cluny pours out for Héloise his unbounded admiration of her mind, her intellect, her dedication to religion. Then he turns to Abelard:

"Brief words will not tell of that Godlike blessing which at the end of his life on earth Peter Abelard, holy, humble and devoted, gave to Cluny. I do not remember ever having met one like him in humility of bearing, of character. High was his rank, as ordered by me, amid the great community of our brethren, yet in his shabby clothing he looked lowest of all. Words often failed me for wonder when I saw him, a man of so great fame, walking before me with the sacred relics. His habit was of the simplest kind; he would have nothing for his body—clothing, food, drink—but what absolute necessity demanded. Reading, study, prayer, filled his days, spent in silence, only interrupted when our monks asked him to instruct them in some matter of theology. Whenever his health allowed he was at Mass, offering the Holy Sacrifice.

"Steadily he grew weaker as the days went by, consecrated to God. The trouble was largely scabies, disease of the skin, but there were other worries as well. At last I sent him to Chalon-sur-Saône, which lies in one of the loveliest regions of Burgundy. There I found him hospitality in a house near the city, on the bank of the river Arar" (it was the monastery of Saint-Marcel, a daughter-house of Cluny).

"There he died, on April 21, 1142, sixty-three years of age. Death found him wide awake, his lamp, like those of the wise virgins, full of oil. His passing was brief; he made confession of his sins, received viaticum, and entrusted for ever his soul to the Lord Who dwelt within him."

The letter ends with words that must have been of comfort to her who read them:

"This Peter, my sister Héloise, reverend and most dear to me, you held, first in union of the flesh, then in the stronger and holier bond of Divine love; with him and under him you served the Lord. Now God holds him, and of His own Divine grace He will give him back to you at His coming, when the Lord shall descend from heaven, when shall sound the voice of the Archangel and the trumpet of God.

"So be mindful of him in the Lord."

The cemetery of Saint-Marcel first received his body in burial; but it did not remain there long. Years before this time Abelard had asked of Héloise that they both rest in the same place, the burial-ground of the Paraclete. This fact Peter the Venerable remembered, and he promptly acted, as he himself told:

"I, Peter, Abbot of Cluny, who received Peter Abelard as monk of Cluny, and yielded his body, carried away in stealth and secrecy, to Héloise, Abbess, and the nuns of the Paraclete, by the authority of Almighty God and of all the saints, do absolve him from all his sins."

The parchment on which these words were carefully inscribed was taken by Peter the Venerable himself to Héloise. We still have the letter in which, with gratitude and deep affection, she described his visit and its effect:

"Far from putting into words, I cannot even imagine in my thoughts how valuable, how happy your visit was for me. You, our Abbot, our head, on that day of last year, November 16, celebrated for us a Mass in which you commended us to the Holy Spirit; in Chapter you nourished us with counsel Divine; you gave to us the body of our Father: a gracious favor from Cluny. As for me myself, not even worthy to be called your handmaid, your wonderful humility brought you to call me 'sister,' both in letter and in talk; your love and true friendliness also gave me another gift: a gift of thirty requiem Masses which the abbey of Cluny is to offer for me after my death.

"You did say, too, that you would confirm this gift by sealed letter, and so, my brother—or, rather, my authority—would you do this for me, your sister—No! for her who serves you? And would you send me the Absolution of my director, Abelard, written in clear script, that it may be placed above his grave? Would you for the love of God keep also in mind my son Astrolabe, and win for him office in the Church as Prebend, from the bishop of Paris or some other prelate?

"Farewell. May the Lord protect you and at some time allow me your presence here again!"

Answer came from Peter the Venerable in words equally warm:

"I was so happy, and I mean really happy, when I read the letter of your Reverence. From it I learned that my coming to you had not been a mere matter of a moment of time, that I had not been just a visitor for you; but that since my visit I had been ever present in your mind. I was for you no stranger, no alien, but a fellow-citizen of the saints and—may it be true!—a servant of God. All that happened was so clearly printed upon your kindly spirit, all that I said in that swiftly passing stay, all that I did; not only my words spoken in serious earnest, but even a word carelessly uttered! Nothing fell forgotten to the ground. You kept all in your memory, as though my words, my acts, were great, were sacred, were Divine; as though they were the very words or acts of Jesus Christ Himself!

"I make to you such return as I can. Long before I saw you, and certainly from the time when I first heard about you, I put aside for you a special place in my innermost heart, and it was no place of false affection. It was I who planned for you this gift of thirty Masses, and I will send the script and the seal, as also the Absolution of Father Peter, written on parchment and sealed in the same manner. As soon as I get the opportunity I will do my best to secure a Prebend office for your Astrolabe in one of our well-known churches, for your sake and his. It is not an easy matter, because, as I have often found, bishops, on various pretexts, are very reluctant to bestow Prebends in their churches. However, I will do what I can, as soon as I can."

Two epitaphs for Abelard are also said to be the work of this Abbot of Cluny. The first, in Latin, runs in English translation:

"A Socrates of France, a Plato famous in the West,
Our Aristotle, in logic equal or superior to all,
Whosoever they were; known to the world of learning
As chief of all; in genius varied, subtle and most keen,
Conquering all things by power of reason, skill of argument,
Was Abelard. But rather did he conquer all at last,
When, vowing himself a monk, of Cluny's rule a follower,
He passed to own the true philosophy of Christ.
In this he ended well the years of a long life.
That sometime he might join the throng of good philosophers
He gave us hope when April called him home."

The second ends with praise rare indeed:

"Here lies Peter Abelard,
To whom alone whatever could be known was known."

His name lived on. As his pupil, John of Salisbury, declared (*Metalogicus* II, c. 10):

"In the year" (1136) "after the Lion of Justice, Henry, that renowned king of England, died, I went to study in France, under the Peripatetic Palatine" (Peter Abelard), "who was then a noted professor at Mont Sainte-Geneviève, directing everything and everyone with marvelous skill. There at his feet I received my first lessons in philosophy and, so far as my mind allowed, I learned in all eagerness all that he let fall from his mouth." Later on, in 1159, John wrote: "Abelard, my professor, left many followers and witnesses of his lecturing; he still has some."

Many were his "adversities," many his flights for refuge, from place to place; intense were his ambition and his pride, numerous his enemies. As a younger man he delighted in soaring above all, in his glory as the great scholar and teacher of his time. Yet in his last years, mellowed by age and infirmity, every one at Cluny loved him, for his humility, his charity, his love of the Church, his devotion to prayer, to study, to teaching those who willed to learn. There he cast aside his "revolutionary" thought. In this he went too far, no doubt; yet he was ever earnest in seeking to follow the pattern of the Christ. And here he was a forerunner of twentieth-century procedure.

Héloise, wife and "sister," lived on in the convent of the Paraclete some twenty-one years; she died on Sunday, May 16, 1164. Her life as Abbess was magnificent. She maintained in constant vigor for her community the discipline of the Rule given by Abelard; she cared for all, nuns and visitors; she founded daughter-houses; she was dear to all and all mourned her death.

Both Abelard and Héloise sinned; he in ordering one united with him by the sacrament of Holy Matrimony, through his own desire to find refuge from shame in monastic vow, to dedicate herself in the same for the duration of her life; she in thus yielding her soul, mind, and body: a yielding for which she had no vocation, but endured splendidly until her death, supported by her never-failing love for her husband. If she could not have him in this world of fleeting time, she would be united with him for all eternity, was her hope and her support.

It is good to think of them, then, as Peter the Venerable thought, united at last, not merely in the tomb within the Père Lachaise cemetery of Paris, but kneeling hand in hand before the throne of God.

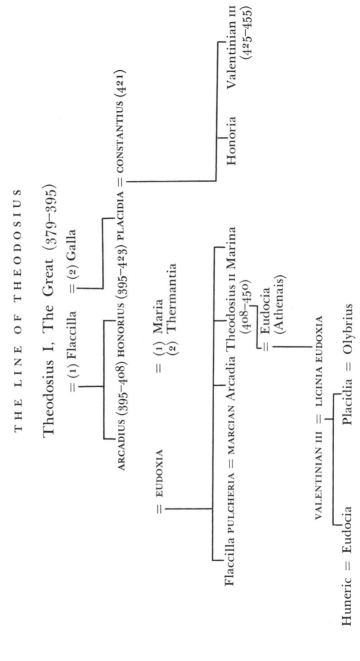

THE LINE OF THEODOSIUS

Theodosius I, The Great (379–395)

SOURCES

Selected, Primary and Secondary

Abbreviations

Auct. Ant.: Auctores Antiquissimi
CSEL: Corpus Scriptorum Ecclesiasticorum Latinorum
CSHB: Corpus Scriptorum Historiae Byzantinae
DCB: Dictionary of Christian Biography
DHGE: Dictionnaire d'Histoire et de Géographie Ecclesiastique
FHG: Fragmenta Historicorum Graecorum IV–V, ed. C. Müller
MGH: Monumenta Germaniae Historica
MSPIT: Mediaeval Studies: Pontifical Institute of Mediaeval Studies,
    Toronto
PG: Patrologia Graeca
PL: Patrologia Latina
ROC: Revue de l'Orient chrétien
SRG: Scriptores rerum Germanicarum
SRM: Scriptores rerum Merovingicarum

Abelard, Peter: *Opera,* ed. V. Cousin, 1840; *PL* CLXXVIII, CLXXX, CLXXXII, CLXXXIX; ed. J. T. Muckle, *Abelard's Letter of Consolation to a Friend. (Historia Calamitatum) MSPIT* XII, 1950, 163ff.; "The Personal Letters between Abelard and Héloïse: Introduction, Authenticity, and Text," *MSPIT* XV, 1953, 47ff.; "The Letter of Héloïse on Religious Life, and Abelard's First Reply": *ibid.,* XVII, 1955, 240ff.; ed. T. P. McLaughlin, *ibid.,* XVIII, 1956, 241ff.

Agnellus: *Raccolta degli Storici Italiani: Muratori II, 3,* 1924

Agobard, Archbishop of Lyons: *Flebilis Epistola: De Divisione Imperii Francorum inter Filios Ludovici Imperatoris: PL* CIV, 287ff.; *De Comparatione Regiminis Ecclesiastici et Politici: ibid.,* 291ff.; *Liber Apologeticus pro Filiis Ludovici Pii Imperatoris adverus Patrem: ibid.,* 307ff.

Altheim, F.: *Attila et les Huns:* trans. French, Jacques Marty, 1952.

Ambrose, Saint: *Imperatori Theodosio Epistola, scripta c. 390: PL* XVI, No. 51, 1209ff.

Analecta Bollandiana: Vita S. Melaniae Junioris, VIII, 1889 (Latin); XXII, 1903 (Greek).

Angus, S.: *The Environment of Early Christianity,* 1914–1915.

Annales Altahenses Majores: SRG, MGH, ed. E. Oefele, 1891.
Annales Bertiniani: SRG, MGH, ed. G. Waitz, 1883.
Annales Fuldenses: ed. F. Kurze, 1891.
Annales Mettenses Priores: ed. B. De Simson, 1905.
Annales Regni Francorum: ed. F. Kurze, 1895.
Annales Xantenses, ed. B. De Simson, 1909.
Apollinaris Sidonius: *Epistulae et Carmina,* ed. C. Luetjohann, *MGH, Auct. Ant.* VIII, 1887; trans. English, W. B. Anderson, I–II, 1936–1965, Loeb Classical Library; and by O. M. Dalton, I–II, 1915.
Asmus, Rudolf: *Hypatia in Tradition und Dichtung: Studien zur vergleichenden Literaturgeschichte* VII, 1907, 11ff.
L'Astronome: *Hludovici Pii Vita: PL* CIV, 927ff.; trans. English (see Cabaniss, Allen)
Aurelius Augustinus, S.: *De Civitate Dei* V, c. 25, ed. E. Hoffmann, *CSEL* 40, i, 1899; *Epistulae,* ed. Al. Goldbacher, *CSEL* LVII, 1911
Auzias. Leon: *L'Aquitaine carolingienne* (778–987), 1937

Bardenhewer, Otto: *Geschichte der altkirchlichen Literatur,* IV, 1924
Baur, Dom Chrysostom, O. S. B.: *John Chrysostom and his time,* I–II, 1959–1960
Becker, Ph. Aug.: *Duodas Handbuch: Zeitschrift für Romanische Philologie,* XXI, 1897, 73ff.
Bernard, St., First Abbot of Clairvaux: *Opera omnia: PL* CLXXXII, CLXXXV
Bethune-Baker, J. F.: *An Introduction to the Early History of Christian Doctrine,* eds. 1–8, 1903–1949
————: *Nestorius and his teaching,* 1908
Bondurand, E.: *Le Manuel de Dhuoda,* 1887
Boutruche, Robert: *Seigneurie et Feodalité,* 1959
Bovini, G.: *Ravenna Mosaics,* 1956
————: *Les monuments antiques de Ravenne,* ed. 2, 1960, trans. French, M. Vieillefond
Brière, Maurice: "La légende syriaque de Nestorius": *ROC* XV, 1910, 1ff.
Burger, A.: "Les vers de la Duchesse Dhuoda et son *poème, De temporibus suis:* Mélanges J. Marouzeau, 1948, 85ff.
Bury, J. B.: *History of the Later Roman Empire,* I–II, (395–565), 1923
————: "Justa Grata Honoria": *Journal of Roman Studies,* IX 1919, 1ff.

Cabaniss, Allen: *Agobard of Lyons, Churchman and Critic,* 1953
————: *Son of Charlemagne: A Contemporary Life of Louis the Pious* (trans. English), 1961
————: *Charlemagne's Cousins: Contemporary Lives of Adalard and Wala* (trans. English), 1967
Calmette, Joseph: *De Bernardo sancti Guillelmi filio,* Toulouse, 1902
————: *L'Effrondrement d'un Empire et la Naissance d'une Europe,* IXe et Xe siècles, 1941
————: *La Question des Pyrénées et la Marche d'Espagne au Moyen-Age,* 1947

Cambridge Medieval History, The: vols. I–V, ed. Gwatkin, H. M.; Whitney, J. P.; Tanner, J. R.; Previté-Orton, C. W.; Hussey, J. M.; Brooke, Z. N., 1922–1966

Cambridge Medieval History, The Shorter: vols. I–II, ed. C. W. Previté-Orton, revised by Philip Grierson, 1952

Caspar, Erich: *Geschichte des Papsttums* I, 1930

Cassiodori-Epiphanii: *Historia Ecclesiastica Tripartita,* ed. W. Jacob: *CSEL* LXXI, 1952

Cassiodorus, Senator: *Chronica: Chronica Minora* II, 109ff.

———: *Varia, MGH, Auct. Ant.* XII, 1894, 328f.

Cedrenus: *Historiarum Compendium* I–II, ed. I. Bekker, *CSHB* 6–7, 1838–39

Celestine I, Pope (422–432): *Epistulae et Decreta: PL* L, 417ff.

Chadwick, Nora K.: *Poetry and Letters in Early Christian Gaul,* 1955

Charrier, Charlotte: *Héloïse dans l'histoire et dans la légende,* 1933

Christ, W. von: *Geschichte der griechischen Litteratur,* ed. G. W. Schmid and Otto Stählin, Teil 2, 1924

Chronica Gallica: Chronica Minora I, 615ff.

Chronica Minora, saec. IV–VII, ed. Theodore Mommsen, I–III, *MGH, Auct. Ant.* IX, XI, XIII, 1892–1898

Chronicon Paschale: ed. L. Dindorf, *CSHB* IX–X, 1832

Claudian: *Poems,* text and trans. English, Maurice Platnauer I–II, 1922 (Loeb Classical Library)

Codex Theodosianus, ed. Th. Mommsen and P. M. Meyer, II, 1905

Corpus Inscriptionum Latinarum, ed. E. Bozmann and G. Henzen, VI, i, 1749; IX, 1371; X, 1485; XI, i, 276

Courcelle, Pierre: *Histoire littéraire des grandes invasions germaniques,* 1948

Cross, Frank L.: ed. *The Oxford Dictionary of the Christian Church,* 1957

Cyril, St., Patriarch of Alexandria: *Epistulae-PG* LXXVII

Cyrus, Praetorian Prefect of the East: *The Greek Anthology,* vol. III, Nos. 136, 808 (Loeb Classical Library)

Dalton, O. M.: *Byzantine Art and Archaeology,* 1911

Daniel, Pillar Saint: see H. Delahaye: "Une Epigramme de l'Anthologie grecque," *Revue des Études grecques* IX, 1896; *Greek Anthology,* vol. I, Book I, No. 99, trans. W. R. Paton (Loeb Classical Library)

Daniel-Rops, H.: *The Church in the Dark Ages,* trans. English, Audrey Butler, 1959

Dawes, Elizabeth, and Baynes, Norman H.: *Three Byzantine Saints,* 1948

Delahaye Hippolytus: ed. *Vita S. Danielis Stylitae: Analecta Bollandiana* XXXII, 1913, 121ff.

Demougeot, E.: *De l'Unité à la Division de l'Empire romain,* 1951

Diehl, Charles: *Ravenna,* 1907

Driver, G. R. and Hodgson, Leonard: trans. English: *The Bazaar of Heraclides,* 1925

Du Cange: *Glossarium* s.v. *Parabolani*

Duchesne, Louis: *Early History of the Christian Church*, vol. III, *The Fifth Century:* trans. English, Claude Jenkins, 1924
Duckett, Eleanor: *Carolingian Portraits*, 1962

Ennslin, W.: "Aelia Galla Placidia," Pauly-Wissowa, *Real-Encyclopädie der classischen Altertumswissenschaft*, XX, ii, 1910ff. (1950)
Eunapius of Sardis: *Historia Romana: FHG*, ed. Müller IV, 7ff., 1928
Evagrius: *Historia Ecclesiastica: PG* LXXXVI, 2

Fasti Consulares Imperii Romani: ed. W. Liebenam, 1909
FitzGerald, A.: *The Letters of Synesius of Cyrene*, trans. English, 1926
Fletcher, C. R. L.: *The Making of Western Europe*, I, 1912

Ganshof, François L.: *Feudalism*, trans. English, Philip Grierson, 1952
Gibbon, Edward: *Decline and Fall of the Roman Empire*, ed. J. B. Bury, III, 1908
Gildae Sapientis De Excidio et Conquestu Britanniae: Chronica Minora III, *Auct. Ant.* XIII, 1898, c. 20
Gilson, Étienne: *Héloïse et Abélard*, 1948; trans. English, L. K. Shook, 1951 (University of Michigan paperback, 1960)
Glover, Terrot R.: *Life and Letters in the Fourth Century*, 1901
Gordon, C. D.: *The Age of Attila*, 1960
Gore, C.: *Leo I, Pope: DCB* III, 452ff., 1882
Greenslade, S. L.: trans. and ed. *Early Latin Theology:* Library of Christian Classics V, 1956
Gregoire, H. and Kugener, M-A.: ed. *Marc Le Diacre, Vie de Porphyre, évêque de Gaza*, 1930
Gregory IV, Pope (827–844): *Epistola ad Episcopos Regni Francorum: PL* CIV, 297ff.
Gregory of Tours: *Opera*, ed. W. Arndt and B. Krusch, *SRM* I, 1885, page 72; *History of the Franks*, trans. O. M. Dalton, 1927
Guizot, M. et Madame: *Abailard et Héloïse*, 1853

Halphen, Louis: *Charlemagne et l'Empire Carolingien*, 1947
Hardy, Edward Rochie: *Christian Egypt: Church and People*, 1952
——— in collaboration with Cyril C. Richardson: *Christology of the later Fathers:* Library of Christian Classics III, 1954
Haskell, Henry C.: *The Morning Star*, 1953
Hefele, C. J. and Leclercq, H.: *Histoire des Conciles* II, i, 1908
Hesychius of Miletus (on Hypatia): *FHG* IV, 176
Histoire de l'Église, IV: Labriolle, P.; Bardy, G.; Brehier, L.; de Plinval, G., 1948
Hodgkin, Thomas: *Italy and her Invaders*, I–II, 1880
Hodgson, Leonard: "The Metaphysics of Nestorius": *Journal of Theological Studies* XIX, 1917, 46ff.
Hydatius: *Continuatio Chronicorum Hieronymianorum: Chronica Minora* II, 1ff., 1894

Isidore Junior: *Historia Gothorum, Wandalorum, Sueborum: Chronica Minora* II, 241ff.

Jaffé, P. and W. Wattenbach: *Regesta Pontificum Romanorum* I, 1885

Jalland, Trevor: *The Life and Times of St. Leo the Great*, 1941

Jerome, Saint: *Epistulae* I–LXX, ed. I. Hilberg, *CSEL* LIV, 1910

John of Antioch: *Excerpta Historica iussu Imp. Constantini Porphyrogeniti*, II, i, ed. Th. Büttner-Wobst, fragments 193f., pp. 204f.; III, ed. K. De Boor, fragments 82–85, 88, pp. 123–127, 129, 1905–1906; *Fragmenta Historicorum Graecorum* IV, ed. K. Müller, fragments 193–196, 198, 199, ii, 201, 204, pp. 612–616, 1928

John, Patriarch of Antioch: *Epistulae, PG* LXXVII, 1449ff.

John Chrysostom, Patriarch of Constantinople: *Opera, PG* vols. XLVII–LXIV

John Lydus: *De Magistratibus* (II, 12): Teubner, ed. R. Wuensch, 1903

John Malalas: *Chronographia*, ed. I. Bekker and L. Dindorf, *CSHB* XXVIII, 1831

Jones, A. H. M.: *The Later Roman Empire*, 284–602, I–III, 1964

————: *The Decline of the Ancient World*, 1966

Jordanes: *De Origine Actibusque Getarum; De Origine Actibusque Romanorum:* ed. Th. Mommsen, *MGH Auct. Ant.* V, i, 1882

Kelly, Thomas A.: *Sancti Ambrosii Liber De Consolatione Valentiniani:* text and translation, 1940

Kleinclausz, Arthur: *L'Empire carolingien*, 1902

Knowles, Dom David: *The Evolution of Medieval Thought*, 1962

Lassere, P.: *Le Sécret d'Abélard*, 1926

Leo I, Pope and Saint: *Epistulae, PL* LIV, 551ff.

Levillain, L.: *Annales du Midi* XLIX, 1937, 337ff.; L, 1938, 5ff.

Lexicon für Theologie und Kirche, 1957–1965, ed. Josef Höfer and Karl Rahner

Libanius: *Orationes*, ed. R. Foerster, II, 1904, No. XX, pp. 424f. c. 7

Lloyd, Roger: Peter Abelard: *The Orthodox Rebel*, ed. 2, 1947

Loofs, Friedrich: *Nestorius and his Place in the History of Christian Doctrine*, 1914

Lot, Ferdinand, and Halphen, Louis: *Le Règne de Charles le Chauve*, I, 1909

Ludwich, A.: "Eudokia, die Gattin des Kaisers Theodosius II, als Dichterin": *Rheinisches Museum für Philologie* XXXVII, 1882, 206ff.

————: ed. *Eudociae Augustae Carminum Graecorum Reliquiae*, 1807 (Teubner)

McLeod, Enid: *Héloïse: A Biography*, 1938

Mannix, Sister Mary Dolorosa: ed. *S. Ambrosii Oratio de Obitu Theodosii*, 1925

Mansi: ed. *Sacrorum Conciliorum Nova et Amplissima Collectio* III–VI, 1759–1761

Marcellinus Comes: *Chronicon: Chronica Minora* II, 37ff.

Martroye, F.: *Genséric: La Conquête Vandale en Afrique et la Destruction de l'Empire d'Occident*, 1907

Merobaudes, Fl.: *Reliquiae,* ed. F. Vollmer: *MGH, Auct. Ant.* XIV, 1961, *Carmen* I; *Panegyricum* II, 27ff.

Mommsen, Theodor: *Historische Schriften* I, 516ff. (Stilicho und Alarich); 531ff. (Aetius)

Monjo, Nicolas: *The edge of perfect; the tragedy of Abelard and Héloïse: A play,* 1956

Moore, George. *Héloïse and Abelard,* I–II, 1921

Nau, François: trans. French: *Le Livre d'Heraclide de Damas,* 1910
————: *Nestorius d'après les sources orientales,* 1911

Nestorius: To Cyril: *Epistulae* III, V: *PG* LXXVII, 43f., 49ff.

Nithard: *Histoire des Fils de Louis le Pieux:* ed. and trans. French, Ph. Lauer, 1926

Nordström, Carl-Otto: *Ravennastudien,* 1953

Olympiodorus: Fragmenta: *FHG* ed. K. Müller, IV, 57ff., 1928

Orosius: *Historiae adversum Paganos,* ed. C. Zangemeister: *CSEL* V, 1882; trans. English, Raymond, Irving W., 1936

Ostrogorsky, George: *History of the Byzantine State,* trans. English, Joan Hussey, 1956

Palladas of Alexandria: *The Greek Anthology,* vol. III, No. 400 (on Hypatia; Loeb Classical Library)

Palladius: *Dialogus de Vita S. Joannis Chrysostomi,* ed. P. R. Coleman-Norton, 1928

Paschasius Radbert: *De Vita S. Adalhardi: PL* CXX, 1507ff.
————: *Epitaphium Arsenii seu Vita Venerabilis Walae:* ibid., 1557ff.

Paulinus Pellaeus: *Eucharisticus,* ed. W. Brandes: *CSEL* XVI, *Poetae Christiani Minores* I, 263ff., 1888; trans. English. Hugh G. Evelyn White (with Ausonius, vol. 2), pp. 293 ff., 1921

Peter the Venerable, abbot of Cluny: *Epistulae: PL* CLXXXIX, 61ff.

Pharr, Clyde: trans. English: *The Theodosian Code and Novels,* 1952

Philostorgius: *Kirchengeschichte (Historia Ecclesiastica),* ed. J. Bidez, 1913

Pope, Alexander: *Eloisa to Abelard*

Possidius, bishop of Calama, N. Africa: *Vita S. Augustini,* ed. text, with trans. English, Herbert T. Weiskotten, 1919

Priscus: Fragmenta, *FHG* IV, ed. K. Müller, 69ff., 1928

Procopius of Caesarea: *History of the Wars* I–II: *The Persian War; The Vandalic War:* ed. Greek text, with trans. English, H. B. Dewing, 1916 (Loeb Classical Library)

Prosper Tiro: *Epitoma Chronicon: Chronica Minora* I, 341ff.

Prudentius: *Carmina,* ed. J. Bergman, *CSEL* LXI, 1926

Rampolla: *Vita Melaniae Junioris,* trans. E. Leahy, ed. H. Thurston, 1908

Ricci, Corrado: *Art in northern Italy,* 1911

Runciman, Steven: *Byzantine Civilisation*, 1933
Rutilius Namatianus: *De reditu suo*

Salvian: *Opera omnia*, ed. F. Pauly: *CSEL* VIII, 1883
Schmidt, Ludwig: *Histoire des Vandales*, ed. 2 (trans. French from German), 1953
Seeck, Otto: *Studien zu Synesius: Philologus* LII, 1894, 442ff.
————: *Geschichte des Untergangs der antiken Welt*, V–VI, 1920–1921
Sellers, R. V.: *The Council of Chalcedon*, 1953
Shepherd, William: *Historical Atlas*, ed. 8, 1956
Sikes, J. G.: *Peter Abailard*, 1932
Simson, Bernhard: *Jahrbücher des frankischen Reiches unter Ludwig dem Frommen*, I–II, 1874–1876
Socrates: *Historia Ecclesiastica: PG* LXVII
Sozomen: *Historia Ecclesiastica: PG* LXVII
Stein, Ernest: *Histoire du Bas-Empire*, trans. French from German. I–II, 1959
Strecker, K.: *Rhythmi ex libro manuali Dhuodanae deprompti: Poetae latini aevi Carolini* IV, 2–3, 1923, 703ff.
Suidas: *Lexicon* I–II, ed. Ada Adler, 1928–1938
Sundwall, J.: *Weströmische Studien*, 1915
Synesius, bishop of Ptolemais: *Opera: PG* LXVI, 1859–1864

Thegan: *Vita Ludovici Imperatoris: PL* CVI, 401ff.
Theodoret: *Historia Ecclesiastica*, ed. L. Parmentier, 1954
Theophanes: *Chronographia* I–II: ed. C. De Boor, 1963

Vacandard, E.: *Vie de Saint Bernard, Abbé de Clairvaux*, I–II, 1910
————: *Abélard, DHGE* I, 1912
Vasiliev, A. A.: *History of the Byzantine Empire, 324–1453, University of Wisconsin Studies in the Social Sciences*, 13–14, 1952
Victor, Episcopus Tonnennensis: *Chronica, Chronica Minora* II, 178ff.
Victor, Episcopus Vitensis: *Historia persecutionis Africae*, ed. M. Petschenig: *CSEL* VII, 1881

Waddell, Helen: *Peter Abelard: A Novel*, 1947
Walden, John W. H.: *The Universities of Ancient Greece*, 1909
Whitman, Cedric: *Abelard*, 1965
William of Saint-Thierry: *Letter to Geoffroy of Chartres and Bernard of Clairvaux: PL* CLXXXII, Epist. 326

Zananiri, Gaston: *Histoire de l'Église byzantine*, 1954
Zonaras: *Epitome Historiarum*, ed. L. Dindorf, III, 1870
Zosimus: *Historia Nova*, ed. I. Bekker, *CSHB* XLV, 1837; ed. L. Mendelssohn, 1963; trans. English, *The Decline of Rome*, Buchanan, J. J., and Davis, H. T., 1967

INDEX